The Yachtsman's Pilot to the
West Coast of Scotland
Castle Bay to Cape Wrath

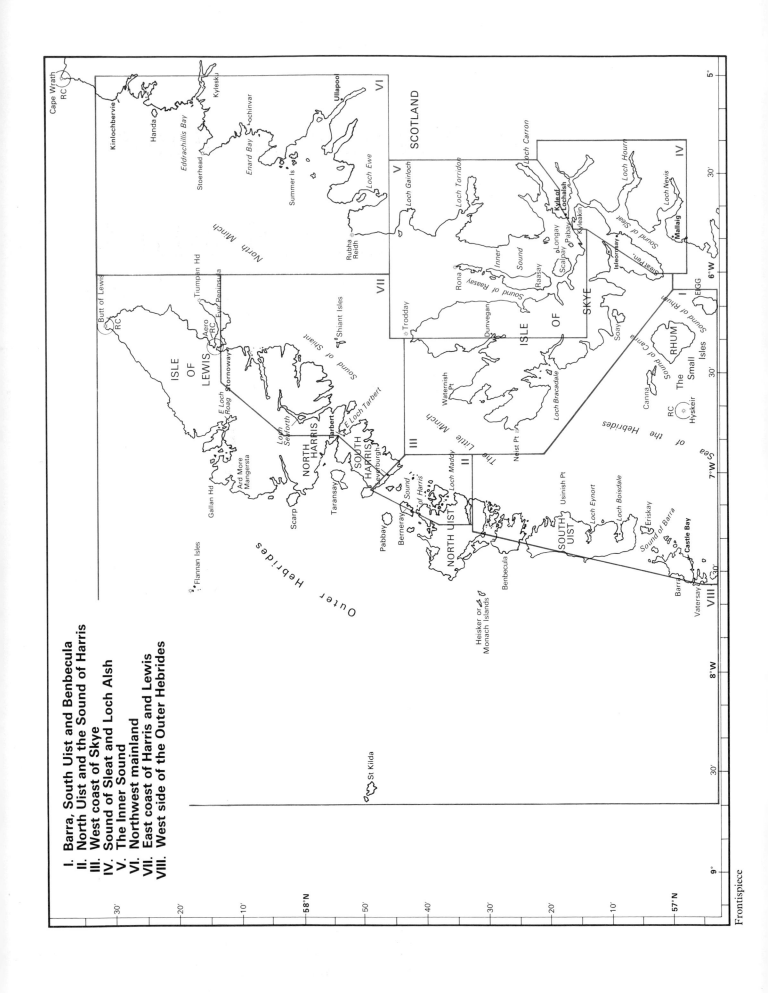

I. Barra, South Uist and Benbecula
II. North Uist and the Sound of Harris
III. West coast of Skye
IV. Sound of Sleat and Loch Alsh
V. The Inner Sound
VI. Northwest mainland
VII. East coast of Harris and Lewis
VIII. West side of the Outer Hebrides

The Yachtsman's Pilot to the West Coast of Scotland
Castle Bay to Cape Wrath

MARTIN LAWRENCE

Imray Laurie Norie & Wilson Ltd
St Ives Cambridgeshire England

Published by
Imray, Laurie, Norie & Wilson Ltd
Wych House, St Ives, Huntingdon,
Cambridgeshire, PE17 4BT, England.

© Martin Lawrence 1990
Lawrence, Martin, *1939–*
    Castle Bay to Cape Wrath.
    1. Scotland. Western Scotland. Coastal waters – Pilots' guides
    I. Title   II. Series
    623.89′29411

    ISBN 0 85288 144 4

CAUTION
Whilst every care has been taken to ensure accuracy, neither the Publishers nor the Author will hold themselves responsible for errors, omissions or alterations in this publication. They will at all times be grateful to receive information which tends to the improvement of the work.

PLANS
The plans in this guide are not to be used for navigation. They are designed to support the text and should at all times be used with navigational charts.

The last input of technical information was June 1990.

Printed at The Bath Press, Avon

Contents

Preface

The first pilot book specifically for yachts cruising on the west coast of Scotland was *Volume 5* of Frank Cowper's *Sailing Tours* written nearly 100 years ago. Cowper had no great enthusiasm for the Outer Hebrides or the northwest mainland: 'As regards a cruise among the Outer Hebrides...I do not think unless one has unlimited time the scenery is worth the trouble. Rocks, endless rocks; land barren, bleak, mountainous here and there, but with mountains of no great height.... Of all the shelters none is better than Stornoway and everything worth seeing can be visited from there....' Certainly there is little 'worth seeing' in the way of monuments or artificial entertainments; if you need more than the sea and the hills, seabirds, seals and porpoises, plants and 'endless rocks' for entertainment, and the constant inconstancy of the weather, and solitude (perhaps more highly regarded now than in Cowper's time), you may be disappointed.

A meticulous survey of the Outer Hebrides was carried out between 1845 and 1860 under the command of Captain Henry Otter and Captain F.W.L. Thomas, and the accuracy achieved with the methods available to them is almost incredible. A few areas such as the Sound of Harris have been resurveyed more recently but most current charts are derived from these old surveys.

The northwest of Scotland and the Outer Hebrides is a marginal area, not well enough known for every detail to have been precisely described, and referred to by one yachtsman as 'here-be-dragons country'. An article by Michael Gilkes in the Royal Cruising Club *Journal* led me to the old Admiralty surveys at a time when I had undertaken to redraw the plans for the Clyde Cruising Club's *Sailing Directions*, to correspond with the 'metrication' of Admiralty charts.

Since 1976 I have been gathering information from many sources previously unexamined, such as the surveys described above, and RAF survey photographs which have provided detail available in no other way. The initial product of these investigations was the Clyde Cruising Club's *Outer Hebrides Sailing Directions* of 1979, the first of a series of volumes to replace the classic *Sailing Directions West Coast of Scotland*. Others followed, and a new edition of the *Outer Hebrides* has since been produced by the current editor, Dempster Maclure.

An initiative by Nigel Gardner led to this present series of yachtsmen's pilots, using the more comprehensive resources available to Imrays to include photos, and plans with colour and shading. Incidentally, Imray's involvement on the West Coast is of long standing: a chart of precisely the area covered by this book was published by Laurie and Whittle, a predecessor of Imray, Laurie, Norie and Wilson, in 1794, about 50 years before the first Admiralty chart of the West Coast.

While I have sailed on the West Coast for nearly 30 years I make no claim to personal knowledge of every anchorage described, and I regard my purpose as gathering information from every available source and presenting it in the clearest possible way. Many people know far more about individual areas than I do, and some of them have generously given me the benefit of their experience and taken a great deal of time to discuss their observations. However, the greatest single source of value which this book has must be the unpublished Admiralty surveys. In return I have only been able to supply a few observations to the Hydrographic Department, which have always been gratefully acknowledged. I do urge any yachtsman who knows of uncharted hazards or features which would be of use to other mariners, to supply the fullest details to the Hydrographic Department. The Department relies heavily on information from users, particularly for less-frequented areas, and is not sufficiently well funded to be able to update its surveys except for some very pressing commercial or military purpose.

It is the constant complaint of writers of pilot books, whether published commercially or by clubs, that they receive little support from users. As Honorary Editor of *Sailing Directions* of the CCC I received about 15 letters a year (other than from people whom I had asked for specific information). Of those 15 at least half were from people who were not members of the club; some were from commercial operators wishing to publicise their services, and some were reporting items which had already been published as amendments to the *Sailing Directions*.

Ideally photos should be taken at low spring tides to reveal as many hazards as possible. However it takes many years to visit each place at a specific time of day and month, whether by sea, land or air – with no guarantee that conditions will be suitable for photography when one gets there, so that coverage isn't as comprehensive and some of the photos not as clear as I would like. Most of my photos were taken during cruises (and visits by land) in 1988 and 1989. I have also used more photos by other yachtsmen for this volume than previous ones.

While this book was in page-proof stage I was able to take air photos of the Outer Hebrides and Inner Sound, and some of these have been inserted, although not always close to the text to which they relate, but cross-references to detached photos are given. Apart from this, however, it is not always possible to present all relevant information on facing pages, and plans and photos should be looked for on pages preceding and following the text.

Acknowledgements

Valuable help was provided by Captain Robert Frater, the Harbourmaster of Comhairle nan Eilean (Western Isles Council), and the Assistant Harbourmaster, Captain Calum Macleod, and detailed information about new harbours was provided by Waterman Partners, civil engineers, and the engineer responsible for these works, Joe Magee. Margaret Wilkes and the staff of the Map Room of the National Library of Scotland have been patiently dealing with my requests for obscure information for many years.

I am particularly grateful to the following for various help, ranging from reading through the text and making constructive suggestions, and providing the results of their own observations, to helping to keep my boat in commission: Robert Arnold, Mike Balmforth, Charles Barrington, Nigel Gardner, Stuart Harris, Ben Kaner, Heather and Phil Lyon, Bill Neate, Norman and Gillian Smith, Bill Speirs, Anna Stratton, and Pat Thomas. As usual Harriet Lawrence made the drawings of views (apart from those which have been reproduced direct from old charts); my wife Jean tidied up the text (and took some of the photos); some other photos are by Mike Balmforth, Wallace Clark, and Joe Magee.

Nell Stuart, Imray's editor, meticulously checked every detail, and the final form of the plans is due to Imray's cartographers, working from outline drawings which I had provided.

Many of the plans in this book are based on British Admiralty charts with the permission of the Hydrographer of the Navy and the sanction of H.M. Stationery Office, but above and beyond that I am extremely grateful to the Hydrographer and many of his staff who have taken time to search through archives and reply to requests for information.

There is much that is not fully known about parts of the West Coast and in spite of checking by many people it cannot be certain that errors have been eliminated. The fact that an anchorage or passage is described is no guarantee that it is usable by you on the day you are there. There could well be hazards which I have missed by luck rather than good management, and in spite of all the efforts of Imrays and others, there may be simple errors which have been overlooked – even the supplements to the Admiralty *Pilot* contain the occasional comment 'for E read W'. Scepticism and checking against all other information available is the safest course to adopt – with any directions. Before following the directions plot the course on a large-scale chart and if you are confident that any errors will not be fatal, proceed; and if you disagree with what I have written, or find mistakes or changes, then please let me know, through the Publishers.

The Publishers are grateful to Elizabeth Cook who compiled the index.

Martin Lawrence
Edinburgh
May 1990

Mol Mor, Shiant Isles.

Caolas Scalpay from southeast.

Introduction

Most of the area described in this volume lies within a rectangle 100 miles by 80, equivalent to the English Channel between Cap de la Hague and Dover, or the southern North Sea between Ramsgate and Den Helder. There are many islands, many inlets, no marinas, almost no commercial harbours, few services and supplies, and fewer organised entertainments, but the natives are friendly. Daylight in summer is longer than in the Channel owing to being 400–500 miles further north, and the weather is on the whole less settled. But if you are prepared for the conditions which this paragraph merely hints at, you may experience unique and memorable cruising. The whole area is increasingly at risk from fish farming, and future oil development.

This pilot sets out to provide as much information as may be useful to small-boat visitors to the waters of northwest Scotland, clearly and concisely. The upper limit of size for which it caters is a draught of 2 metres, and it includes information applicable to shoal-draught boats – centreboarders, trailer-sailers, twin-keel boats and multihulls, and motor cruisers. In many anchorages there are parts which are only accessible to shoal-draught boats, particularly those which can dry out fairly upright.

However, while the smallest boats, even cruising dinghies, may be at home in much of the area described in this pilot, they must be soundly equipped and competently handled by experienced crews. The West Coast is no place for anyone who is unable to deal with adverse conditions which may arise unexpectedly. A good way to gain experience on the West Coast is to take a berth on one of the skippered charter yachts or instructional courses which are available.

Some of the waters covered by this volume are sheltered by islands or are within lochs which penetrate far among some of the highest hills in Britain. This shelter creates problems of its own, particularly the squalls which are generated in the lee of hills as well as the higher rainfall. Anyone who is capable of managing a yacht at a comparable distance from the shore whether in the North Sea, the Baltic, the English Channel, the Atlantic coast of France or the Irish Sea should have little problem on the west coast of Scotland. However, the lack of navigational marks (and the number of unmarked rocks), and the strong tides in some passages will require some adjustment on the part of the navigator. To set against these are the relative absence of commercial shipping and also the visibility which is usually good – except in rain; fog as such is fairly rare. To complete a round of generalisations, the climate is wetter and cooler than, for example the south coast of England (although the further west you go, out of the lee of the hills, the drier the weather), but a compensating factor is the longer daylight in summer, so that you rarely need to sail at night.

Equipment should be as robust and reliable as for a yacht going a similar distance offshore anywhere in the English Channel or the North Sea, and a more comprehensive stock of spare parts carried, owing to the remoteness from sources of supply.

So many yachts are now kept in marinas and only sail to another marina, or to a harbour, that anchoring is no longer an everyday operation, but on the West Coast it is essential that the crew is thoroughly familiar with anchor handling. You should have at least two anchors, of the sizes recommended by anchor manufacturers or independent reference books, rather than those supplied as standard by boat builders which are often on the light side. Chain rather than rope will restrain a yacht from roving around in gusts, but if you do use rope it will help to have an 'angel', a weight which can be let down to the seabed on a traveller. Whatever the design of the anchor there is no substitute for weight and I suspect that the reputation some anchorages have for poor holding may be due to many yachts having inadequate anchors. Attention should be devoted to ease of handling – unless you stick to places with visitors' moorings (and there's no guarantee that one will be free) you will be using the anchor frequently.

Chartering Charter boats are available, both for bareboat and skippered charters, within the area of this volume from Armadale and Badachro, as well as from further south. Many of the operators are members of the Association of Scottish Yacht Charterers, whose brochure can be obtained from the Scottish Tourist Board, 23 Ravelston Terrace, Edinburgh EH4 3EU, ☎ 031-332 2433. Most operators, including some owners of individual yachts, also advertise in yachting magazines.

Charts This pilot is not intended as a substitute for Admiralty charts. Although many of the plans in the book are at a larger scale than the charts, and include more detail, they only cover small areas, and it is essential to have a comprehensive set of charts at both small and large scales. A complete list of current charts and Ordnance Survey maps, is given in Appendix II.

Some obsolete charts show more detail than any current one and sometimes at a larger scale, but the soundings are in feet and fathoms. They should of course only be used to supplement current charts, not as a substitute for them; although it has been observed that 'rocks don't move', new hazards are discovered (sometimes the hard way), buoys are moved around, and new features are constructed.

Imray's charts *C65* and *C66* at 1:150,000 give better coverage for passage making than any current Admiralty charts and are more convenient to use.

The Clyde Cruising Club publish a folio of sketch charts which may be found convenient although they show less detail than the Admiralty charts.

Maps published by Ordnance Survey at 1:50,000 or Bartholomew at 1:100,000 provide topographical detail absent from current charts (see Appendix II). Where the charts are at small scale the Ordnance Survey maps may also be some help for navigation.

Travel

Transport There are good roads to those places on the mainland coast where one might make crew changes, although they are often narrow and patience needs to be exercised on touring coaches, caravans and heavy lorries.

Car ferries to Skye run from Mallaig to Armadale and from Kyle of Lochalsh to Kyleakin, as well as a more remote one across Kyle Rhea (there is sometimes a delay of several hours on the Kyle ferry). Car ferries to the Outer Hebrides operate from Oban to Castlebay and Lochboisdale; from Uig on Skye to Lochmaddy and Tarbert (Harris), and from Ullapool to Stornoway.

Trains to Mallaig run from Glasgow via Fort William, and to Kyle of Lochalsh from Inverness. Air services to the Outer Hebrides operate from Glasgow and Inverness. A variety of long distance and local bus services reach most places eventually.

Details of all public transport services (as well as local boat and car hirers) north and west of the Clyde and for the whole of the rest of the Highlands and Islands are included in a combined timetable with the title *Getting Around the Highlands and Islands*, published by FHG Publications in association with the Highlands and Islands Development Board annually; available from FHG Publications, Seedhill, Paisley PA1 1JN, ☎ 041-887 0428, and bookshops.

Trailed boats may be launched at Plockton, Gairloch, Kylesku, and at Arisaig, which is a few miles south of Mallaig. For Arisaig, phone Arisaig Marine ☎ (06875) 224; the others are not under the control of a specific authority.

Passage making

Unless you are crossing the Minch the distance between the entrances of sheltered anchorages is rarely more than 12 miles. Serious navigation is still necessary, but for much of the time it is a matter of pilotage by eye and satisfying yourself that what you see corresponds to the chart. The most useful position lines are transits such as tangents of islands, or beacons in line with headlands and these should be picked out on the chart in advance. Compass bearings should of course be taken as well, if only to avoid wrongly identifying a whole group of islands.

Some light beacons are inconspicuous structures and not mentioned as daymarks where they are not easily seen and identified.

At night salient points and hazards in the Minches, Sound of Sleat and Inner Sound, and in the approaches to lochs and inlets used by naval and commercial traffic, are well enough lit but in these latitudes there is little darkness in the summer months.

Radiobeacons are located at Barra Head, Hyskeir, Eilean Glas, Stornoway (aero), Butt of Lewis, Cape Wrath. Unfortunately, quite apart from Stornoway aero beacon, they are in three separate chains. Details are given in the appropriate chapters.

Visibility is commonly good and fog as such is rare (the Admiralty *Pilot* says that 'visibility of less than ½ mile may reach 3 days per month in midsummer' and visibility of less than 2 miles 'does not average more than 3 days per month during the worst summer weather at Stornoway and Tiree'. The words 'may', 'reach', and 'average' should be carefully noted.

Lobster and prawn creel floats are often encountered even in the middle of the Minch and in the fairway of approaches to anchorages. Often floating lines lie upstream of the float, especially at low tide, and sometimes stray lines lie downstream.

Weather

Weather is extremely variable and any statistics can be interpreted so widely as to be of little help. After visibility the aspects of most concern are wind speed and direction, and rainfall. Rainfall is greatly affected by the proximity to high ground, and annual figures vary from less than 1,000mm at the south end of the Outer Hebrides to between 1,250 and 1,800mm in the Sound of Sleat and Inner Sound, and between 2,300 and 3,000mm at the heads of Lochs Hourn, Nevis and Torridon.

Forecasting schedules vary from year to year and a current almanac should be consulted. Apart from the shipping forecasts on BBC Radio 4 and inshore waters forecasts on Radio 3, general weather forecasts are often equally relevant where land and sea are so much intermingled. Marinecall inshore weather forecasts are currently broadcast on VHF Ch 67 by Oban Coastguard at (or soon after) 0240, 0640, 0840, 1040, 1440, 1840, 2240, and by Stornoway Coastguard at 0110, 0510, 0910, 1310, 1710, 2110 (local time).

Tides

The spring range varies from 3.6 metres at Barra to 4.9 metres at Broadford in the Inner Sound. Tidal streams are strong wherever the movement of a large body of water is constricted by narrows, and there are often overfalls at the seaward end of narrow passages, particularly with wind against tide. Overfalls also occur off many headlands, and eddies are formed, usually down-tide of a promontory or islet or even a submerged reef, but sometimes in a bay up-tide of the obstruction. There are also usually overfalls wherever two tidal streams meet.

Anchorages

A few very general observations may be helpful. Steep high ground to windward is unlikely to provide good shelter – in fresh winds there may be turbulent gusts on its lee side, or the wind may be deflected to blow from a completely different direction, or funnel down a valley. After a hot windless day there may be a strong katabatic wind down the slope, usually in the early morning – such conditions are by no means unknown in Scotland. Trees to windward will absorb a lot of wind and provide good shelter.

Within some anchorages there are often several suitable berths depending on conditions and it may not be practicable to describe them all, nor to mark each one on the plans. In any case, an anchorage suitable for a shoal-draught boat 6 metres long may be inaccessible to a 15-metre yacht with a draught of 2 metres, and a berth which would give shelter for the larger yacht might be uncomfortably exposed for the smaller.

Rivers, burns and streams generally carry down debris, often leaving a shallow or drying bank of stones, sand or silt, over which the unwary may swing – frequently in the middle of the night. The heads of lochs and inlets commonly dry off for more than ½ mile.

Drying area head of Loch Shieldaig.
The heads of lochs dry out, anything up to
half a mile.

Within any anchorage the quality of the bottom may vary greatly. Mud is common (usually where there is little current), but its density may not be consistent and there are likely to be patches of rock, boulders and stones; also clay which tends to break out suddenly. Sand is also common, but sometimes it is so hard that an anchor, particularly a light one, will not dig in. Weed of all kinds appears to be on the increase, but it does vary from year to year.

Fish farms are increasing at an alarming rate, usually outwith the most popular places, but attempts are sometimes made to establish them in recognised anchorages as well. There are two main forms: cages for 'fin fish', (usually salmon), and rows of buoys from which ropes are suspended, on which shellfish are 'grown'. These buoys may have ropes between them on or close to the surface. Fish cages may be moved around within a bay or inlet, often because they have created so much pollution that the fish can no longer live in the original location, so that they may not be found where shown on a chart or plan. The boundary of an area licensed for fish farming is sometimes marked by buoys, usually yellow and sometimes lit. These are often a long way from the cages, and there may or may not be moorings or other obstructions within the area marked out by the buoys.

Beacons are often not at the extreme end of the hazard which they mark.

Car ferries run to very tight schedules and the space to manoeuvre at a ferry terminal is often restricted. Yachts must leave clear turning space near ferry terminals; apart from the safety aspect they may be disturbed by the wash from a ferry's bow thruster. Ferry schedules differ from day to day, especially those to Castle Bay, Lochboisdale, Lochmaddy, and Tarbert (Harris). If you intend to cruise in the Outer Hebrides you should have a copy of Caledonian MacBrayne's current timetable (easily obtained from tourist offices and ferry offices or by post from Caledonian MacBrayne Ltd, The Ferry Terminal, Gourock PA19 1QP) to avoid conflict in the often very constricted space around terminals.

Ferry at Loch Maddy. Car ferries have little room to manoeuvre in the approach to the terminals.

Moorings for fishing boats are laid in many anchorages, but many are not used in summer as their owners are often working on the Atlantic coast of the Outer Hebrides, and you may be invited to use a fisherman's mooring. Do not pick up a buoy unless you are sure that it is a mooring buoy and not marking creels for storing live prawns – or another yacht's anchor buoy!

Visitors' moorings are provided by local hotels free of charge to yachts whose crews patronise their establishments, as well as by HIDB (Highlands and Islands Development Board). They are arranged (as they have to be) to suit the largest boats likely to use them, and a boat on a mooring behaves differently from a boat at anchor. The effect is often to reduce the number of visiting boats which can use an anchorage. There is no guarantee that the mooring is suitable for any boat intending to use it.

HIDB moorings have been laid in several locations to attract more business to local traders. These moorings have large blue buoys marked 'HIDB visitors 15 tons'. There is no pick-up, and a rope has to be fed through a ring on top of the buoy. If your bow is so high that the buoy is out of reach and you cannot pass your rope through the ring, the best way to secure to one of these moorings is to lead a rope from the bow to the lowest point amidships, pick up the buoy there and take the end of the rope back to the bow. Two turns should be taken round the ring, and an appropriate knot formed to avoid the chafe which would occur with a slip rope.

"are you sure ...?" (Grey Horse Channel, Sound of Harris)

Visiting yachts are expected to raft up together on these moorings within the limits of the capacity of the mooring; no yacht can expect the exclusive use of an HIDB mooring if it has the capacity to hold another yacht.

Quays, piers, jetties, slips, linkspans and related structures are in need of some definition, as the categories overlap and a structure identified on the chart may have fallen into disuse, or been replaced by one of a different type, or have a description well above its status. The definitions used in this book are as follows, and give some indication of what you may expect to find.

A quay, wharf or pier is used by fishing boats and occasional coasters, and usually has at least 2 metres of water at its head at chart datum. It is often constructed of piles or open framing, or stone or concrete with vertical timber fendering, alongside which it is difficult for a small yacht to lie without a robust fender board. A pier projects from the shore, but a quay or wharf is either part of a harbour or parallel to the shore. Many of these structures were erected or extended by the Admiralty 40–50 years ago and some which have not been maintained are in very poor condition.

Ferry terminals serving the Outer Hebrides all have a linkspan for a bow-loading car ferry. The inner end is hinged and the outer end, supported between concrete towers, is raised or lowered to match the height of the ramp on the ferry, according to the state of the tide. The linkspan is usually at one end of a quay alongside which the ferry lies.

A jetty is smaller and, for yachts, more user-friendly but often dries alongside. Newer jetties are constructed of more or less smooth concrete, older ones of stone, often with a very uneven surface; a few are of timber.

A slip runs down at an angle into the water, although its outer end may be above water at low tide and it may be used by a ferry to an inshore island. There is sometimes sufficient depth for a yacht to go alongside a slip for a brief visit ashore for stores.

With the enormous growth in inshore fishing and fish-farming many of these structures are in regular use by fishermen whose livelihood depends on being able to land their produce quickly, and yachts should take care not to obstruct them.

Dues are charged at some piers and harbours, even for a brief visit to take on water. While this may be seen as a way in which yachtsmen can contribute to the local economy, the charges sometimes appear disproportionate to the service obtained. Some authorities offer a sort of 'season ticket' for a yacht to use two or several of their piers or harbours over a period of time.

Facilities

Considerable time, resourcefulness and imagination needs to be devoted to obtaining supplies or services but local people are, as it were, in the same boat and usually go out of their way to be helpful. Ferrymen, piermasters, hotel keepers, postmistresses and fishermen are all willing and useful sources of information, and there are many services and sources of supply that are too irregular or ephemeral or unknown to be listed here.

There are few yachting services as such, although yacht chandlers at Badachro, Ullapool and Portree will advise. Sailing clubs are at Plockton, Gairloch and Ullapool. Caley Marine at Inverness ☎ (0463) 236539 operate a mobile repair service.

Showers or baths are often available at hotels. Mobile banks operate widely throughout the Highlands and Islands. Bicycles are available for hire at Lochboisdale, Lochmaddy, Castlebay, Kyle.

Diesel is often more easily available by hose in small fishing harbours, but do not expect quick service; fuel is supplied to yachts as a favour, although usually very willingly, but the person dispensing it may have better things to do than turn out to supply a relatively small quantity.

Water supplies at the quayside are fairly rare, and a yacht with built-in tanks should have a portable container or two, together with a straight-sided funnel, with which to fill the tank. A 20-metre hose of the flat variety on a reel, with a universal coupling to fit on any sort of tap is also well worth carrying, as several small jetties have taps but no hoses. These small jetties, although they may only be approachable above half tide, are usually more convenient than the massive piled ferry piers, where the only hose may be too large to serve a yacht.

Eating ashore A reasonably varied selection of eating places is scattered throughout the area, one or two aspiring to gourmet status, and many at which you will eat well if unadventurously, whether in a restaurant or a bar. No recommendations are made as establishments change hands and standards change rapidly. *A Guide to Restaurants, Pubs and Hotels of the West Coast of Scotland* is published by Clyde Marine Press, Westgate, Toward, Argyll PA23 7UA.

Communications

Phone boxes are fairly well distributed and are referred to where known, but the 'rationalisation' of the telephone service may lead to a reduction in their numbers.

Post offices Many now have very restricted hours of opening.

VHF radiotelephones The mountainous nature of this coast puts some areas out of range of either the coastguard or coast radio stations. The west side of Harris, for instance, is a blind spot for Stornoway Coastguard.

Emergencies

Serious and immediate emergencies (including medical ones) are usually best referred to the coastguard. If you don't have VHF R/T but are able to get ashore (for example, if a crew member is ill), phone the coastguard or police. For less serious problems, such as a mechanical breakdown out of range of a boatyard, mechanics experienced at least with tractor or fishing-boat engines, will often be found locally.

Coastguard The Maritime Rescue Sub Centres for the area are at Oban ☎ (0631) 63720 and Stornoway ☎ (0851) 2013.

Lifeboats are stationed, within the limits of this volume, at Castlebay, Mallaig, Loch Inver and Stornoway.

Notes on plans and pilotage directions

Generally the conventions used on Admiralty charts have been followed so that this pilot may be used in conjunction with them. See also *Charts* on page 1.

In each chapter information about charts, tides, dangers and marks, relevant to the whole, comes first; then any passage directions, sometimes including certain anchorages where it is necessary to relate these to plans associated with the passages; then any branches from the main passage; and finally individual anchorages, usually in the same sequence as the passages described.

Conspicuous features are listed to help identification in poor visibility.

Lights, and any directions for making a passage or approach by night, are separated from the description of dangers and marks, as most of us sail mainly by day, and this reduces the information to be absorbed.

Bearings are from seaward and refer to true north. A few of the plans are not orientated with north at the top, in order to make the best use of the space available, but reference to the north point on the plan will make this clear.

Distances are given in nautical miles and cables (tenths of nautical mile); a distance of less than ¼ cable is generally expressed in metres.

Coordinates to locate anchorages are approximate – not waypoints for entrance.

Depths and heights are given in metres to correspond with the current Admiralty charts. Depths are related to the current chart datum which is generally lower than that on older charts. It is the lowest level to which the surface of the sea is expected to fall owing to astronomical causes. If high barometric pressure and/or strong offshore winds coincide with a low spring tide the water may fall below this level, in which case there will be less depth than shown on the chart or sketch plan.

Tides Heights of tides are represented by five sets of figures; these are: Mean High Water Springs, Mean High Water Neaps, Mean Tide Level, Mean Low Water Neaps, Mean Low Water Springs. The word *Mean* is important because (for example) Low Water Springs in any particular fortnight may be substantially higher or lower than the mean. If you have tide tables which give heights of tides at Ullapool you will be able to relate the tide on any particular day to the equivalent figures there (5·2 3·9 3·0 2·1 0·7) and judge whether the rise and fall will be greater or less than the mean.

The difference between times of tides at Ullapool and at Dover may vary by as much as 40 minutes, so that tide tables for Ullapool will give more accurate results than those for Dover. Tide tables for Ullapool are included in all almanacs but are not published separately; but the constant for that port is +0110 relative to Oban, for which a booklet of tables is widely available.

The Yachtsman's Almanac – Malin, Hebrides and Minches Edition available from chandlers or from the publishers, Clyde Marine Press, Westgate, Toward, Argyll PA23 7UA, ☎ (036 987) 251.

Shelter The heading *Shelter* at the beginning of each chapter implies an anchorage for which to run in reasonable visibility if the wind is increasing.

Place names are a frequent source of confusion and there are often differences between the name used on a current chart, on an older chart, by local people, and by yachtsmen. Anglicisations or translations are sometimes used quite arbitrarily on current charts among a nest of Gaelic names. The name on the current chart (or in the absence of a name on the chart, the OS map) is always given in this pilot, together with a popular name if the chart name is unpronounceable. As place names often need to be spoken the following approximate pronunciation of common words in names may be helpful: *Bagh* – Bay; *Bogha* – Bo'; *Caol* – Kyle; *Caolas* – Kyles; *Dubh* – Doo; *Mhor* – Vore; *Rubha* – Ru'.

Names of lochs, etc., are normally written as two words (e.g. Loch Boisdale), but the name of a settlement beside the loch as a single word (Lochboisdale).

Photographs and views from sea level are used to illustrate transits and clearing marks, or to help identify landmarks, while air and hilltop photos often show more detail than can be included in the plans. Transits are in some cases more clearly illustrated when the marks used are not actually aligned; where this is done the marks are indicated by pointers.

Key to symbols used on plans

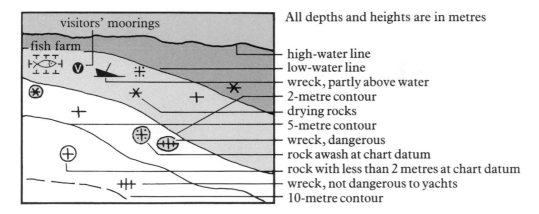

All depths and heights are in metres

— high-water line
— low-water line
— wreck, partly above water
— 2-metre contour
— drying rocks
— 5-metre contour
— wreck, dangerous
— rock awash at chart datum
— rock with less than 2 metres at chart datum
— wreck, not dangerous to yachts
— 10-metre contour

I. Barra, South Uist and Benbecula

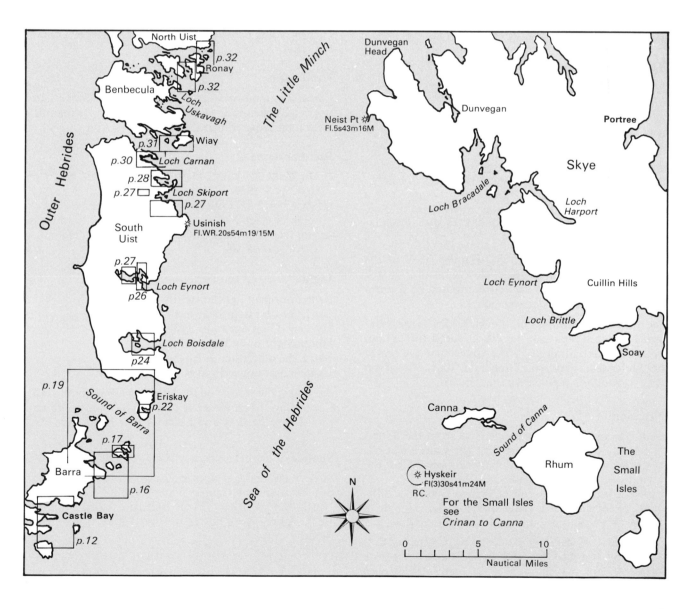

Map labels:

North Uist
p.32
Ronay
p.32
Benbecula
Loch Uskavagh
p.31
Wiay
p.30 Loch Carnan
p.28
p.27 Loch Skiport
p.27
✷ Usinish
Fl.WR.20s54m19/15M
South Uist
p.27
Loch Eynort
p26
Loch Boisdale
p24
p.19
Sound of Barra
Eriskay
p.22
p.17
Barra
p.16
Castle Bay
p.12
Outer Hebrides

Sea of the Hebrides

The Little Minch

Dunvegan
Head
Dunvegan
Neist Pt ✷
Fl.5s43m16M
Portree
Skye
Loch
Harport
Loch Bracadale
Loch Eynort
Cuillin Hills
Loch Brittle
Soay

Canna
Sound of Canna
Rhum
The
Small
Isles

✷ Hyskeir
Fl(3)30s41m24M
RC.
For the Small Isles
see
Crinan to Canna

N

0   5   10
Nautical Miles

9

The southern islands of the Outer Hebrides have a maze of channels among them with a wide choice of anchorages and some spectacular sandy beaches.

Crossing the Sea of the Hebrides to Barra and the Uists

Charts

1795, 1796 (1:100,000).

Tides

Tidal streams in the Sea of the Hebrides are generally weak except around Hyskeir. The north-going stream begins +0550 Ullapool (+0130 Dover). The south-going stream begins −0010 Ullapool (−0430 Dover).

Around Humla the spring rate is 2½ knots with overfalls over all the rocks around Hyskeir, and the sea breaks heavily up to 15 miles southwest of Hyskeir particularly in heavy weather and when wind and tide are opposed.

Dangers and marks

Cairns of Coll, above water and drying, extend 1½ miles north of Coll. A white tower, 8 metres in height, stands on Suil Gorm an islet ½ mile north of Coll, but the Cairns of Coll, a reef which dries 4 metres, lies ½ mile further NNE.

Hyskeir (Oigh Sgeir), a rocky islet 5 miles southwest of Canna with a white lighthouse 39 metres in height. Mill Rocks, awash and submerged, lie up to 2¼ miles southwest of Hyskeir; the north point of Eigg open south of Rhum bearing 085° leads 1½ miles south of Mill Rocks.

Humla, a rock 5 metres high, 2 miles SSW of the west end of Canna, with rocks close west of it as well as between Humla and Canna, is marked by a green conical light buoy on its west side.

The bottom of the Sea of the Hebrides is very uneven and steep seas may be encountered throughout the area. The Admiralty *Pilot* states that the sea of the Hebrides, between Tiree and Barra 'is about twice as rough in a given wind as the Minch'.

Directions

From Gunna Sound the passage is as from the Sound of Mull, without the hazard of the Cairns of Coll, but heavy overfalls may be encountered at the windward end of Gunna Sound.

Returning by this route, Gunna Sound is difficult to locate, but a radio mast on Ben Hough, 8 miles WSW of the sound makes a good landmark.

From Sound of Mull to Castle Bay, Cairns of Coll must be watched for and the passage lies across Hawes Bank which rises to 18 metres from over 100 metres. Barra is identified by Heaval, which is

382 metres high. In poor visibility the 30-metre contour is absolutely as close as it is safe to approach Barra without being certain of your position.

From Sound of Mull to Loch Boisdale, in good visibility three groups of three hills are visible on South Uist. From south to north these are: south of Loch Boisdale, the Boisdale Hills between Loch Boisdale and Loch Eynort, and the more massive Beinn Mhor range at the north end of South Uist.

From Sound of Mull to Loch Maddy pass north of Hyskeir to avoid Mill Rocks. Eaval, south of Loch Eport, is noticeably wedge-shaped, and the prominent North Lee and South Lee, south of Loch Maddy help to identify the landfall. Canna, about halfway across, has good shelter and access is easy. The passage east and north of Rhum may be preferred for shelter and interest and is only about a mile longer. If passing between Muck and Eigg, note that drying rocks lie ¼ mile southwest of Eigg and that magnetic anomalies occur in that area.

See Chapter III for the passage along the southwest side of Skye and at Neist Point. For anchorages in the Small Isles including Canna see the companion volume Crinan to Canna.

Landmarks

Prominent landmarks when returning are: Small Isles (especially Rhum), Hyskeir lighthouse, Ardnamurchan lighthouse, Cairns of Coll light beacon.

Radiobeacons

Barra Head 308 kHz BD (−···/−··) 200/70M Seq 1
   56°47′N 7°39′W
Hyskeir 294·2 kHz OR (−−−/·−·) 50M Seq 5
   56°58′N 6°40′W
Eilean Glas 294·2 kHz LG (·−··/−−·) 50M Seq 6
   57°51′N 6°38′W

Lights (relevant to passage only)

Ardnamurchan lighthouse Fl(2)20s55m24M
Cairns of Coll light beacon Fl.12s23m10M
Hyskeir (Oigh Sgeir) Fl(3)30s41m24M
Humla light buoy Fl.G.6s
Barra Head lighthouse Fl.15s208m21M
Usinish lighthouse Fl.WR.20s54m19/15M

At night the most easily approached harbours are Castle Bay, Loch Boisdale and Loch Maddy; the approaches to Eriskay and Loch Carnan are also lit.

Shelter

Shelter and ease of approach in reasonable visibility can be found at Canna, Vatersay Bay, Castle Bay, North Bay, Eriskay, Loch Boisdale, Loch Skiport, Loch Eport (given power to stem 3-knot tide), Loch Maddy.

Islands south of Barra

A chain of islands extends about 10 miles SSW of Castle Bay to Berneray. Strong tides run through the sounds between them, with overfalls and eddies. Occasional anchorages may be found at some islands in quiet weather.

Chart

2769 (1:30,000).

Tides

In the passages between Mingulay, Pabbay, Sandray and Vatersay, tidal streams run at up to 4 knots. The east-going stream begins +0505 Ullapool (+0045 Dover). The west-going stream begins −0140 Ullapool (−0600 Dover).

Constant −0110 Ullapool (−0530 Dover)

Height in metres

MHWS	MHWN	MTL	MLWN	MLWS
4·1	3·0	2·4	1·6	0·7

Passages between the islands south of Vatersay

In each of the sounds the tidal stream runs at between 2½ and 4 knots with turbulence at the downtide end of the sounds and heavy overfalls with an opposing wind.

Chart

2769 (1:30,000).

Sound of Berneray is only ¼ mile wide at its west end, and Shelter Rock which dries 2·4 metres lies a cable off the north side of Berneray.

Tides

Tidal streams in the Sound of Berneray and close south of Berneray run at 2–2½ knots; the east-going stream begins −0600 Ullapool (+0205 Dover), and runs for 4¼ hours. The west-going stream begins −0145 Ullapool (−0605 Dover) and runs for 8¼ hours. 3½ miles south of Berneray the east-going stream begins an hour earlier and and runs for 6½ hours, and the rate in each direction is 1½ knots.

Constant −0105 Ullapool (−0525 Dover)

Height in metres

MHWS	MHWN	MTL	MLWN	MLWS
4·0	3·0	2·4	1·8	0·8

Anchorage

Berneray, 56°47′N 7°38′W, has an occasional anchorage off the jetty and store house on the north side of the island east of Shelter Rock, which dries 2·4 metres, and lives up to its name, usually keeping the anchorage remarkably free from swell.

The Sounds of Mingulay and Pabbay

Clean, and at the west end of each sound there are islets with a passage about ¾ mile wide between them. In the Sound of Pabbay reefs which are partly above water lie 2 cables off the west side of Sandray and must be watched for if heading northwest by the east side of Flodday. A submerged spit at a depth of 2·2 metres extends 2 cables southwest from Vatersay.

Tides

The east-going stream begins +0505 Ullapool (+0045 Dover). The west-going stream begins −0140 Ullapool (−0600 Dover). In both sounds the east-going stream is the stronger, up to 3 knots at springs in Sound of Mingulay, and 4 knots in Sound of Pabbay with races and overfalls at the east ends of the sounds.

Sound of Sandray

Partly blocked by a line of rocks which extend south from the east end of Vatersay to Sgeir a' Chlogaid, 3 metres high, in the middle of the east end of the sound. A drying rock lies ¾ cable off the north side of Sandray south of Sgeir a' Chlogaid, and a 2-metre patch lies in the middle of the fairway. At the west end of the sound a rock which dries 1·1 metres lies in mid-channel. This passage needs more care than the other sounds.

Tides

In the Sound of Sandray tides turn at the same times and run at the same rate as in the Sound of Mingulay.

Lights

Barra Head lighthouse (Berneray) Fl.15s208m21M

At night there are no lights to assist a passage between the islands.

Anchorages

Mingulay, 56°49′N 7°37′W, has occasional anchorage off the middle of a sandy beach on the east side of the island, but in the most apparently calm weather there is often enough swell to capsize a dinghy; even if you can get ashore there may be difficulty in launching a dinghy. The west side of Mingulay is very impressive and worth sailing round the island in moderate weather.

Vatersay Bay, 56°55′·5N 7°32′W, on the east side of Vatersay, has a clean sandy beach at its head partly sheltered by Muldoanich. Sgeir Vichalea, a detached drying rock 2 cables from the south side of the bay, is unmarked. The holding is good on

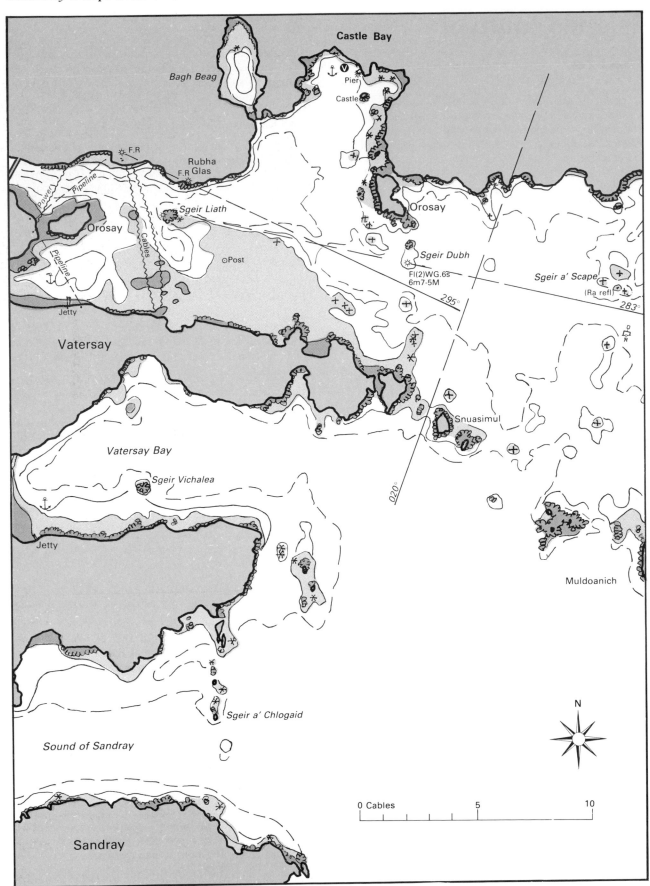

Castle Bay

Bagh Beag

Pier

Castle

F.R

Rubha
Glas
F.R

Power
Pipeline

Cables

Sgeir Liath

Orosay

Pipeline

Jetty

Orosay

○Post

Sgeir Dubh

Fl(2)WG.6s
6m7.5M

295°

283°

Sgeir a' Scape

(Ra refl)

R

Vatersay

Snuasimul

020°

Vatersay Bay

Sgeir Vichalea

Jetty

Muldoanich

Sound of Sandray

Sgeir a' Chlogaid

N

Sandray

0 Cables   5   10

Castlebay and Vatersay Bay

clean sand. From the open sea the bay should be approached by the south side of Muldoanich as rocks are scattered northwest of that island. The best shelter is in the southwest corner of the bay, where there is a jetty, but this is uncomfortable in winds between southeast and northeast.

Passages

From Castle Bay a fishermen's passage leads west of Snuasimul, a 17-metre islet east of the northeast point of Vatersay. A drying rock in the middle of the passage is avoided by keeping closer to a rock which stands above water on a drying reef northwest of Snuasimul. Drying rocks extend over 3 cables north from the east end of Uinessan, the islet west of Snuasimul, towards Sgeir Dubh light beacon.

Approaching from Castle Bay continue ESE on the line of the fairway for ¼ mile from Sgeir Dubh beacon and approach the passage on a heading of 200°. Passing northwards through the passage steer 020° towards Beinn nan Carnan on Barra until on the leading line for the fairway to Castle Bay.

Vatersay Bay, looking south towards Barra Head.

Fishermen's passage from northwest; note drying rocks in foreground.

Castle Bay

56°57′N 7°29′W

Heaval, the main hill on Barra, and Muldoanich assist identification on approaching. The open bay provides less shelter than might be expected, and the holding is poor unless the anchor has been very well dug in, but HIDB visitors' moorings have been laid to the west of the pier. Vatersay Sound has been closed by a new causeway across its west end.

Chart

2769 (1:30,000). OS map *31*.

Tides

Streams are probably insignificant on account of the new causeway.

Constant −0110 Ullapool (−0530 Dover)

Height in metres

MHWS	MHWN	MTL	MLWN	MLWS
4·3	3·0	2·4	1·6	0·5

Dangers and marks

Bo Vich Chuan, in a depth of 0·7 metre 1½ miles southeast of Barra, is marked by a south cardinal light buoy which serves as a landfall buoy (in poor visibility Curachan east cardinal, or Perch Rock south cardinal buoys in Sound of Barra might be mistaken for this if your navigation is adrift).

A red can light buoy 2 miles west of Bo Vich Chuan light buoy marks rocks on the south side of the channel.

Sgeir a' Scape 2 cables north of the red light buoy has the stump of a thin cylindrical beacon (or thick post) on it with a radar reflector.

Sgeir Dubh light beacon, a mile west of the red light buoy, is a conspicuous cylindrical tower with a platform at the top, near the south end of a drying reef. Drying rocks lie on the south side of the channel south of Sgeir Dubh, as well as west of Orosay and the shore of Barra north of Sgeir Dubh.

Sgeir Liath light beacon, a white rectangular building 6 metres in height, stands on a reef a mile west of Sgeir Dubh.

Castle Bay from north; visitors' moorings at right foreground.

Leading beacons (inconspicuous white lattice towers 4 metres in height with red triangular topmarks) stand on the south shore of Barra north of Sgeir Liath.

Directions

Pass south of Bo Vich Chuan light buoy, and steer to bring Sgeir Dubh light beacon in line with Sgeir Liath 283° and pass a cable north of the red light buoy. Pass south of Sgeir Dubh and continue WNW for ½ mile before turning north towards the head of the bay. The pier open west of the castle by the width of the castle rock leads clear of rocks east of Orosay.

For an inshore passage from North Bay and Sound of Barra see page 16.

Lights

Bo Vich Chuan Q(6)+LFl.15s
Red light buoy Fl(2)R.8s
Sgeir Dubh Fl(2)WG.6s6m7·5M
Sgeir Liath Fl.3s7m8M
Leading beacons Rubha Glas 295° F.R.9/22m4M

At night pass south of Bo Vich Chuan light buoy and steer with Sgeir Dubh and Sgeir Liath light beacons in line 283°. After passing north of the red light buoy steer to port until the Rubha Glas leading lights are in line bearing 295°. Keep them on that bearing to pass south of Sgeir Dubh and continue for ½ mile before turning north towards the lights of the village.

Anchorages

The bay northeast of the castle is full of fishing-boat moorings and drying rocks. The pier beside the ferry terminal is often busy with fishing boats at night.

HIDB visitors' moorings have been laid west of the ferry terminal. If no mooring is available, particular care must be taken to dig the anchor in as the bottom is soft mud over hard sand. Space must be left for ferries to manoeuvre at the terminal. There is a good landing slip behind the linkspan. The space north of a reef on the west side of the bay is occupied by local fishing boats.

Bagh Beag on the west side of Castle Bay has a narrow entrance with a sill which dries about 1·5 metres at its east side, on which a rock which dries 2·9 metres stands slightly west of mid-channel. Shellfish rafts are moored outside the entrance and numerous floats are moored inside and outside, as well as fish cages within, and a rock which dries 1·7 metres lies near the head of the inlet; apart from these obstructions there is nothing to prevent a yacht anchoring in Loch Beag.

Cornaig Bay, south of the new causeway, has a pipeline across its mouth whose ends were unmarked in 1989 but are being reinstated; the north end is close to a cable beacon and the south end about ½ cable east of a concrete jetty. Drying rocks lie up to a cable off the northwest shore. A drying patch lies 1½ cables west of Sgeir Liath. With sufficient rise of tide the bay may be approached by the south of Sgeir Liath, passing north of a post ¼ mile off the Vatersay shore which marks a drying rock. At the time of writing the jetty is floodlit at night, but may not continue to be lit when the causeway is in use.

The bay on the east side of the causeway may be a convenient anchorage, and a slipway is incorporated in the causeway.

Supplies

Diesel and petrol at pumps in main street, water from hose at pier, *Calor Gas* ½ mile west from pier.

Shops (some hardware at Crofters' Co-op close west of ferry terminal; another hardware shop in the main street). Some shops are open in the evening when supplies arrive by a late ferry (which is the best time to buy fresh bread and milk). Post office, telephone, hotels. Showers and baths at Castlebay Hotel. Bank, doctor, tourist office, cycle hire.

Harbourmaster's office beside CalMac ticket office (VHF).

Coastal passage from Castle Bay to Sound of Barra

Chart

2770 (1:30,000).

Dangers and marks

A thin red and white radio mast on Barra 120 metres high, as shown on the plan, is a useful reference mark.

Curachan (56°58′·3N 7°21′·3W), a rock 10 metres high 9 cables southeast of Bruernish, together with Red Rocks, a patch of submerged and awash rocks NNE of it, and *Curachan* light buoy (56°58′·6N 7°20′·45W) are, rather perversely, outwith both of the large-scale charts, but could be plotted on the margins in order to lay bearings on them. The plan here is at the same scale as the current charts.

Many rocks lie inshore and the safe course is to pass southeast of Bo Vich Chuan and steer to pass east of Curachan and *Curachan* light buoy. Ben Scrien on Eriskay open east of Gighay 015° leads east of Curachan and surrounding dangers. However a course further inshore as described below has been taken at a suitable rise of tide, in quiet weather and good visibility and with no swell. It would be as well to plot the passage on the chart before attempting it.

From Castle Bay pass south of Sgeir Dubh and a cable southeast of Rubha Charnain and Rubha Mor, keeping Sgeir Dubh beacon just in sight for the next ½ mile and then steer for Curachan until the reefs inshore of Curachan have been identified. Some of them appear to cover more than the figures on the chart indicate, so that a passage at the top of springs would be hazardous, although the clear passage between the reefs and Curachan is ½ mile wide.

From north to south pass a cable west of Curachan and a cable southeast of Sgeir Fiaclach Beag; steer to pass a cable southeast of Rubha Mor with Am Meall at the southeast point of Vatersay just open of Rubha Mor, and when Sgeir Dubh comes open of Barra head towards it, keeping a cable offshore.

Lights

Curachan light buoy Q(3)10s
Eriskay leading lights 285° both Oc.R.6s10m4M

North Bay

57°00′N 7°24′W

Tides

Constant −0110 Ullapool (−0530 Dover)

Height in metres

MHWS	MHWN	MTL	MLWN	MLWS
4·3	3·1	2·4	1·7	0·6

Dangers and marks

Curachan, Red Rocks, and *Curachan* light buoy are described above.

Beatson's Shoal, 4 cables south of Flodday, has a depth of 2·1 metres.

The tall chimney at a fish processing factory (currently disused) on the north point of Bay Hirivagh is conspicuous.

Directions

From south pass east and north of Curachan light buoy and steer for the tall chimney keeping in midchannel. Alternatively pass 1 cable west of Curachan heading for the east side of Fuiay 356° until the chimney is open of the southwest side of the channel. From north Beatson's Shoal is a hazard if a heavy sea is running and the tide is low.

When Bay Hirivagh opens up keep to the north side to avoid drying reefs off the south point and anchor as convenient in the north part of the bay. If the fishmeal factory should reopen the smell is said to be a real deterrent to using this anchorage. A stone jetty which dries alongside stands at the head of Bagh Hirivagh.

Lights

Curachan light buoy Q(3)10s
Ard Veenish Oc.WRG.3s6m9/6M (due 1990)

Supplies

Castlebay is accessible by postbus. Water tap at fishmeal factory jetty.

Sgeirislum

57°00′N 7°22′·5W

North of Fuiay, Sgeirislum is enclosed by islands and partly occupied by fish cages. From south approach between Fuiay and Flodday, keeping to the west side

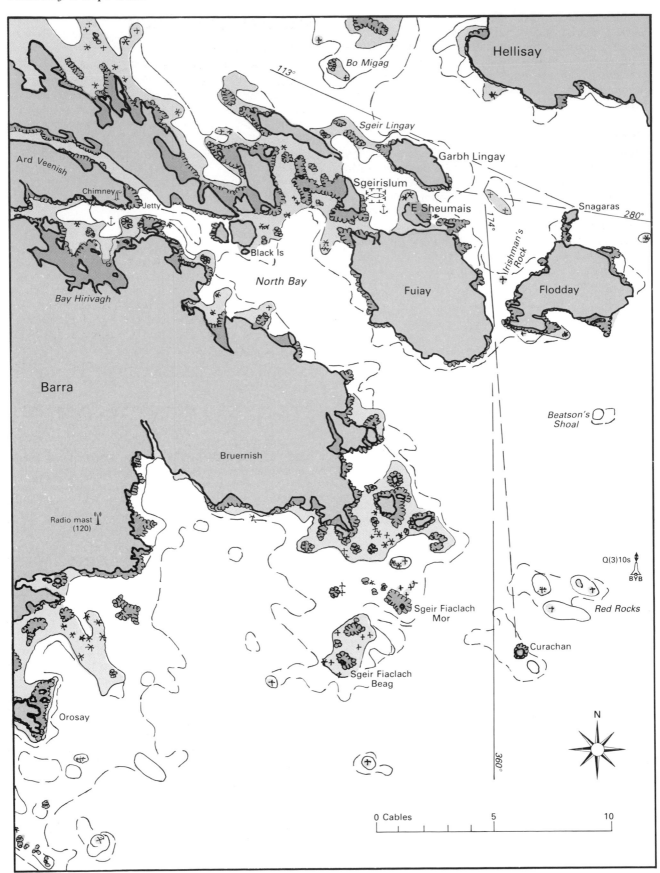

Curachan and North Bay

of the passage at its north end to avoid Irishman's Rock which has a depth of 1·8 metres. A drying reef east of Eilean Sheumais is avoided by keeping Curachan open of the east shore of Fuiay 174°. Turn to port and pass close south of Garbh Lingay to avoid drying rocks north of the west end of Eilean Sheumais.

Directions

From east pass midway between Hellisay and Snagaras with the south side of Garbh Lingay open north of Snagaras 280° to pass north of a rock 1½ cables northeast of Flodday which dries 0·3 metre. Steer for the north side of Garbh Lingay until Curachan is in line with the east side of Fuiay to clear submerged rocks northwest of Flodday and pass south of Garbh Lingay as above.

From North Bay a narrow passage between reefs leads north of Black Isles and between Sgeirislum island and Fuiay, but may not be usable at low water.

To pass through Sound of Hellisay keep Snagaras in line with the north side of Garbh Lingay 113° to avoid Bo Migag and Sgeir Lingay.

Hellisay and Gighay

57°01'N 7°20'W

A secluded sound between two islands both entrances of which are choked with rocks; part of the attraction is the challenge of finding the way in without touching any of them. Once inside, each visiting yacht seems to find more rocks, or perhaps the same rocks in different positions, in spite of which a few boats find it worthwhile to go in. The plan is based on a survey by E.L.F. Mucklow in the 1930s, supplemented by other observations.

Tides

There is some uncertainty about the direction of tidal streams in this sound. From most observations it appears that the flood tide enters through both channels at 1½–2 knots at springs, although it has been stated to run right through from southeast to northwest, and may perhaps do so at neaps. The best time to approach is either at dead low water or about an hour before high water when the strength of the flood stream has eased but there is still some rise to lift a yacht off a rock; it should be considered only if no sea is running.

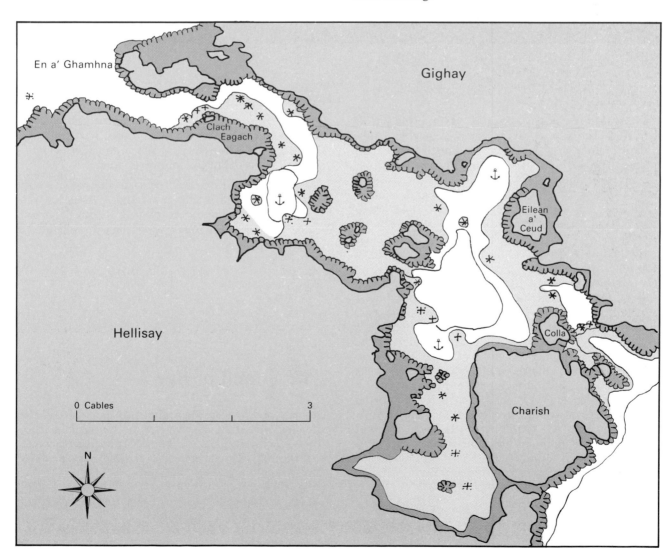

Gighay Sound, northwest entrance.

Directions

The southeast entrance is relatively straight, but a rock in mid-channel east of Colla just dries with a submerged rock at a depth of 1 metre east of it. Another drying rock lies in mid-channel north of Colla with others on the north side of the channel. A sandbank across the inner end is awash at chart datum. This entrance might best be used above half flood on a rising tide and only if there is no onshore sea. Two drying rocks ½ cable west and southwest of Eilean a' Ceud cover at about ¼ flood.

The northwest entrance winds between drying rocks and is best picked out at slack low water with a lookout at the bow. The clear passage shows pale over sand below water. Steer initially for Clach Eagach, then northwest of it passing south of the reef which extends southeast from Eilean a' Ghamhna. Close the shore of Gighay to avoid rocks northeast of Clach Eagach before turning southeast to avoid a drying rock ½ cable west of the cairn on Gighay. Turn to head southwest, keeping ½ cable from the west side of the bay on Hellisay, to avoid drying rocks both inshore and further east. Anchorage can be found in this bay, but it should be examined carefully. If you find any more rocks do let me know.

Anchorages

The two most suitable anchorages at the east end are northwest of Eilean a' Ceud, and northwest of Charish. At the west end of the sound there should be swinging room in the southwest pool.

There is a relatively clear passage along the south shore south of the islets. A through passage on the north side is a matter of picking a way between rocks, although this is no worse than the northwest entrance itself.

The Sound of Barra

The passage through the sound is tortuous but all the anchorages in this chapter can be approached from the east without using it. The chart has an elaborate sequence of courses for deeper-draught vessels which depend on the correct identification of a variety of natural features, but by keeping ¼ mile from Fuday yachts can avoid the rocks further east as described below. Overfalls occur northeast of Fuday with a southeast-going tide, that is, the in-going tide referred to below.

Gighay anchorage from Gighay; note the two drying rocks at the right.

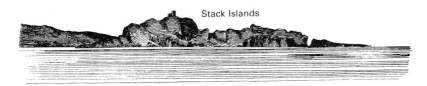

Stack Islands

Weaver's Castle 290° leads eastward of Binch Rock

Lingay

View D   Ben Scrien over south side of Lingay 87°

View B   Corran Ban just open of Ru Hornish 277°

View A   Fuiay over Dunan Ruadh

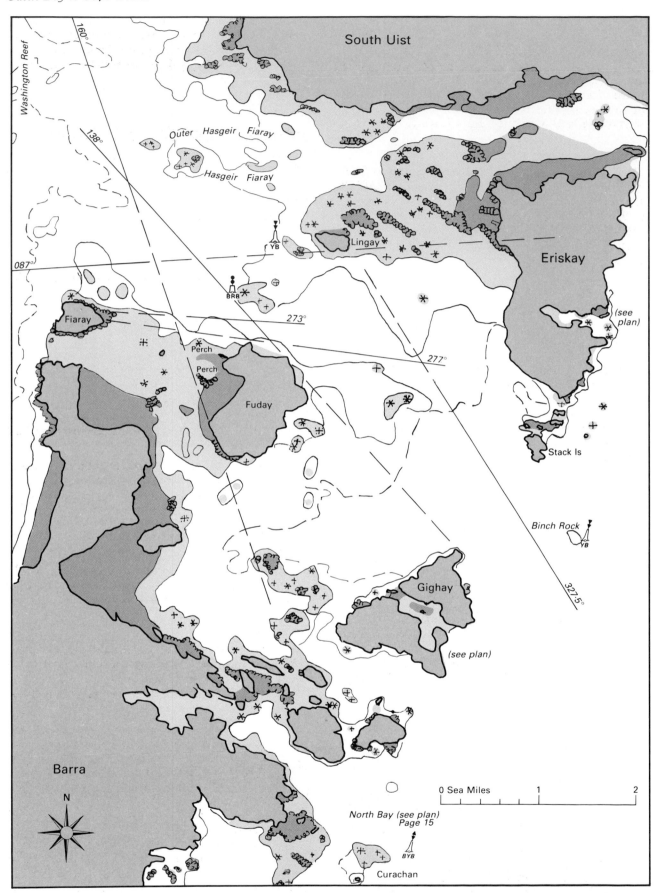

Sound of Barra.

Buoys have recently been installed in the Sound of Barra on the route used by the ferry between Barra and South Uist and some of these will be useful to boats passing through the sound. The most useful are: an isolated danger buoy west of Drover Rocks north of Fuday; a perch on Old Woman's Rock west of the north point of Fuday; a west cardinal buoy west of Big Rock which is west of Lingay.

Tides

Tidal streams in the Sound of Barra run inward from both ends at once beginning +0530 Ullapool (+0110 Dover) and outward beginning −0045 Ullapool (−0505 Dover). They meet and separate in Oitir Mhor, east of Fuday, and west of Eriskay. Transits should be watched at all times to avoid being set off course.

Directions

From southeast approach between Stack Islands and Gighay heading for Fuday (if coming from Stack Islands do not head directly to pass north of Fuday). Pass ¼ mile northeast of Fuday until two prominent stone beacons on Fiaray are in line bearing 273°. Keep on that line until Gighay has disappeared behind Fuday 135° astern and begin to come round to northwest – not too promptly, to avoid Drover Rocks – until the south side of Lingay is in line with the peak of Ben Scrien (on Eriskay) bearing 087°, see *View D* (the views are taken from a 19th-century chart).

If conditions are such that the overfalls northeast of Fuday might be troublesome, pass ¼ mile southwest of Stack Islands with the east side of Lingay touching the west side of Orosay 327·5° until Corran Ban shows north of Fuday 277° (*View B*). Steer on that bearing for ½ mile then northwest to pick up the beacons on Fiaray 273° as above.

Washington Reef, on which the sea usually breaks although its least depth is 3·7 metres, lies around 2 miles north of Fiaray. Outer Hasgeir Fiaray which dries 2·4 metres lies 2 miles NNE of Fiaray but depending on the state of the sea a passage between Outer Hasgeir Fiaray and Washington Reef may be made by keeping the summit of Fuiay over the west side of Fuday 160° (see *View A*). The northeast points of Gighay and Fuday in line 138° and the southwest points of Lingay and Eriskay in line 124° provide additional checks on position, and the current chart recommends a bearing of 150° on the summit of Fuday. If the marks can be identified this passage will probably give an easier ride than by going outside Washington Reef.

From northwest if the marks (*View A*) can be identified take the passage east of Washington Reef, otherwise keep outwith the 20-metre contour until Lingay and Ben Scrien, Eriskay have been identified, and bring them into line bearing 087°. Keep on this line until past Fiaray then steer southeast toward the summit of Fuday until the beacons on Fiaray are in line astern 273°. Follow

round the northeast side of Fuday at a distance of about ¼ mile and steer for the northeast point of Gighay. As with all pilotage on the west side of the Outer Hebrides this depends heavily on good visibility.

Passage from Barra to South Uist

Chart

2770 (1:30,000). OS map *31*.

Tides

The northeast-going stream begins +0530 Ullapool (+0110 Dover). The southwest-going stream begins −0045 Ullapool (−0505 Dover).

Constant −0032 Ullapool (−0442 Dover)

Height in metres

MHWS	MHWN	MTL	MLWN	MLWS
4·2	3·2	2·5	1·8	0·6

Dangers and marks

Curachan, Red Rocks, and *Curachan* east cardinal light buoy (see above).

Binch Rock, at a depth of 3 metres 1½ miles south of Eriskay, is marked by a south cardinal buoy.

Galeac, 3 metres high, lies a mile north of Binch Rock buoy.

Roderick Rock, 3½ cables NNE of Galeac, dries 0·6 metre.

Hartamul, 25 metres high, lies 7 cables south of Ru Melvick, South Uist, with drying rocks up to 5 cables SSW and 2 cables northeast of it.

Directions

Pass ½ mile east of visible dangers and marks to clear those unseen; however the west side of Hartamul is cleaner and it can be passed on that side. Passages closer inshore are described in relation to individual anchorages.

Acairseid Mhor, Eriskay

57°04′N 7°18′W

Eriskay is a well populated island with a sheltered natural harbour on its east side. The main settlement at Haun at the north end of the island is difficult to approach through rocks and sandbanks in the Sound of Eriskay although there are light beacons for the benefit of the car ferry from South Uist; with the large-scale chart it might be possible to approach in quiet weather, but directions are only given for Acairseid Mhor.

Leading lights

Approach to Acairseid Mor, Eriskay.

Rock dr. 3·0m

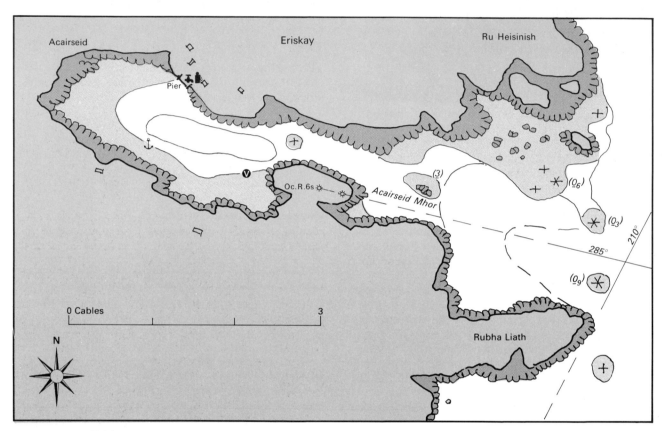

Acairseid Mor, Eriskay

Dangers and marks

Roderick Rock, south of the entrance, dries 0·6 metre.

Drying rocks in the entrance are shown on the plan.

Leading lights on columns which are not conspicuous by day lead between these rocks. Comhairle nan Eilean intend to incorporate daymarks on these beacons, probably by the time this is published.

At the narrows a reef dries along the south shore and a submerged rock lies in the middle of the west end at a depth of 1·2 metres.

Approach

From south either keeping at least ½ mile offshore until the leading beacons are identified, or pass west of Galeac and steer to pass ½ cable east of Grey Point (Rubha Liath) taking care not to stray

to the east, to avoid Roderick Rock. On passing Rubha Liath keep Rubha Meall nan Caorach and the east point of Stack Islands open of Rubha Liath astern 210° until on the leading line to avoid the rock which dries 0·9 metre. A traditional course is to keep close (30 metres) to Rubha Liath to pass south of the drying rock, then head for the north side of the promontory on which the leading beacons stand.

From north pass west of Hartamul, identify the entrance by houses but keep Stack Islands open of Rubha Liath 210° until the leading beacons are in line 285° to avoid drying rocks on the north side of the entrance.

Approach with the leading beacons in line 285° until close to the promontory on which they stand, and pass round its north side avoiding the rock which dries 3 metres. At low spring tides the rock in the middle of the narrows may be a hazard, at which time it is best passed on its north side.

Anchorage

Anchor as convenient clear of moorings and shoal water, but the bottom is soft mud and is reputed to be foul with old moorings. Long lines of floating boxes of shellfish are left swinging around moorings. HIDB visitors' moorings have been laid on the south side of the harbour. Landing is not easy from a dinghy, either on rocky shore or at ladders at the pier. Fishing boats lie at the pier at night.

Lights

Leading lights 285° Oc.R.6s4M
Flood lights at pier.

At night approach on leading lights 285°, beyond which (with care) the floodlight at the pier shows the way in.

Supplies

Shop, post office, pub/restaurant, telephone, all at Haun more than 1½ miles from the pier. Water tap and diesel at pier (it may be difficult to find anyone to dispense diesel fuel). Rubbish bins.

South Uist

Passage notes for the east shore of South Uist

Tides

Off Loch Boisdale tidal streams run at up to 2 knots off salient points. The north-going stream begins +0520 Ullapool (+0100 Dover). The south-going stream begins −0040 Ullapool (−0500 Dover).

At Rubha Melvick a tidal eddy causes a permanent set to southwest.

Dangers and marks

Clan Ewan Rock and other rocks extend ¼ mile off-shore ½ mile north of Rubha na h-Ordaig, which is 1¼ mile NNE of Ru Melvick.

McKenzie Rock, a mile north of Rubha na h-Ordaig, is marked by a red can light buoy. A rock at a depth of less than 2 metres lies ½ cable east of a direct line from Rubha na h-Ordaig to the light buoy.

Calvay Island, on the south side of the entrance to Loch Boisdale, has a white rectangular light beacon near its east end.

Stuley Island and rocks 3 cables east of the island lie 3 miles north of Calvay Island.

Usinish lighthouse, a white tower 12 metres in height, stands on a 40-metre cliff 10 miles north of Calvay Island.

Loch Boisdale

57°09′N 7°18′W

Charts

2770 (1:12,500). OS map *31*.

Tides

In Loch Boisdale the in-going stream begins +0530 Ullapool (+0110 Dover). The out-going stream begins −0045 Ullapool (−0505 Dover).

Constant −0045 Ullapool (−0455 Dover)

Height in metres

MHWS	MHWN	MTL	MLWN	MLWS
4·3	3·0	2·4	1·6	0·5

Dangers and marks

McKenzie Rock, ½ mile offshore, at a depth of 2·4 metres, is marked by a red can light buoy.

Calvay Island light beacon is a white rectangular structure. Drying rocks lie southeast and south of Calvay Island and submerged rocks lie up to 1½ cables WNW of the island.

Gasay Island, a mile WNW of Calvay Island has a white rectangular light beacon on its northeast side. Gasay Rock, nearly a cable east of Gasay Island, dries 0·9 metre.

Sgeir Rock, on the north side of the fairway north of Gasay at a depth of 1·2 metres, is marked on its south side by a green conical light buoy.

Rocks on the south side of the loch are described separately.

Lights

McKenzie Rock light buoy Fl(3)R.15s
Calvay Island light beacon Fl(2)WRG.10s16m7-4M, showing red over McKenzie Rock, and a narrow green sector towards submerged rocks at the north side of the entrance.
Gasay light beacon Fl.WR.5s10m7/4M shows red over Gasay Rock.
Light beacon on N shore, ENE of Gasay Q.G.3m3M
Sgeir Rock light buoy Fl.G.3s
Ferry terminal pier head Iso.RG.4s12m2M
Ferry terminal linkspan 2F.G(vert)

At night, approach in the white sector of Calvay light beacon, and in the white sector of Gasay light beacon, passing south of the Q.G light beacon and Fl.G.3s light buoy, then head towards the lights at the pier.

Anchorages

Bagh Dubh, southwest of the ferry terminal, is surrounded by drying reefs, occupied by moorings which sometimes cause foul anchors, and the bottom is soft mud. It is best used as a temporary anchorage to go ashore for stores. Take care to avoid obstructing approach to the ferry terminal. HIDB

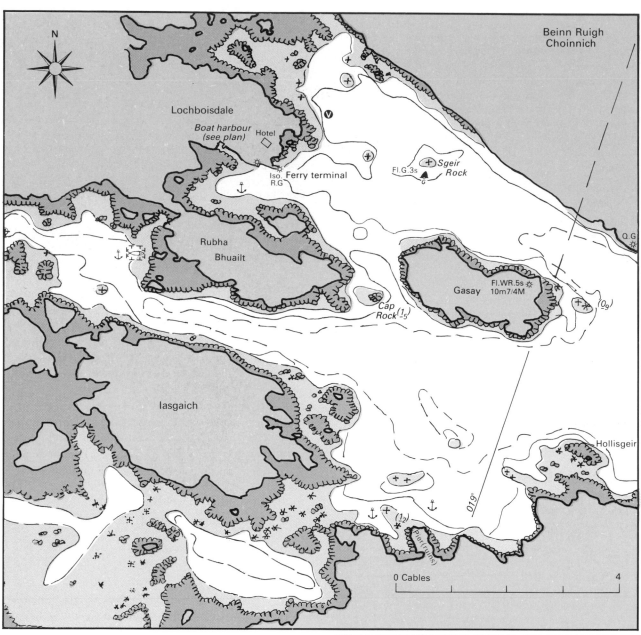

N

Beinn Ruigh
Choinnich

Lochboisdale

*Boat harbour
(see plan)* Hotel

Iso.
R.G Ferry terminal

Fl.G.3s *Sgeir
Rock*
G

Rubha
Bhuailt

Cap
Rock (1₅)

Gasay Fl.WR.5s
10m7/4M

(0g)

Q.G

Iasgaich

Hollisgeir

(1₂)

Pier (ruins)

019°

0 Cables   4

Loch Boisdale

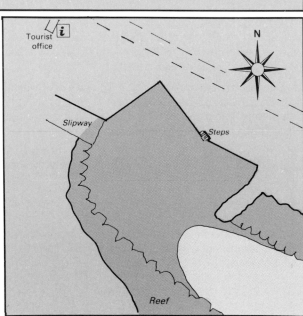

Tourist
office

N

Slipway

Steps

Reef

Lochboisdale boat harbour

Bagh Dubh, Loch Boisdale, from southeast showing reefs and, at top, the channel to the boat harbour.

visitors' moorings have been laid northeast of the ferry terminal.

A fishery pier stands in the northwest corner of the bay behind a breakwater the head of which dries at chart datum; a yacht of moderate draught might go alongside there at half flood. A reef extends on the southeast side of the approach as far as the west end of the linkspan leaving a narrow channel on its northeast side. Approach on a northwest course parallel to the face of the head of the breakwater.

Shop (including hardware), post office, telephone, hotel, bank. Petrol, diesel and car hire at garage (¼ mile). Water at boat harbour or from a large hose at the main pier. Cycle hire (cycles may be returned to Lochmaddy depot). Rubbish bins. Tourist information office.

Rubha Bhuailt A new fish cage has been moored in the anchorage west of the promontory and holding has been found to be poor. In the passage from Bagh Dubh, Cap Rock which dries 1·5 metres lies in mid-channel. Keep to Gasay side of channel until the south side of Gasay is open to avoid Cap Rock.

South Lochboisdale. Submerged and drying rocks lie up to ¾ cable off the south shore east of Hollisgeir, an extensive reef part of which is just above water. The east end of Gasay under the peak of Beinn Ruigh Choinnich 019° leads close west of rocks west of Hollisgeir.

A ruined jetty lies 3 cables WSW of Hollisgeir, with a drying rock close northwest of it, a shoal ¾ cable north of the jetty, and a 2-metre patch 1½ cables NNE of the jetty. Fish cages lie 1 cable east of the jetty. Anchor southeast of the fish cages or northwest of the ruined jetty.

Loch Eynort

57°13′N 7°16′W

A landlocked loch with a tortuous entrance in which the tide runs strongly and which should be treated with the greatest respect, although the scenery of the upper loch is worth the effort.

Chart

2825 (1:25,000). OS map *22*.

Tides

In the narrows of Sruthan Beag tidal streams run at up to 7 knots with eddies along both sides and overfalls in the channel. The in-going stream begins −0605 Ullapool (+0200 Dover). The out-going stream begins −0010 Ullapool (−0430 Dover). Both flood and ebb tides set obliquely across Bogha Dearg when it is covered.

Constant −0045 Ullapool (−0455 Dover)

Height in metres

MHWS	MHWN	MTL	MLWN	MLWS
4·3	3·0	2·4	1·6	0·5

Dangers and marks

In the outer loch, Na Dubh-sgeirean are islets above water off Eilean nan Gamhna off the south point of the entrance, with a drying reef ¼ cable northeast of them. Bogha Carrach which dries 3·5 metres, together with a patch of submerged rocks, lie 1½ cables offshore 4 cables WNW of Na Dubh-sgeirean. Still Rocks which dry 1·4 metres lie 4 cables further west.

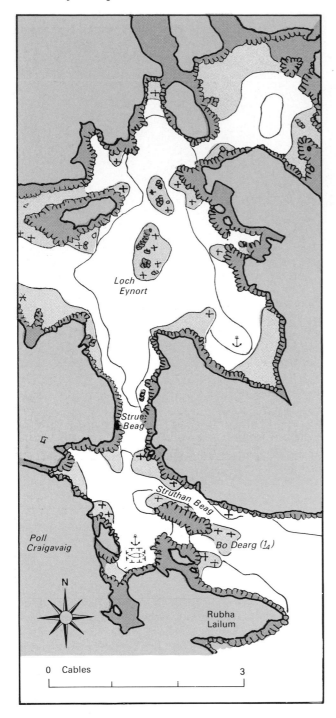

Anchorage

Anchor anywhere in the inner loch clear of rocks and fish cages, and in Poll Craigavaig at the narrows, but this is rather restricted by fish cages. Occasional anchorage in the outer loch on sand at Cearcdal Bay, in the southwest corner.

Loch Skiport

57°20′N 7°14′W

A popular, well sheltered and easily entered loch in spectacular surroundings under the slopes of Hecla.

Chart

2904 (1:25,000), *2825* (1:12,500). OS map *22*.

Tides

Tidal streams are slight except in narrow channels, including the entrance to Linne Arm. The in-going stream begins +0545 Ullapool (+0125 Dover). The out-going stream begins −0035 Ullapool (−0455 Dover).

Constant −0052 Ullapool (−0602 Dover)

Height in metres

MHWS	MHWN	MTL	MLWN	MLWS
4·6	3·3	2·5	1·7	0·5

Anchorages

Wizard Pool is the first anchorage on the south side. Float Rock between Shillay Mor and Ornish dries 2·3 metres. To avoid it steer towards Shillay Mor until within less than a cable. Pass the east end of Shillay Beag to the west of mid-channel to avoid drying rocks off Ornish and then closer to Wizard Island to avoid a drying rock east of the south end of Shillay Beag. Anchor anywhere around the sides of the pool. The bay on the southeast side of Shillay Beag provides some shelter from northeasterly swell; in southerly gales fierce gusts come down from Hecla. Water may be had from a burn south of Wizard Island.

Caolas Mor, otherwise known as Little Kettle Pool, has submerged rocks at a depth of about 1 metre in the middle and on the west side (about 0·3 metre), and fish cages on its south side. The pool can be entered from the west or by the narrow channel from Wizard Pool, but a depth of only 1·3 metres is shown on the chart at the south side of its west end.

Bagh Charmaig on the north side of the loch to the west of Shillay Mor has a bottom of soft mud. When visited in 1989 the southwest side was obstructed by fishing floats. An old stone slip stands in the northwest corner.

Poll na Cairidh in the southwest corner of the loch has drying rocks over a cable from the shore but they are easily avoided by keeping outwith the 5-metre line; this bay has been found to provide excellent shelter in a southerly gale.

Bogha Coilenish, ½ cable southeast of Rubha Coilenish on the north side of the loch opposite Bogha Carrach, dries 0·5 metre.

In the narrows Bogha Dearg dries 1·4 metres. Drying rocks extend from the east side of Strue Beag.

Directions

The narrows should only be attempted at or just before high or low slack water; the deeper and cleaner passage is to the north of Bogha Dearg.

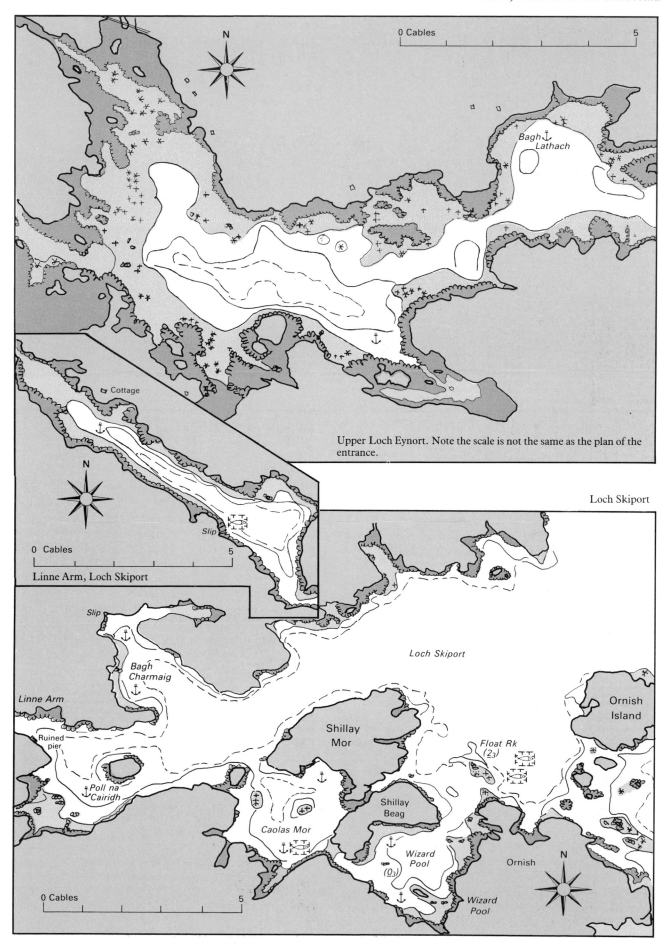

N

0 Cables   5

Bagh Lathach

Upper Loch Eynort. Note the scale is not the same as the plan of the entrance.

Cottage

N

0 Cables   5

Slip

Linne Arm, Loch Skiport

Loch Skiport

Slip

Loch Skiport

Bagh Charmaig

Linne Arm

Ornish Island

Ruined pier

Shillay Mor

Float Rk (2₃)

Poll na Cairidh

Shillay Beag

Caolas Mor

Wizard Pool (0₃)

Ornish

N

Wizard Pool

0 Cables   5

27

Loch Skiport from east side of Wizard Pool; Wizard Island in foreground and Caolas Mor beyond.

Loch Sheilavaig and Caolas Luirsay

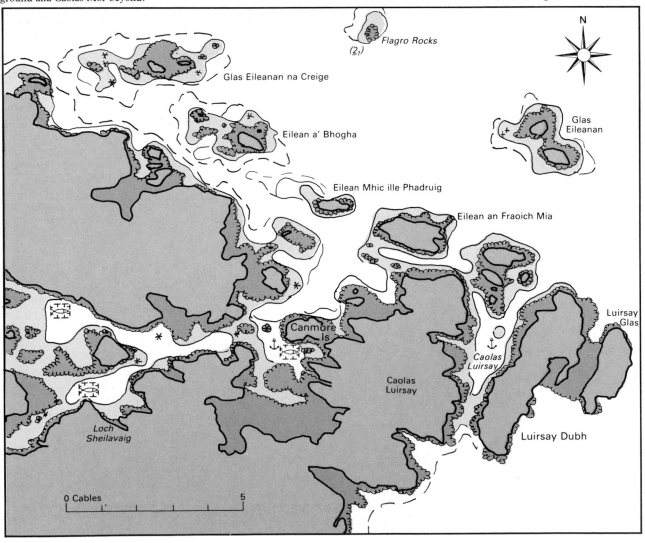

Linne Arm is virtually landlocked but the surroundings are less shut in by hills. The pier at the entrance is ruined and there are extensive fish cages on the south shore with a new slip from which they are serviced; water might be had there. A phone box stands ¼ mile from the slip. Holding in Linne Arm has been found to be poor.

Caolas Luirsay, a pool on the west side of Luirsay Dubh at the north entrance to Loch Skiport, can be entered from south or by a narrow channel from northeast, but is affected by swell in northerly winds. A submerged rock at the north end of the pool extends over a considerable area and is best passed on its east side.

Loch Sheilavaig, ½ mile west of Caolas Luirsay, is a rather featureless loch with many fish cages in it, but it is full of rocks and provides an interesting challenge. The fish farm operators regard the loch as their private property. The entrance, between Eilean Mhic ille Phadruig and Eilean an Fraoich Mia, is most easily found by taking a bearing astern on Glas-Eileanan (062°). Pass about 50 metres west of Canmore Island to pass east of a drying rock ½ cable from the island as well as a shallow rocky patch which extends almost to the west shore of the narrows, and anchor south of the island.

Passage notes – South Uist to North Uist

Tides

The north-going stream begins +0550 Ullapool (+0130 Dover). The south-going stream begins −0010 Ullapool (−0430 Dover) at a spring rate of 1½ knots off salient points.

Dangers and marks

The principal landmarks are the hills: Hecla (606 metres) on South Uist, Beinn a' Tuath, Wiay (102 metres), Beinn a' Charnain, Ronay (115 metres), and Eaval (347 metres) on North Uist, conspicuously wedge-shaped from east, provide some guide as to position.

A landfall buoy (RW pillar, 57°22'·3N 7°11'·4W) lies in the mouth of Bagh nam Faoileann between South Uist and Wiay. The power station at Loch Carnan with two chimneys is conspicuous.

Greanamul Deas, a prominent islet 10 metres high is 6 cables north of the northeast point of Wiay; Bo Greanamul with a depth of 2·1 metres lies 4 cables ESE of Greanamul Deas. Luirsay Glas well open of Wiay 193° leads east of Greanamul Deas.

Ritchie Rock lies 3½ cables off the east side of Ronay at a depth of 0·6 metre. Rueval, a prominent hill on Benbecula, 123 metres high, open south of Rubha na Rodagrich 263° leads south of Ritchie Rock, and Madadh Mor, off the entrance to Loch Maddy, open east of Floddaymore 013° leads close east of it.

Loch Carnan

57°22'N 7°17'W

The power station for the Uists with its oil terminal stands here and it has little other interest, but it does have the merit of a buoyed and lit approach. A few yachts are kept on moorings there. The power station, a long rectangular building with two chimneys, is conspicuous.

Charts

2904 (1:25,000), *2825* (1:12,500). OS map *22*.

Tides

The in-going stream begins +0535 Ullapool (+0115 Dover). The out-going stream begins −0025 Ullapool (−0445 Dover).

Constant −0020 Ullapool (−0440 Dover) at springs; −0110 Ullapool (−0530 Dover) at neaps.

Height in metres

MHWS	MHWN	MTL	MLWN	MLWS
4·5	3·2	2·6	1·9	0·7

Directions

It is possible to approach by the south of Gasay, but each island must be correctly identified to avoid various hazards. The key to this passage is the most southerly islet on the north side of the passage, 3 metres in height and well separated from the other islets south of Gasay. The main hazards are a rock which dries 0·6 metre a cable northeast of Glas-Eilean na Creig and a submerged rock at a depth of 1·2 metres a cable southwest of the 3-metre islet.

Pass south of Glas-Eileanan and ¼ mile outside the string of islands along the south shore heading towards Gasay, to pass between Flagro Rocks, ½ mile WNW of Glas-Eileanan, and drying reefs north of Glas-Eilean na Creig. Steer for the 3-metre islet and pass south of it, and from there towards the oil wharf.

For the buoyed channel identify *Outer No. 1* buoy, pass north of it and pass subsequent buoys on the appropriate hand. Approaching from north keep 2 cables off Dubh Sgeir a' Tuath and Dubh Sgeir a' Deas, each 1 metre high and lying 2 cables from the southeast shore of Wiay, to avoid drying and submerged rocks to seaward of them.

Buoys further north and northwest in Bagh nam Faoileann are for the use of army landing craft which operate from South Ford, and should not be confused with the Loch Carnan approach buoys.

The oil terminal wharf is piled, but a little to the west is a plain concrete jetty which may be easier to go alongside. Anchor clear of the fairway and moorings; the inlets west and southwest of Direy are beset by drying rocks, but space can be found among them further from the industrial surroundings. HIDB visitors' moorings have been laid south of Direy.

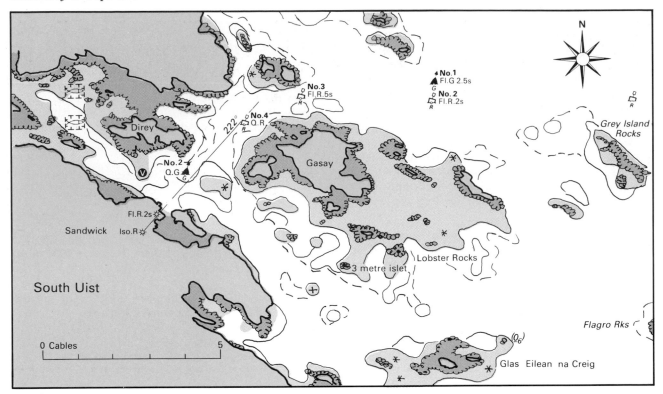

Loch Carnan

Lights

Landfall buoy LFl.10s
Outer No. 1 Fl.R.3s
Inner No. 1 Fl.G.2·5s
No. 2 Fl.R.2s
No. 3 Fl.R.5s
Leading lights 222°
    front Fl.R.2s7m, rear Iso.R.10s11m5M
No. 4 Q.R
No. 2 Q.G (green conical)

At night follow the buoyed channel taking care to avoid confusion with buoys in South Ford, of which the outermost, north of Sgeir a' Choin, is lit Q.R.

Supplies

Diesel is available at the oil terminal wharf; ask at office on the wharf. Phone box by derelict cottage 100 metres up track from pier.

Benbecula anchorages

For a small shoal-draught boat a fascinating network of inner channels extends over a distance of about ten miles from south to north.

Chart

2904 (1:25,000) gives as much detail for many of these anchorages as could be provided by a pilot, so it is not duplicated here except where additional detail can be included, and that chart should be carried. The obsolete fathoms chart *3168*, a fine 19th-century engraving, shows some further detail. OS map *22*.

Tides

Constant −0052 Ullapool (−0602 Dover)

Height in metres

MHWS	MHWN	MTL	MLWN	MLWS
4·6	3·3	2·5	1·7	0·5

Peter's Port

57°23'·4N 7°14'·4W

Directions

Identify by reference to Beinn a' Tuath on Wiay, the highest hill on the east shore between South Uist and Ronay. Approaching from north keep 2 cables off both Dubh Sgeir rocks, both 1 metre high, to avoid drying and submerged rocks to seaward of them.

Bogha Ruadh at the east side of the entrance lies a cable southwest of a group of islets and reefs south of Wiay and Cleit nan Luch is a small islet on the west side of the entrance. The south tangent of Lingay open south of Cleit nan Luch 286° clears Bogha Ruadh. Pass north of Cleit nan Luch and Lingay and south of Cleit Charmaig and anchor as convenient clear of the approach to the new slip which is used by fishing boats. A reef lies parallel with the south face of the slip and 15 metres from it.

The wreck shown on the plan appears to be on the southeast side of the rock which dries 1·4 metres and not as shown on the Admiralty chart, and it would be unwise to pass west and north of the rocks west of Cleit Charmaig even if the wreck is uncovered, without careful investigation.

Sruth Chomhraig, on the north side of Peter's Port, is lined with fish cages on its west side and drying rocks on the east side.

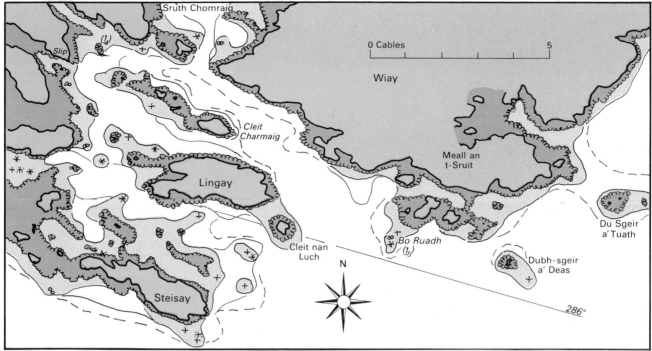

Peter's Port

Loch a' Laip

57°24'·7N 7°12'W

Identify by reference to Greanamul Deas (see *Passage notes* above, page 29) and enter by the north side of Bo' Carrach heading 230° for the south shore to avoid rocks on the north side of the entrance. A submerged rock north of the drying rock in the mouth of Bagh a' Bhraoige is avoided by keeping Rubha Cam nan Gall open north of the un-named point 3 cables west of it 090°. There are fish cages in several parts of the loch, in particular in Bagh a' Bhraoige, formerly the most suitable anchorage; otherwise there is nothing to add to the information on the chart.

Loch Keiravagh

Entered ¼ mile north of Loch a' Laip and more straightforward. Apart from obvious drying rocks, submerged rocks showing on the chart on either side of the entrance should be noted.

Loch Uskavagh

57°26'·5N 7°13'W

It may not be possible to identify the 'white house (ruins)' shown on the chart, and the approach is best made at low tide when some of the most hazardous rocks show. Sgeir na Geadh at the north side of the narrows is fairly easy to identify; approach with Sgeir na Geadh bearing 270°. Once through the narrows the tangents of Orasay Uskavagh and Maaey Riabhach on the south side of the loch in line astern 105° lead clear of hidden dangers. Neavag Bay on the north side of the loch is well sheltered but the bottom is very soft mud. Other anchorages can be found in moderate depths around the shores of the main part of the loch.

Kallin

57°29'N 7°12'W

A small community principally occupied with lobster fishing; boats from Kallin pass regularly under a bridge in the causeway at North Ford to work on the Atlantic coast except for the newest and largest boats which have to go round by the Sound of Harris.

Tides

The in-going stream begins +0535 Ullapool (+0115 Dover). The out-going stream begins −0025 Ullapool (−0445 Dover).

Constant −0040 Ullapool (−0500 Dover)

Height in metres

MHWS	MHWN	MTL	MLWN	MLWS
4·8	3·6	2·8	1·9	0·7

Dangers and marks

Bogha Mor, 4 cables SSW of Rubha na Rodagrich on Ronay, dries 3 metres, and Morrison's Rock lies 3 cables ESE of Bogha Mor at a depth of 2·8 metres. Other drying rocks lie 2 cables south and southwest of Rubha na Monach, the southwest point of Ronay, and drying reefs extend ½ cable southwest of that point.

Light buoys have recently been installed approximately as shown on the plan. Their actual positions may differ from those shown, as the plan is based on advance information.

White cottage

Garbh Eilean Beag

Garbh Eilean Mor

Vallastrome and approach to Kallin harbour.

Kallin harbour.

Kallin from Ronay. The pool north of St Michael's Point is at upper left, and Vallastrome upper right. Sugar Bay is left of islands
in foreground.

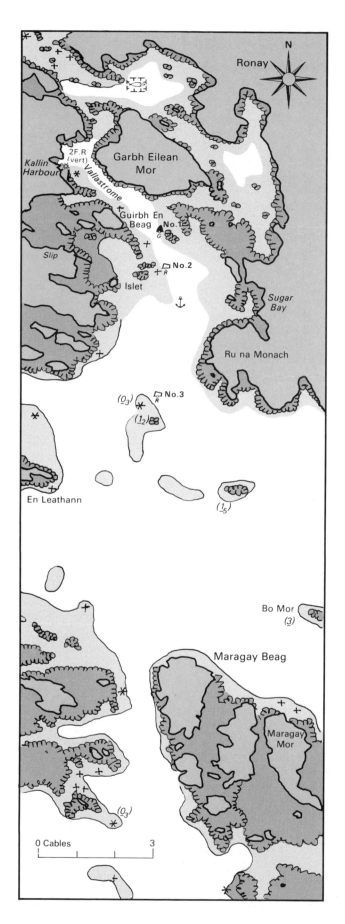

Approaches to Kallin.

Directions

From south keep the summit of Beinn a' Tuath open of the east side of Greanamul astern 200° to clear Morrison's Rock. Turn to pass 1 cable off the south points of Ronay to avoid the detached drying rocks and the reef southwest of Rubha na Monach. Pass northeast of *No. 3* red can light buoy.

Alternatively pass west of the Maragay islands heading for the east end of Eilean Leathann, but the clear passage is only ½ cable wide, and a submerged rock lies a cable east of Eilean Leathann. Pass midway between *No. 3* red can light buoy and islets off St Michael's Point to port.

From north keep ½ mile off the east side of Ronay to avoid Ritchie's Rock (for clearing marks see *Passage notes* above, page 29) and pass a cable south of Ronay as above.

Lights

No. 3 light buoy
No. 2 light buoy
No. 1 light buoy
Harbour entrance, southeast side, 2F.R(vert)

Anchorages

Anchor in the basin between Ronay and Grimsay. Shoal-draught yachts, and others at neaps, might anchor in a pool north of the islet north of St Michael's Point; pass 20 metres northeast of the islet to avoid the drying reef which extends south from Gairbh-Eilean Beag. Land at a slip WNW of the islet. In easterly winds yachts can anchor close to Ronay in the mouth of Sugar Bay.

The small harbour in the southwest corner of Vallastrome, the channel north of Gairbh-Eilean Beag, has depths of 2·5 metres inside and 1·7 metres in the entrance; drying rocks lie on both sides of the entrance to Vallastrome, marked by light buoys as above. A conspicuous white cottage open northeast of Gairbh-Eilean Beag 309° leads between these rocks, but after passing the rock to starboard keep in mid-channel. The tide runs strongly in Vallastrome and care is needed when turning in to the harbour; it is very small and often becomes full to capacity and a yacht is unlikely to be able to remain overnight, but it is a useful source of water and fuel. It is possible to anchor in Vallastrome, but the tide runs strongly and the fairway must not be obstructed.

Supplies

Water tap at harbour. Diesel at harbour, enquire locally but don't expect anyone to be waiting to serve you. Yachts are supplied as a favour, although local fishermen are far too courteous to make you aware of this. Limited fishermen's chandlery. Mains electricity outlet at harbour. Travelling shop twice weekly.

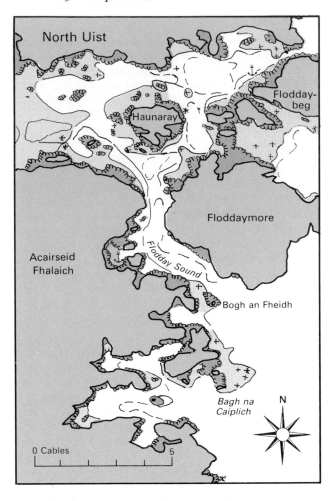

Flodday Sound

Flodday Sound

57°30′N 7°10′W

Directions

Approaching from south keep ½ mile off Ronay to avoid Ritchie Rock (for clearing marks see *Passage notes* above, page 29). Enter by the channel southwest of Floddaymore. The tide runs briskly in Flodday Sound.

Anchorages

Acairseid Fhalaich on the west side of the sound can be entered through a narrow steep-sided channel between the two islets at the entrance, and there appears (from a brief visit) to be clear depth and swinging room within. Although the current chart shows the entrance to be blocked by drying rocks, the previous chart showed depths of 2 fathoms there, which appears to be correct. The bottom is probably very soft mud as there is no scour to disturb it.

Anchorages east of Haunaray are reasonably straightforward to approach, but at low tide two submerged rocks in the passage southeast of Haunaray could be a hazard.

Fishing boats use the channel north of Floddaybeg but a rock in the middle of its west end just dries, and submerged rocks lie further west.

Entrance to Flodday Sound from southeast; Acairseid Fhalaich is at top left.

II. North Uist and the Sound of Harris

For crossing from Mull and the mainland see Chapter I.

North Uist

Tides

The north-going stream begins −0550 Ullapool (+0215 Dover). The south-going stream begins +0035 Ullapool (−0345 Dover) at a spring rate of 2 knots off salient points.

Dangers

The coast is free from hidden dangers.

Loch Eport

57°33′N 7°10′W

The position of Loch Eport is found by reference to Eaval, the wedge-shaped hill 1½ miles south of the entrance.

Charts

2825 (1:15,000) does not cover the head of the loch and that section of the plan here is taken from a 19th-century chart, and a recent survey by the Brathay Exploration Group. OS map *18*.

Tides

The in-going stream begins +0550 Ullapool (+0130 Dover). The out-going stream begins −0020 Ullapool (−0440 Dover).

Constant −0040 Ullapool (−0500 Dover)

Height in metres

MHWS	MHWN	MTL	MLWN	MLWS
4·8	3·6	2·8	1·9	0·7

Dangers and marks

Bo Lea, 2 metres high, stands on the south side of the entrance with drying rocks further west. The entrance channel is clean but the inner parts of the loch are full of rocks.

Directions

The north point of the entrance just open of McCalter Island (Eilean Mhic Shealtair) on the south side of the channel 082° astern clears all rocks as far as One Stone Rock.

Anchorages

The principal anchorages are on either side of the loch immediately west of the narrow entrance channel.

Bagh a' Bhiorain on the south side is entered between Riffag Mhor, at the west end of which lies a drying wreck, and Riffag Beag, a drying reef at the west side of the entrance with an islet on its east end. A cairn on a rock near the head of the bay in line with a white boulder on the hillside 129° leads between these obstructions, but if this line is not seen pass close northeast of Riffag Beag. Anchor between the cairn and the east shore of the bay.

Acairseid Lee on the north side of the loch is less sheltered. It is best approached when Sgeir n' Iolla which dries 4 metres, about 1¼ cable southwest of the east point of the entrance, is showing. A rock drying 2·7 metres stands at the south end of a reef which extends ½ cable south from the shore northeast of Deer Island. Anchor near the east shore, or either side of Deer Island. The holding has been found to be poor, with weed and soft mud.

Upper loch

To go further up the loch needs great care: if One Stone Rock is showing it may be passed on its south side; then keep about half a cable off the south shore as far as Eilean Fhearghuis, after which keep about half a cable from the north side. A drying reef extends south from the east end of Steisay over halfway across the channel. After Steisay there are patches with depths of 1 metre but no submerged rocks in the fairway as far as Locheport pier.

It is possible to anchor 2 cables from the pier at the head of the loch in a small pool in 2 metres, soft mud, or to the northeast of Eilean a' Cairidh in 4 metres. Other anchorages may be found with chart *2825*, although it does not cover the head of the loch.

Supplies

Shop at Clachan, 1 mile west from pier.

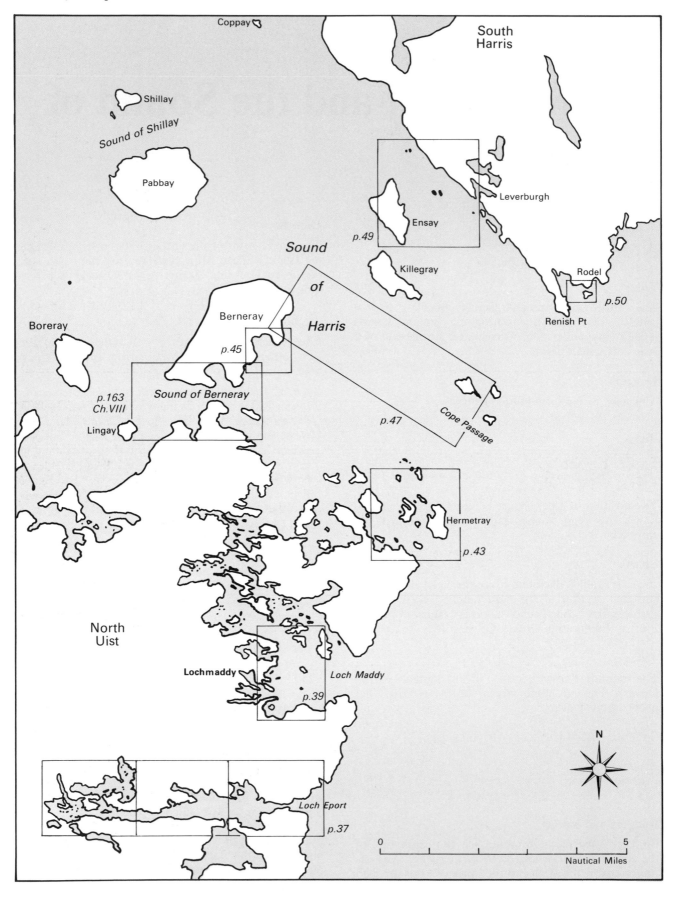

Coppay

South
Harris

Shillay

Sound of Shillay

Pabbay

Leverburgh

Sound

Ensay

p.49

of

Killegray

Rodel

Harris

p.50

Boreray

Berneray

Renish Pt

p.45

p.163
Ch.VIII

Sound of Berneray

Cope Passage

p.47

Lingay

Hermetray

p.43

North
Uist

Lochmaddy

Loch Maddy

p.39

N

Loch Eport

p.37

0   5

Nautical Miles

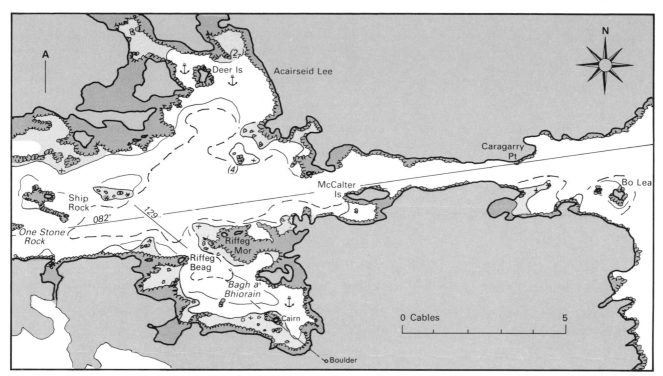

Loch Eport entrance

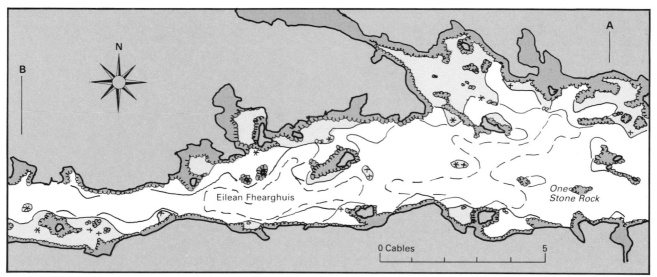

Loch Eport middle part

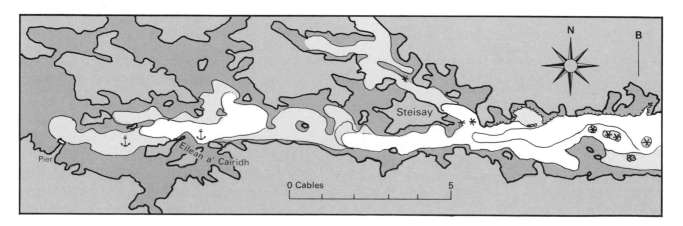

Loch Eport head

Loch Maddy

57°36′N 7°08′W

A broad loch littered with islands and rocks but well marked and lit for the needs of car ferries. Loch Maddy is identified by the gap in the hills at the entrance, and the conspicuous angular islets, Madadh Mor and Madadh Gruamach on the south side of the entrance and Madadh Beag on the north side, as well as the small light beacon on Weaver's Point at the north of the entrance.

Chart

2825 (1:12,500). OS map *18*.

Tides

The in-going stream begins +0555 Ullapool (+0135 Dover). The out-going stream begins −0025 Ullapool (−0445 Dover). Owing to the influence of the tidal streams along the coast, the in-going stream turns to run northeast between Weaver's Point and Madadh Beag, and the out-going stream sets strongly along the south shore.

Constant −0040 Ullapool (−0500 Dover)

Height in metres

MHWS	MHWN	MTL	MLWN	MLWS
4·8	3·6	2·8	1·9	0·7

Approach

Heavy seas may be encountered off the entrance when wind and tide are opposed, especially close to either point, and it is best to approach in mid-channel.

Dangers and marks

A small white light beacon stands on Weaver's Point, the north side of the entrance. Other light beacons are so inconspicuous that they do not serve as useful daymarks.

Glas Eilean Mor, within the south side of the entrance, has drying reefs up to a cable off its west side.

Faihore and Ruigh Liath lie about a mile west of Glas Eilean Mor with reefs all round them. The main fairway is south of these islets and an unlit red perch stands at the outer edge of reefs off the south shore of the loch. A red buoy lies northwest of Faihore.

Directions

For the anchorage at the ferry terminal, pass either south or not less than a cable north of Glas Eilean Mor and either south of Ruigh Liath or north of the red buoy which lies northwest of Faihore.

Loch Maddy entrance from southwest; Ardmaddy Bay in foreground.

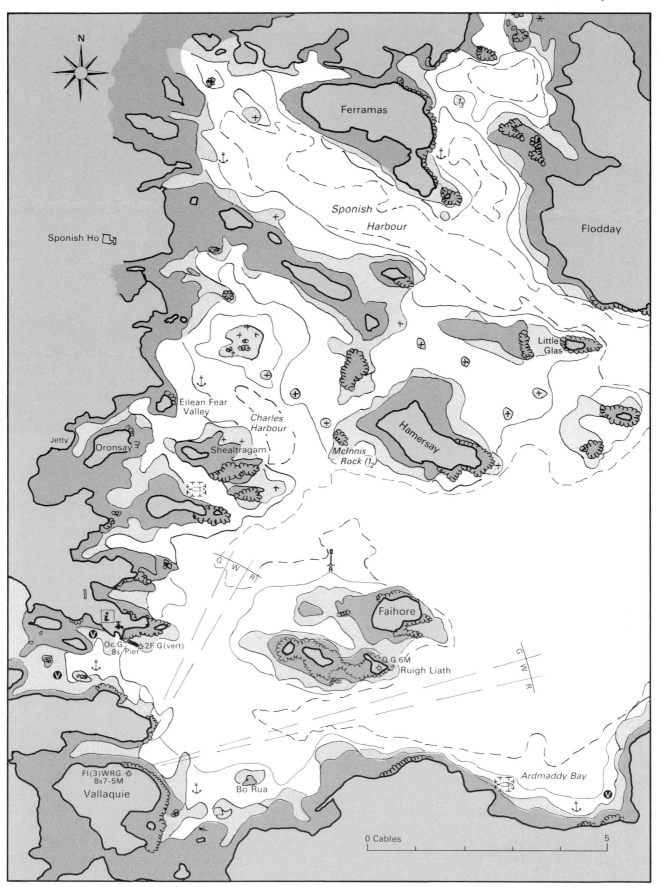

Loch Maddy inner part

Loch Maddy from south; Faihore and Ruigh Liath left of centre.

Lights

Weaver's Point light beacon Fl.3s21m7M
Glas Eilean Mor Fl(2)6s8m
Ardmaddy Point light beacon Fl.R.4s7m5M
Ruigh Liath light beacon Q.G.6m
Vallaquie Island light beacon Fl(3)WRG.8s11m7-5M
Ferry terminal leading lights 298° 284°-vis-304°
   front 2F.G(vert)8m4M
   rear Oc.G.8s10m4M

Anchorages

South of the pier clear of approach to the linkspan, or southwest of the nearest islet, clear of the two drying reefs. HIDB moorings have been laid; 2 in Ardmaddy Bay, 2 west of the ferry terminal, and 4 south of the island west of the terminal. Landing at concrete steps west of the linkspan.

Shops, post office, telephone, bank, hotel (showers/ baths). Petrol and diesel at garage, water hose at pier, *Calor Gas* (ask at tourist office). Cycle hire (cycles may be returned to Lochboisdale). Piermaster (VHF Ch 12).

Ardmaddy Bay (Bagh Aird nam Madadh) on the south shore tends to be squally in southerly winds, and fish cages lie on the west side of the bay.

Vallaquie, 4 cables SSE of ferry terminal. An old large mooring buoy lies in the middle of the bay northeast of Vallaquie Island, with Bo Rua, which dries 0·8 metre, to the east of it. A wreck which covers, and two drying rocks, lie towards the head of the bay; there is space to anchor between the mooring buoy and the wreck, but a submerged reef extends a cable north from the east end of Vallaquie, and fish cages lie at the west side of the bay.

Charles Harbour, northwest of Hamersay, is obstructed by drying and submerged rocks and fish cages and much of the bottom is either rock or soft mud; the best anchorage is northeast of Eilean Fear Vallay. Approach from southeast, keeping 1½ cables off Hamersay to avoid McInnis Rock which dries 3·2 metres, heading for Sponish House a conspicuous 3-storey building until east of Eilean Fear Vallay, then turn west towards anchorage.

Oronsay Island shelters a pool with a stone jetty where local boats are moored but there is little space for visiting yachts; those prepared to take the ground on soft mud might anchor southwest of the moorings. Approach by the north of Shealtragam and between Eilean Fear Vallay and Oronsay. Water at jetty.

Sponish Harbour is cleaner than Charles Harbour, but the holding is also poor. Enter between Flodday, a large island on the northeast side of the loch, and Little Glas, less than a cable off its south side.

Ferramas On the west side of the pool between Flodday and Ferramas. The best shelter is northeast of Ferramas, but drying reefs extend over 1½ cables northwest from Flodday, and a submerged rock lies ½ cable east of the northeast point of Ferramas.

Loch Portain (Partan), the northeast arm of Loch Maddy is well sheltered, especially east of the islet but the bottom is soft mud in which some boats find it difficult to get an anchor to hold, and all sides are shoal. Approach by the east side of Flodday; Mackay Rock ¾ cable from the east side of the channel dries 0·7 metre but it is well clear of the fairway. At the northeast point of Flodday the channel is a cable wide, but drying boulder banks reduce it to 1/3 cable. The channel is again reduced to ¼ cable between the northeast shore and a small islet ½ mile further northwest, and a drying bank extends ½ cable west from Rubha nan Gall, the southeast point of Loch Portain, which lies ENE of the point.

A submerged rock spit extends over ¾ cable south from the shore north of Rubha nan Gall, leaving a clear passage less than ½ cable wide south of it. An islet in the middle of the loch 3 cables northeast of Rubha nan Gall is connected to the north shore by a drying reef; drying and submerged rocks lie 1 cable west of the islet; pass south of the islet and anchor not more than 2 cables beyond it, south of a small stone slip.

Post office, telephone, small shop.

Oronsay pool from south.

Lochmaddy Pier from southeast; note drying rocks in bay at left.

Sound of Harris

Caution

The Sound of Harris is a maze of rocks and islets and shallow passages; neither of the two through passages should be taken by yachts except in settled moderate weather using a large-scale chart, and even in light winds a very heavy sea may be met at the northwest end of the sound.

Charts

2642 (1:20,000). Hermetray anchorages could be approached with chart *1795* (1:100,000). *2481* (1:50,000) serves for the Stanton Passage and the northwest end of the sound. OS map *18*.

Tides

Tidal streams throughout the Sound of Harris are very variable not only between springs and neaps, but also between day and night and between summer and winter. The notes here should only be taken as a rough guide.

Passage notes between Skye and the Sound of Harris

Crossing the Little Minch from Skye to the Sound of Harris is straightforward in moderate weather. For Neist Point on the WSW of Skye see Chapter III, and for Rubha Hunish at the north point of Skye see Chapter V. Shelter on the west side of Skye may be found at Loch Dunvegan, Loch Snizort and, in some winds, Duntulm Bay. Prawn creel buoys are scattered all over the Minch. International traffic uses the Minch, and a good lookout should be kept for commercial vessels.

Tidal streams in the Little Minch

Off Vaternish Point tidal streams run at a maximum of 2½ knots; the northeast-going stream begins −0350 Ullapool (+0415 Dover), the south-going stream begins +0235 Ullapool (−0145 Dover).

Off the east coast of North Uist the tidal streams run at a maximum of 2 knots; the north-going stream begins −0550 Ullapool (+0215 Dover), the south-going stream begins +0035 Ullapool (−0345 Dover).

Constant −0040 Ullapool (−0500 Dover)

Height in metres

MHWS	MHWN	MTL	MLWN	MLWS
4·6	3·5	2·6	1·9	0·6

Dangers and marks at the southeast entrance to the Sound of Harris

Although there are many drying and submerged rocks further west, no concealed dangers extend beyond ½ cable from any of the islands at the southeast

end of the sound. The individual islands however are not easy to distinguish. Crogary na Hoe, the northeast point of North Uist, is conspicuous. Cope Passage *Fairway* buoy (RW) is 2¼ miles northeast of Crogary na Hoe. Dun-aarin on the east side of the southeast approach to the Stanton Channel is conspicuously angular.

Lights

Weaver's Point, Loch Maddy Fl.3s21m7M
Fairway Buoy LFl.10s
Eilean Glas, Scalpay Fl(3)20s43m23M

Light beacons at Leverburgh (see page 50 below) may provide some guidance.

Anchorages and passages on the southwest side of the sound

Hermetray Group

57°39′·5N 7°04′W

Hermetray is the most southeasterly island in the Sound of Harris with Vaccasay on its west side. Several sheltered and easily accessible anchorages lie within a mile of Vaccasay. Tahay (64 metres), west of Vaccasay is the highest island of the group.

Tides

Tidal streams among the Hermetray Group run as follows: the southeast-going stream begins about −0535 Ullapool (+0230 Dover); the northwest-going stream begins +0035 Ullapool (+0345 Dover).

Directions

Approach from southeast Drying reefs extend a cable south of Hermetray, and Angus Rock, a cable north of Groatay on the south side of the channel, dries 3 metres. Pass midway between Hermetray and Groatay, and when the east end of Groatay is abeam bring the summit of the Righe nam Ban group of islands ahead in line with Beinn Mhor 282° to pass north of Angus Rock as well as Mary Rock over which the depth is 2·1 metres.

From northeast, identify *Fairway* buoy, then Greanem, ½ mile southwest of it. Greanem can be passed on either side. Pass midway between State Rock and Staffin Skerry which, in contrast to other rocks in the area, is sharp and angular. To enter Vaccasay Basin pass west of Staffin Skerry and midway between the skerry and Hulmetray.

Anchorages

Vaccasay Basin Dirt Rock, a cable east of Vaccasay, dries 3 metres, and fish cages are moored south of it. Stanley Rock over which the depth is 1·8 metres lies a cable northeast of Fuam at the south end of

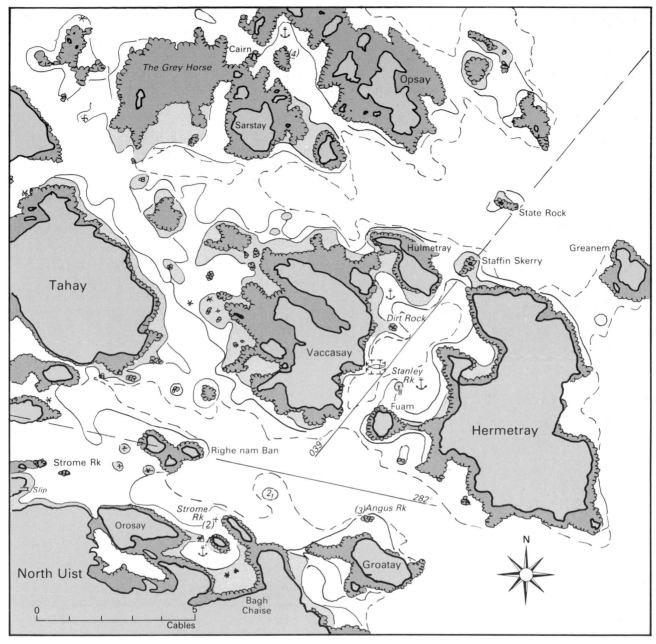

Hermetray Group

the basin. Staffin Skerry in line with the southeast point of Scaravay, the most southeasterly island north of Cope Passage, bearing 039°, clears both these rocks. Anchor in the northwest or southeast corners of the basin; shoal-draught boats can anchor in the inlet on Hermetray known as Acairseid Mor, but this is shallow and rather constricted, with weed on the bottom, although the innermost part of the inlet is said to be free of weed.

Bagh Chaise on North Uist lies southeast of Orasay, south of Righe nam Ban. Drying reefs extend ½ cable east of Orasay; a detached rock which dries 1 metre lies just east of the middle of the entrance, and a reef extends over ¼ cable ESE from Orasay. Drying rocks lie over ½ cable from the south shore. This bay is regarded as having the best shelter and best holding in the area.

Orasay (the Caddy), off a concrete slip on North Uist WNW of Orasay. Approach by the south of Righe nam Ban, keeping closer to Orasay, and look out for Strome Rock which dries 2 metres, over a cable northeast of the slip.

Limited supplies at Loch Portain, nearly 2 miles by road from the slip.

Opsay Basin (57°40′·5N 7°04′·3W), ¾ mile north of Vaccasay, is entered from southeast. All sides of the basin are fringed by drying reefs and the only mark is the cairn on Grey Horse Island at the west side of the basin. The best anchorage is northeast of a drying reef in the middle of the basin east of the cairn.

Bagh Chaise entrance from east.

Southeast end of Grey Horse Channel, looking southeast: Grey Horse Island on the right with the highest point of Hermetray beyond.

Grey Horse Channel

Grey Horse Channel runs through an area of shoals and drying banks and rocks from Opsay Basin towards Bays Loch, Berneray and should only be considered by experienced rock-dodgers. For the first two miles the passage is completely unmarked, after which some guidance may be found from buoys which mark a tortuous channel from Cope Passage to Bays Loch. The existence of these buoys should not be relied on; if using the channel call *Endeavour*, the Berneray ferry, on VHF for advice.

Grey Horse Channel should be taken on a rising tide with no swell, a light, preferably following, wind and the sun (if any) aft of the beam. The tide runs strongly across the passage and such marks as there are must be constantly watched to check that the yacht is not being carried sideways. The passage is easier if started at low water when at least some of the dangers are visible.

From Opsay Basin, pass north of the Grey Horse. A leading line for the next 1¼ miles is the highest point of Hermetray astern over the centre of the channel north of the Grey Horse 135°, but for the first cable keep south of this line to avoid a drying reef on the north side.

Sgeir a' Chruinn, which lies close south of the leading line 1¼ miles northwest of the Grey Horse, is just covered at half tide and shows white under water. After a further ½ mile West Rock (Sgeir a' Siar), which dries 2·1 metres should be left 1½ cables to port and for a mile beyond West Rock the depth varies from nil to 1 metre; after passing West Rock steer to pass south of a starboard-hand light buoy (*No. 3*) ½ mile WNW of West Rock. As one experienced yachtsman put it: 'A moment's lack of concentration could lead to unwanted problems.'

Drowning Rock, nearly a mile northwest of *No. 3* buoy, is marked by a light beacon. Pass 1 cable south of Drowning Rock and continue on the same course to pass south of Catach which dries 1·2 metres, northwest of Drowning Rock. The whole passage is about 4 miles. A red buoy 2 cables southwest of Drowning Rock marks the end of a reef off Rubha Mhanais.

Bays Loch, Berneray

57°43′N 7°10′W

Tides

The southeast-going stream begins +0515 Ullapool (+0055 Dover). The northwest-going stream begins −0125 Ullapool (−0545 Dover).

Constant −0046 Ullapool (−0506 Dover)

Height in metres

MHWS	MHWN	MTL	MLWN	MLWS
3·9	3·5	2·4	1·6	0·7

Directions

For a brief daytime visit to Berneray in settled weather approach by Cope Passage (see below), turn south from *No. 12* buoy and pass a cable from Massacamber, the northeast point of Berneray, between drying reefs off the point, and Cat Rocks which just dry, further off. Anchor off the sandy beach, not too close to the beacons marking the passage through the Reef where the tide runs strongly.

Entrance To enter Bays Loch from the north pass 5 metres east of the two green light beacons and follow the deepest water round to starboard by eye, keeping about ½ cable off the shore, and anchor in the north corner of the bay which is sheltered except from southeast.

To cross Bays Loch to the harbour on the southwest side the following course is taken by local fishermen and has been followed by some yachts although it is not clear how much margin there is for error, and it may not be advisable at low spring tide. Pass close southeast of a spherical pink buoy which lies 2 cables west of the Reef beacons and steer with the ruins of a stone shed known as the 'hen house' in line with the right-hand corner of a house beyond about 230° as in the sketch on the following page. This will take you to the south of the harbour and when within about a cable turn northwest and steer parallel to the face of the breakwater. Although the chart shows a drying spit south of the position of the pink buoy, there is in fact a narrow channel.

Pilotage around Berneray often involves rather ephemeral transits of this sort, but if taken in quiet weather a step at a time it can usually be puzzled out. If stuck, either literally or metaphorically, or even if in doubt, a VHF call to *Endeavour* will bring helpful advice. Berneray is no place to make for in bad weather or poor visibility.

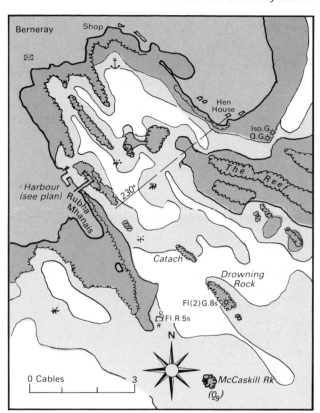

Bays Loch, Berneray

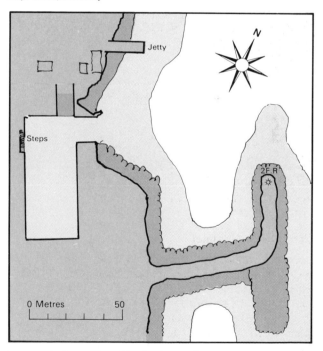

Berneray harbour. Note this plan is not aligned on the meridian.

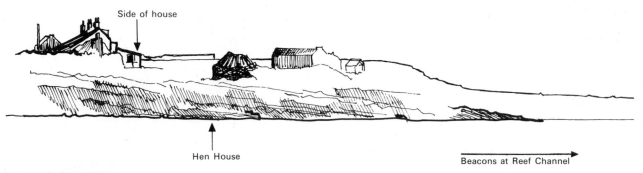

Side of house

Hen House

Beacons at Reef Channel

Bays Loch, Berneray
Line for crossing the bay from the Reef Channel to the harbour.

Berneray harbour from west.

Photo: J. Magee

Lights

Reef Channel *No. 1* Q.G.2m4M
Reef Channel *No. 2* Iso.G.4s2m4M
Drowning Rock Fl(2)G.8s2m2M
Harbour Iso.R.4s

Supplies

Shop at north side of the bay. Post office, telephone, *Calor Gas* at shop. Diesel and water at harbour.

For the anchorage at Loch nam Ban on North Uist, see Sound of Berneray in Chapter VIII, page 164.

Passages through the Sound of Harris

Cope Passage

57°42′N 7°04′W

The channel, which is marked principally for the use of shallow-draught army vessels, winds between drying rocks and is marked by light buoys. If these are passed on the correct hand in the right sequence it should present little problem as far as Berneray and can be used for a visit to that island; for the approach to Bays Loch, see above, page 45. At the northwest end of Cope Passage is a sandbar whose position varies, and which has been known to uncover. The channel is not marked at the bar, which would be dangerous in a westerly swell. For a passage through the Sound of Harris, Stanton Channel, on the northeast side of the sound (page 48 below), is usually better.

Tides

At springs the southeast-going stream begins about +0515 Ullapool (+0055 Dover); the northwest-going stream begins −0125 Ullapool (−0545 Dover), but at neaps in summer the southeast-going stream runs during daytime for 8–9 hours.

Dangers and marks

Gousman, an islet 9 metres high, stands on an extensive drying reef near the southeast end of the passage, 2 miles NNW of Fairway Buoy. From southeast steer with Gousman in line with a cairn on the summit of Killegray about 338°.

Directions

From southeast Pass, leaving light buoy *No. 1* to starboard and light buoy *No. 2* to port, then alter course to pass between light buoys *No. 3* and *No. 4*. Continue on this course to pass between light buoys *No. 5* and *No. 6*, watching the buoys astern to make sure you are not being carried off course. Then steer with Moor Hill at the northeast end of Berneray bearing 297° to pass between light buoys *No. 7* and *No. 8*. Alter course to starboard to leave light buoy *No. 9* to starboard and light buoy *No. 10* to port, and look for light buoy *No. 12*, about a mile ahead under the north end of Pabbay. At the sand bar the best water, with a depth of 3 metres in 1988, lay about 3 cables off the shore of Berneray.

From northwest if any sea is running use Stanton Channel instead. If conditions are suitable at the bar approach with *No. 12* buoy in line with the north side of Groay as above. Pass north of *No. 10* buoy and south of *No. 9*, and reverse the directions above.

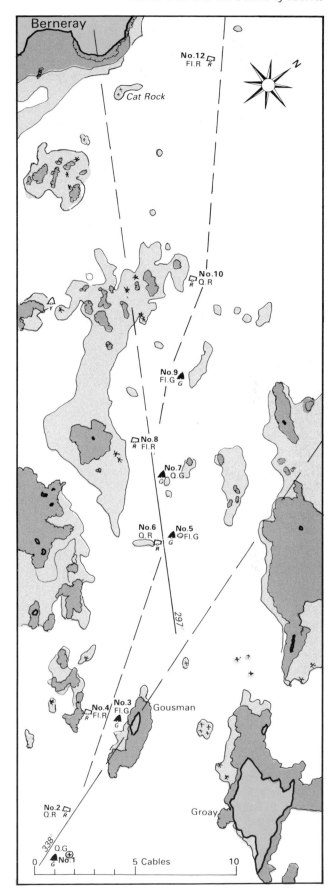

Cope Passage. Note this plan is not aligned on the meridian.

Approach to Sound of Harris from SE.

Approach to Sound of Harris from NW.

Jane's Tower from south with Heb Beacon to the right and the two beacons for the Leverburgh Channel, with a white painted mark above them, to the left.

Lights

The buoys are lit as shown on the plan, but there are no lights northwest of *No. 12*. The passage is not recommended at night.

Caolas Skaari

57°45′N 7°04′W

Not recommended owing to the tidal streams which reach 5 knots, and the drying reefs on either side of the channel, but the channel itself is clear, and might be investigated at low water neaps.

Stanton Channel

57°46′N 7°03′W

This is the main deep-water channel through the Sound of Harris, close to the Harris shore; a safe passage depends on identifying and following a series of transits sometimes at long range, but for a yacht the passage is less complicated than is shown on the Admiralty chart for larger craft.

Very heavy seas may be met at the northwest end of the passage, especially if an Atlantic swell is opposed by a northwest-going tide.

Tides

The southeast-going stream begins +0545 Ullapool (+0125 Dover). The northwest-going stream begins −0025 Ullapool (−0445 Dover); at neaps in summer the tide runs southeast for the whole of the day and northwest during the night. The spring rate is 4 knots southwest of Saghay More.

Dangers and marks

The principal marks are:

Dun-aarin islet at the southeast end of the channel is prominently angular, 26 metres high.

Heb Beacon on Harris (a white tower, 16 metres in height).

Jane's Tower on the northeast side of the channel (off-white with faded green bands).

Dubh Sgeir beacon (red and black bands).

Other beacons are described in relation to each leading line, but there are many of them, and care is needed to be sure that the correct mark has been selected. The transits described must be carefully observed, especially if the course is against the tidal stream.

Directions

The southeast entrance is a mile wide between Renish Point and Dun-aarin, and the first three miles are straightforward. A course of 316° leads in the middle of the fairway to Stumbles Rock buoy, ½ mile short of Dubh Sgeir. The islet of Suem close NNW of Dubh Sgeir in line with Coppay at the northwest end of Sound of Harris is on this bearing.

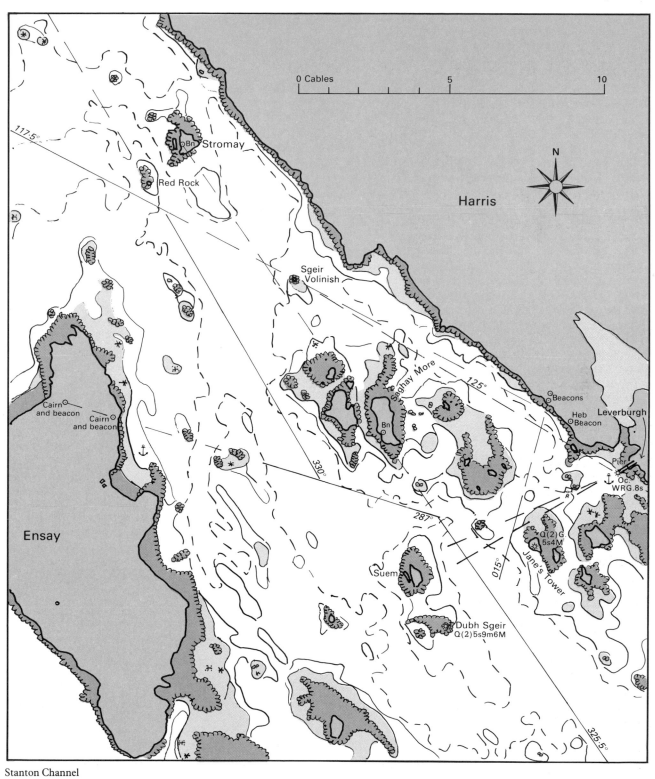

Stanton Channel

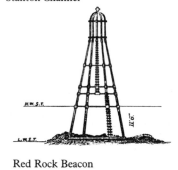

Red Rock Beacon

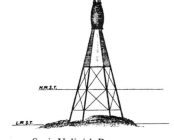

Sgeir Volinish Beacon

From the buoy, a stone beacon on Saghay More in line with a stone beacon on Stromay 325·5° lead clear of dangers between Dubh Sgeir and Jane's Tower; both beacons are similar in height so that the beacon on Stromay is hidden when nearer to Saghay More.

After passing Suem, a pair of cairns and beacons on Ensay 287° in line leads clear of rocks southwest of Saghay More; the rear beacon is on top of the island, the front one black and white striped near the shore.

The next line is a 10-metre conical green beacon on Red Rock which covers, 2 cables southwest of Stromay, in line with a beacon (alternatively if the beacon is not seen, the west end of a ruined chapel) bearing 330°, at Rubh' an Teampuill a little inshore of Cape Difficulty, the southwest tangent of Harris.

The charted line for the northwest entrance to Stanton Channel is Sgeir Volinish beacon (9 metres high, red conical) in line with Heb Beacon at Leverburgh 117·5° and a yacht should not be south of this line for at least a mile northwest of Red Rock. Alternatively if heading north after leaving Sound of Harris, Red Rock beacon in line with the summit of Saghay More 135° leads close south of dangers off the Harris shore.

From northwest keep between ½ and 1 mile off the Harris shore until the marks are identified; Red Rock beacon will probably be seen first. Select one of the transits above and pass 1–2 cables south of Red Rock. Bring Red Rock astern in line with the beacon at Rubh' an Teampuill about 330°, then the beacons on Ensay in line 287°, followed by Saghay More stone beacon in line with Stromay stone beacon astern 325·5°, which leads to Stumbles Rock buoy.

An alternative course close inshore is used by fishermen and there is often less sea there; keep 1–2 cables off Rubh' an Teampuill to pass inshore of Inner and Outer Temple Rocks, then 1 cable off the 24-metre cliffs ¾ mile further southeast and through Sound of Stromay. Submerged rocks extend a cable north from the drying reef at the north end of Stromay.

Lights

Dubh Sgeir beacon Q(2)5s9m6M
Jane's Tower Q(2)G.5s6m4M
Leverburgh Pier head Oc.WRG.8s

Leverburgh Channel

This channel is entered from south by passing a cable west of Jane's Tower with two beacons on Harris in line about 015°; when about a cable from the shore a small iron beacon SSE of Heb Beacon in line with Leverburgh pier head 125° leads to the north of Sgeir Volinish. From there pass south of Red Rock and continue as for leaving Stanton Channel; alternatively take the Sound of Stromay as above.

Leverburgh

57°46′N 7°01′·5W

Tides

Constant −0040 Ullapool (−0500 Dover)

Height in metres

MHWS	MHWN	MTL	MLWN	MLWS
4·6	3·5	2·6	1·9	0·6

Directions

Enter Leverburgh Channel as above and approach with the red buoy in line with the head of the pier. Pass south of the buoy and continue towards the pier; anchor as convenient clear of moorings.

Lights

At night there are lights as above, but it is not practicable for a stranger to approach in darkness.

Supplies

Shop, post office, telephone, *Calor Gas*, petrol, water tap at pier.

Rodel

57°44′N 6°58′W

Poll an Tigh-mhail is completely sheltered, but it is only accessible above half tide.

Chart

Included on *2642* (1:20,000).

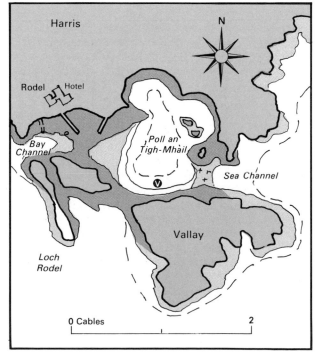

Rodel

Rodel harbour with Bay Channel beyond.

Tides

As Leverburgh.

Dangers and marks in Loch Rodel

Duncan Rock, ½ cable off the southwest shore, has a depth of 0·3 metre.

A submerged wreck lies south of the promontory separating the two arms of the head of the loch, and a drying rock lies off the north side, west of a boulder beach.

Anchorage

Occasional anchorage can be found off the southwest shore, to wait for sufficient water to enter Poll an Tigh-mhail.

Poll an Tigh-mhail appears to have three entrances, but the middle one between the islands is much too obstructed by rocks ever to be considered. Sea Channel partly dries, with a stony bottom, and a boulder spit on the north side covers at half tide; it is dangerous in any swell.

The usual approach is through Bay Channel from Loch Rodel which dries 0·9 metre with large stones on the bottom. Pillar Rock which covers, on the north side of the channel, is marked with a perch; when the base of the perch is covered the depth in the channel is 3·4 metres.

The pool itself is deep with a bottom of soft mud and there are many floats marking shellfish creels. HIDB visitors' moorings are to be laid on the north side of Vallay. The harbour on the north side of Bay Channel dries completely, but a yacht which is able to take the ground might dry out alongside one of its quays. There is an hotel by the harbour.

III. West coast of Skye

Passage notes – Point of Sleat to Soay

Chart

2208 (1:50,000). OS map *32*. OS *Outdoor Leisure Map – The Cuillin and Torridon Hills* (1:25,000).

Tides

The north-going stream begins about +0535 Ullapool (+0115 Dover); the south-going stream begins about −0025 Ullapool (−0445 Dover). There is probably an eddy with the north-going stream on the west side of Point of Sleat and overfalls west and southwest of the point with both flood and ebb tides.

Dangers and marks

Point of Sleat is low and rocky with a 7-metre white light beacon at its southwest tip. Rocks, above water and drying, extend 1¾ cables west of the point to Sgeir Dhubh which is 0·3 metre high.

Lights

Point of Sleat Fl.3s20m9M
Sanday (southeast of Canna) Fl.6s32m9M

Shelter

Shelter may be found in Sound of Sleat, Loch Slapin, Loch Eishort (difficult approach), at Canna, Rhum and Soay Harbour (which has a tidal sill).

Tarskavaig (57°07′N 6°00′W), and Ob Gauscavaig (Tokavaig), a mile northwest, provide occasional anchorages in settled weather.

Supplies

Nearest (limited) at Rhum.

Loch Eishort

57°10′N 5°55′W

Tides

Constant −0040 Ullapool (−0500 Dover)

Height in metres

MHWS	MHWN	MTL	MLWN	MLWS
4·8	3·7	2·8	2·1	0·7

Dangers and marks

Drying reefs extend over a cable southwest of Rubha Suishnish, the north point of the entrance. Two miles further east the loch narrows abruptly with islets and drying rocks up to ½ mile off Rubha Dubh Ard at the south side.

Sgeir an t-Sruith, about 4 cables north of Dubh Ard, stands above water with drying reefs extending from it to the north shore.

A drying reef extends about ¼ cable south of Sgeir an t-Sruith and drying reefs lie up to 2 cables north of Dubh Ard, leaving a passage ¼ mile wide.

Many rocks which cover lie in the next 1½ miles but one, which lies north of Sgeir Gormul on the chart, rarely if ever covers. Sgeir Gormul itself covers at half tide and is not, as shown on the chart, above water.

Directions

Pass 1 cable south of Sgeir an t-Sruith, identify the rock north of Sgeir Gormul and pass within ¼ cable of its south side. If Sgeir Gormul is showing the passage between them is straightforward. Pass either side of the group of rocks 3 cables further east and south of the most southerly rock south of Heast Island. Continue east for ¼ mile before turning north and anchor north of the fish cages in the bay east of the island.

Anchorage

Bagh an Dubh Ard is an occasional anchorage on the south side of the narrows; when approaching from west keep closer to Sgeir an t-Sruith than to Dubh Ard to avoid reefs off Dubh Ard; the bottom shelves steeply.

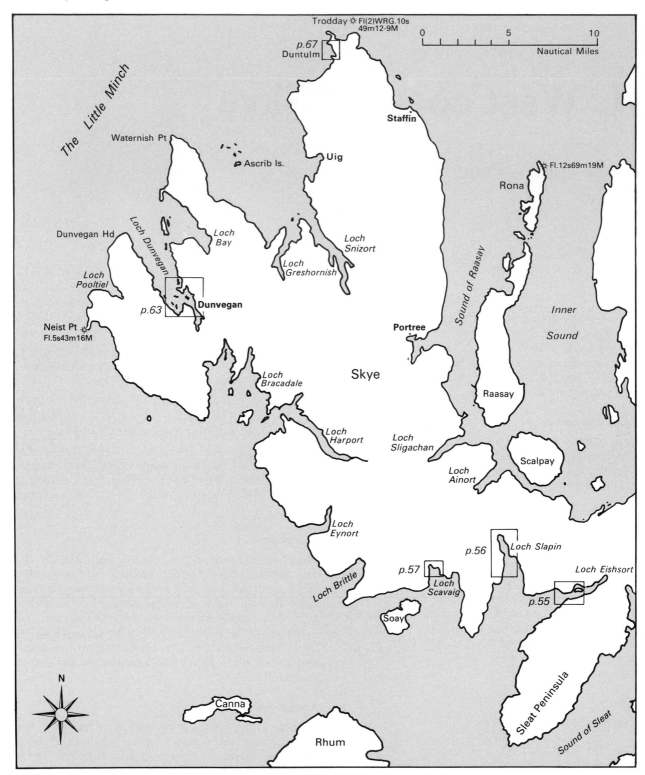

Trodday ☀ Fl(2)WRG.10s
49m12-9M

The Little Minch

Waternish Pt

Ascrib Is.

p.67
Duntulm

Staffin

Uig

0   5   10
Nautical Miles

☀ Fl.12s69m19M

Rona

Dunvegan Hd

*Loch
Bay*

*Loch
Snizort*

*Loch
Dunvegan*

*Loch
Greshornish*

*Loch
Pooltiel*

p.63   **Dunvegan**

*Inner
Sound*

Neist Pt
Fl.5s43m16M

Portree

Sound of Raasay

Skye

*Loch
Bracadale*

Raasay

*Loch
Harport*

*Loch
Sligachan*

Scalpay

*Loch
Ainort*

*Loch
Eynort*

p.56   *Loch Slapin*

Loch Eishsort

p.57

Loch Brittle

*Loch
Scavaig*

p.55

Soay

Sleat Peninsula

N

Canna

Sound of Sleat

Rhum

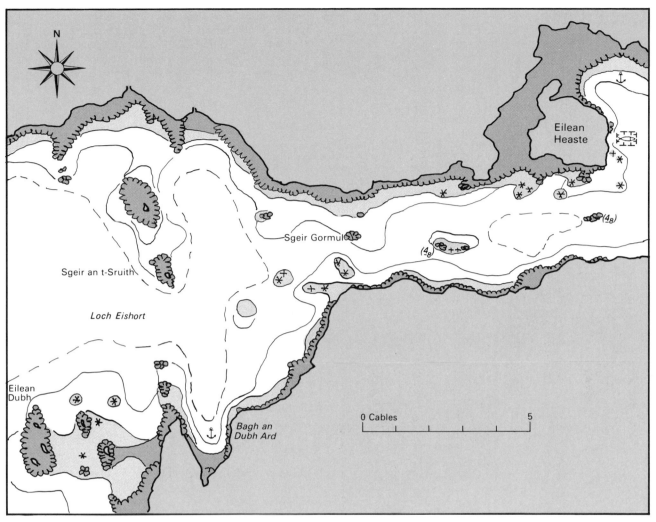

Eilean
Heaste

(4_8)

Sgeir Gormul

(4_8)

Sgeir an t-Sruith

Loch Eishort

Eilean
Dubh

Bagh an
Dubh Ard

0 Cables   5

Loch Eishort

Loch Eishort from south of Sgeir an t-Sruith.

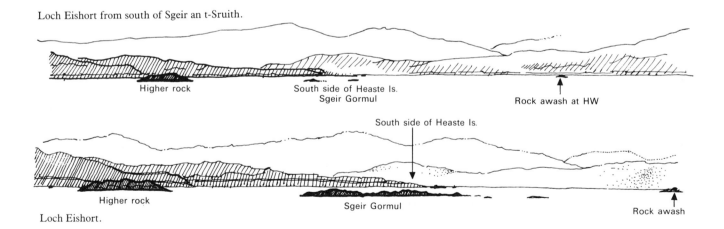

Higher rock

South side of Heaste Is.
Sgeir Gormul

Rock awash at HW

South side of Heaste Is.

Higher rock

Sgeir Gormul

Rock awash

Loch Eishort.

Loch Slapin

57°12′N 6°01′W

Tides

Constant −0040 Ullapool (−0500 Dover)

Height in metres

MHWS	MHWN	MTL	MLWN	MLWS
4·8	3·7	2·8	2·1	0·7

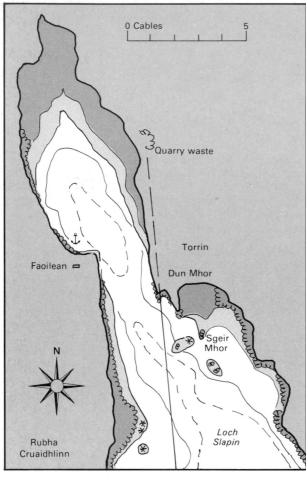

Loch Slapin

Dangers and marks

Fierce gusts can be expected from the hills at the head of the loch and blowing out of the entrance.

Bogha Ailean lies ¼ mile off the west shore 2 miles NNE of Strathaird Point at a depth of 1·8 metres; The southeast point of Rhum open of Strathaird Point 212° clears this rock. Drying reefs extend over a cable southwest of Rubha Suishnish, the east point of the entrance.

Sharp blocks drying and just submerged lie off Rubha Cruaidhlinn. Rocks drying and awash south and west of Sgeir Mhor on the east side of the loch are cleared by keeping a white heap of quarry waste just open west of Dun Mhor, a prominent knob on the east side of the loch (but note that another pile of quarry waste further east is more conspicuous). It would be prudent at low water to keep east of this line while passing Rubha Cruaidhlinn.

Anchorage

The head of the loch dries off ½ mile and the best anchorage is on the west side close to the south shore of Bagh nam Faoilean which is steep-to, or north of the fish cages.

Services

Post office, telephone at Torrin. Water tap at Faoilean.

Loch Scavaig

57°11′N 6°09′W

This anchorage can claim to be the most spectacular on the West Coast, surrounded by the jagged peaks of the Cuillin Hills; however the squalls there tend to be equally spectacular.

Tides

Constant −0040 Ullapool (−0500 Dover)

Height in metres

MHWS	MHWN	MTL	MLWN	MLWS
4·8	3·7	2·8	2·1	0·7

Dangers

Drying rocks lie in the middle of the loch leaving a passage 1¼ cables wide east of Eilean Reamhar which is on the west side of the loch; drying rocks also lie ¼ cable northeast of Eilean Reamhar. Sgeir Doigich 1½ cables north of Eilean Reamhar occasionally covers, and drying rocks lie off the west shore a cable further northwest.

Loch na Cuilce

A shallow pool at the head of Loch Scavaig behind Eilean Glas; the entrance to the pool by the west end of Eilean Glas is ¾ cable wide, but a drying rock lies 55 metres west of Eilean Glas. Another drying rock lies about 10 metres north of the west end of the island and a submerged rock close southwest of it.

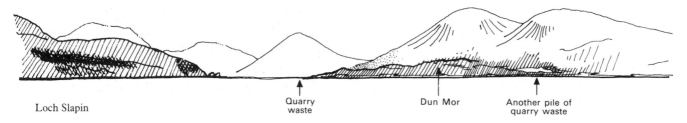

Loch Slapin

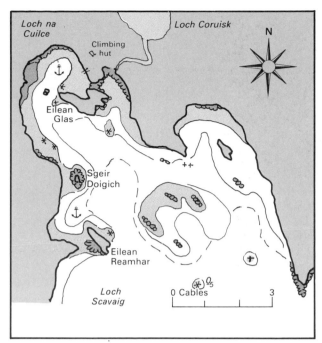
Loch Scavaig

tion round her anchor. There are some mooring rings ashore, but their use may be more of a hindrance than help. An alternative anchorage is west of the north end of Eilean Reamhar.

Landing steps at the northeast side of Loch na Cuilce are used by tourist boats from Elgol, and dinghies should be left clear of the steps.

Soay Sound

57°10′N 6°14′W

Tides

the tidal stream sets permanently to westward. Confused sea is set up at the west end of the sound with south or southwest winds.

Constant −0040 Ullapool (−0500 Dover)

Height in metres

MHWS	MHWN	MTL	MLWN	MLWS
4·8	3·7	2·8	2·1	0·7

Approach

Identify Eilean Reamhar and pass ½ cable east of it and Sgeir Doigich, and 20 metres west of Eilean Glas; if the rock west of Eilean Glas is visible it can be passed on its west side. It is particularly important to leave swinging room clear of other boats already anchored, as squalls may drive a boat in any direc-

Loch na Cuilce, Loch Scavaig.

Soay Harbour

The inlet on the north side of Soay is less than a cable wide and a shingle bar across the entrance dries 0·6 metre in the channel, which lies slightly northeast of the middle of the entrance. Reefs extend ½ cable from the south shore and over a cable northwest from the northeast point of the entrance.

Approach

Approach, not before half flood, heading southeast towards the buildings and jetty on the northeast shore to avoid drying reefs on the east side; two white poles on the southwest shore in line lead through the deepest part of the channel at the bar.

Dangers and marks

A rock which dries 0·6 metre lies less than ½ cable south of the jetty and a drying reef extends towards this rock from the southwest shore, but a narrow passage past the head of the reef leads to an inner pool. Small buoys on either side of the inlet mark lobster storage creels and should be kept well clear of when anchoring.

Services

Telephone by path to cottages at Camas nan Gall.

Soay Harbour entrance from west.

Other anchorages

An Dubh Chamas ¾ mile east of Soay Harbour is well sheltered from southerly winds and free from hazards.

Camas nan Gall, on the south side of Soay, has poor holding on shingle.

Soay Harbour from east. A detached drying rock lies off the promontory in the foreground.

Southwest Coast of Skye from Soay to Neist Point

The shore of this part of Skye consists of cliffs rising to 285 metres with occasional inlets, of which only Loch Bracadale and Loch Harport offer any shelter.

Charts

1795 (1:100,000) (Loch Eynort is on chart *2208*). OS maps *23, 32*.

Tides

Tidal streams between Soay and Loch Bracadale run at up to 1 knot. The northwest-going stream begins +0535 Ullapool (+0115 Dover). The southeast-going stream begins −0025 Ullapool (−0445 Dover).

Off Neist Point the northwest-going stream begins −0405 Ullapool (+0400 Dover). The southeast-going stream begins +0220 Ullapool (−0200 Dover). From +0535 to −0405 Ullapool (+0115 to −0400 Dover) the south-going stream meets a northwest-going stream and is deflected to the west. Thus, effectively, the stream is running northwest or west for nine hours out of twelve.

Dangers and marks

A magnetic anomaly, which is strongest near the northeast point of Canna, affects all of the area between Loch Brittle and Idrigill Point.

An Dubh Sgeir, 5 metres high, 1½ miles from the shore and 3¼ miles west of Idrigill Point at the west side of Loch Bracadale, is the outermost of a line of rocks known collectively as the Mibow Rocks (Mi-bogha), with a passage ¼ mile wide between Mi-bogha Beag and Mi-bogha Mor.

Macleod's Maidens are a prominent group of rock stacks close to the shore southwest of Idrigill Point. To pass between Mibow Rocks keep Macleod's Maidens bearing 112°.

Lights

Neist Point Fl.5s43m16M
Sanday (southeast of Canna) Fl.6s32m9M
Oigh Sgeir (Hyskeir) Fl(3)30s41m24M
Ardtreck Point light beacon, Loch Harport Iso.4s 17m9M

At night Keep Neist Point bearing more than 330° to clear An Dubh Sgeir.

Shelter

Loch Harport or Canna Harbour.

Minor anchorages

Loch Brittle (57°11′N 6°19′W) only very occasional if there is no swell; shop at camp site.

Loch Eynort (57°14′N 6°22′W) occasionally, if no sea from west. Subject to severe squalls from north. An Dubh Sgeir, 5 metres high, off the southeast point has a clear passage inshore. Stac a Mheadais, 24 metres high, stands close to the shore about 1 mile northwest of the entrance. Fish traps extend south from the north point of the entrance. Some shelter will be found beyond the bend, off the northwest shore but the holding here has been found to be poor; good shelter and holding have been found in a gale from east and northeast close to the wooded shore on the east side at the corner.

Idrigill Point and Macleod's Maidens from west.

Loch Harport

57°20′N 6°24′W

A branch of Loch Bracadale for which see below, although Loch Harport is more conveniently described as a separate loch.

Tidal streams are insignificant, and the loch is free from hidden dangers.

Light

Ardtreck Point light beacon Iso.4s17m9M

Anchorages

Loch Beg, north of the entrance is a satisfactory anchorage if there is no sea from the south, although the bottom is soft and the holding has been found to be poor. Several inshore fishing boats lie on moorings, and the end of a concrete slip on the west side is marked by a prominent perch. Shop and post office up hill at the main road.

Gesto Bay, the next bay to the east, is good in offshore winds.

Port na Long, on the south side of the loch, opposite Loch Beg, provides better shelter in southerly winds. Many inshore fishing boats lie on moorings, and the west side is occupied by fish cages. Anchor beyond the jetty which is at the east side of the entrance. Shop, post office, telephone, hotel, all ½ mile along road.

Carbost Anchor near the southwest shore between the pier and the distillery. A shoal area extends out from the distillery burn, and there is a broader area with moderate depth beyond the shoal, below a war memorial, but the head of the loch dries off. The pier has about 2 metres alongside and is sometimes used by fishing boats; a yacht would need fender boards at the pier.

Supplies

Shop at Carbost, post office, telephone up hill. Hotel (meals). Water at the distillery. Tours of distillery Monday, Wednesday and Friday afternoons.

Other shelter

Oronsay gives some shelter on either side of the drying reef which joins the island to Skye, according to wind direction. On the east side a drying reef extends ½ cable southeast from the northeast point of the island.

Loch Harport entrance: Ardtreck beacon on the right with Port na Long beyond.

Loch Beg, Loch Harport from the head. The perch on the submerged end of the slip is on the right.

Loch Bracadale

57°20′N 6°32′W

Tides

Constant −0050 Ullapool (−0510 Dover)

MHWS	MHWN	MTL	MLWN	MLWS
5·1	3·8	2·9	2·1	0·8

Dangers and marks

Rubha nan Clach, the southeast point of the entrance, is a cliff 129 metres high. Wiay, in the middle of the entrance is 60 metres high, flat-topped with cliffs all round. Idrigill Point, the west side of the entrance, is identified by Macleod's Maidens, 3 stacks close southwest of it. The outer part of the loch is free from hidden dangers, and although it has several branches there is little shelter.

Anchorages

Oronsay The bay on its northwest side is clean but very restricted.

Tarner Island gives some shelter on its northeast side.

Loch Caroy, north of Wiay, provides little shelter. Tarner Island, ¾ mile north of Wiay may be passed on either side, but if on the east side, keep closer to Tarner than to Skye as drying rocks lie in the middle and to the east side of the passage. Sgeir a' Chuain, 2 metres high, ¾ mile further north has drying reefs up to a cable round it, but can be passed on either side. About ¼ mile north of Sgeir a' Chuain, drying reefs extend 2 cables from Crossinish Point on the west shore. Anchor near the jetty on the east side, ½ mile from the head of the loch.

Loch Vatten is entered by the west side of Harlosh Island, 1½ miles northwest of Wiay. Harlosh Skerry dries 2 cables west of Harlosh Point.

Poll Roag at the head of Loch Vatten can only be entered near HW by shallow-draught boats, but is traditionally a winter mooring for fishing boats. Holding is poor with weed and patches of soft mud.

Loch Bharcasaig, an inlet on the northwest side of Loch Vatten, with a forestry plantation at its head, is the best anchorage in Loch Bracadale other than Loch Harport; anchor in the southwest corner in 4 metres. Drying rocks lie ¼ cable off the south point of the entrance.

Northwest coast of Skye from Neist Point to Rubha Hunish

The northwest coast of Skye is deeply indented, with extensive groups of lochs between Dunvegan Head and Waternish Point and the west side of Trotternish. There are no hidden dangers on a direct passage between Neist Point and Rubha Hunish.

Loch Bharcasaig, Loch Bracadale.

Chart

1795 (1:100,000). OS map *23*.

Tides

Tides at Neist Point are described at page 59.

Between Neist Point and Ru Bornesketaig, 6 miles southwest of the north end of Skye, the north-going stream begins −0405 Ullapool (+0400 Dover). The south-going stream begins +0220 Ullapool (−0200 Dover). Streams run at up to 1½ knots, but at Waternish Point the tide turns 15 minutes later and runs at 2½ knots.

Dangers and marks

Dunvegan Head is 310 metres high with cliffs on its northwest side sloping down to the north. A conspicuous radio mast stands 3 miles south of the head.

Waternish Point is 15 metres high, with a white light beacon 7 metres in height at the point.

An t-Iasgair, an islet 21 metres high, is 1½ miles NNW of Rudha Bornesketaig.

Lights

Neist Point Fl.5s43m16M
Waternish Point Fl.20s21m8M
Eilean Trodday Fl(2)WRG.10s49m12-9M

Shelter

Loch Dunvegan, Loch Snizort, Duntulm Bay (limited).

Loch Pooltiel

57°28′N 6°45′W

Exposed northwest, but in moderate weather small boats can anchor between the pier at Meanish on the west side of the loch, and Sgeir Mor, which dries, a cable southeast of the pier. The bottom appears to consist of boulders. A rock with less than 2 metres depth lies about 1¼ cable northwest of the pier. Small-boat moorings lie southeast of the pier.

The head of the loch has been found to have good holding in 3–5 metres, but dries off several cables. Many fishing floats and fish cages lie in the loch.

Supplies

Shop, post office, telephone, at Glendale at head of loch. Telephone at Milovaig, up hill from pier. Working water mill at Glendale.

Loch Dunvegan

57°30′N 6°40′W

Chart

2533 (1:25,000). OS map *23*.

Tides

Constant −0045 Ullapool (−0505 Dover)

Height in metres

MHWS	MHWN	MTL	MLWN	MLWS
5·2	3·8	2·9	2·1	0·7

Dangers and marks

A drying reef extends over 2 cables SSW from Lampay Islands, 2 cables west of Groban na Sgeire which separates Loch Dunvegan from Loch Bay. Ard Mor open west of Isay bearing 360° astern leads clear of this reef.

Fishing floats are scattered throughout Loch Dunvegan.

2½ miles SSE of Lampay the channel is reduced to 2 cables between Fiadhairt, a peninsula on its northeast side, and Eilean Grianal 7 metres high with a line of rocks on the southwest side.

Loch Pooltiel: anchorage at the pier from south.

Loch Dunvegan (inner part)

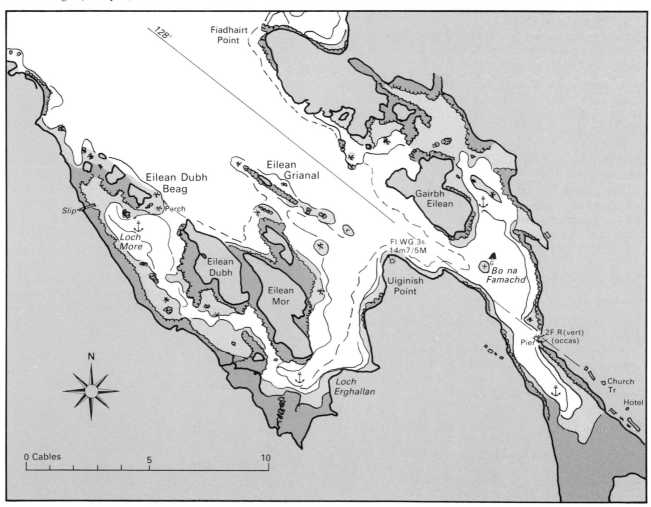

Loch Mor, Loch Dunvegan, from northwest.

Uiginish Point, a mile southeast of Fiadhairt Point, has a white light beacon 5 metres in height at its end.

A white church tower at Dunvegan village in line with the northwest side of Uiginish Point 128° leads along the middle of the channel.

A G conical buoy south of Gairbh Eilean is on the north side of Bo na Famachd over which the depth is 0·9 metre; if passing southwest of it keep closer to the shore than to the buoy.

Lights

Uiginish Point Fl.WG.3s14m7/5M (128°-W-306° but obscured by Fiadhairt Point when bearing more than 148°).
Pier head 2F.R(vert) occasional

At night keep in the white sector of Uiginish Point light, after which the lights of the village and at the pier are the only guide.

Dunvegan

Dunvegan pier is currently unusable, but plans are in hand for its restoration.

A jetty is being constructed at Dunvegan Hotel, from which fuel and water will be available, but the jetty was not finished in June 1990 and dangerous exposed reinforcing rods extended beyond the end of it. Visitors' moorings have been laid for customers of the hotel. If not using a mooring, anchor abreast of the church clear of moorings, but the bottom between the pier and the moorings is very soft, and beyond the hotel it is too shallow for most yachts, but good anchorage can be found and *Thomasina* has ridden out a succession of summer gales there.

Supplies at Dunvegan

Shops, post office, telephone, hotels and restaurants, petrol and diesel at garages; gas and gas fittings at garage. DIY/builders' merchant. Gaeltec, an electronics firm, may be willing to help with electronic repairs and light machining in emergencies. Diver at Stein, marine engineer at Waternish.

Other anchorages

Gairbh Eilean Anchor between the castle and the island clear of rocks above water and drying further north.

Loch More, 57°27′N 6°38′W. Clach a' Charra on the northwest side of the entrance, marked by a red perch with a T-shaped head, rarely covers. Below half tide a drying rock southwest of Eilean Dubh Beag will be visible, and better shelter can be found ESE of the slip at Colbost (which is public although you may be told otherwise). Restaurant 1 mile south from slip.

Loch Erghallan, 57°26′N 6°37′W. Keep on the 128° line until within a cable of Uiginish Point to avoid Bo Channanich; turn to starboard and anchor not more than a cable south of Eilean Mor.

Loch Bay

57°30′·5N 6°35′W

Tides

As Loch Dunvegan.

Dangers and marks

Three islands, Isay, Mingay and Clett, lie in the entrance to the loch. The passage north of Clett is ¾

Stein, Loch Bay, from east. Rubha Maol is on the left and Sgeir nam Biast lies in front of Isay and Dunvegan Head.

mile wide but Sgeir a' Chuain, which dries, extends ¼ mile north of Isay. To clear Sgeir a' Chuain, keep the tangent of Dunvegan Head astern bearing not more than 240°, or Waternish Hall, a low white building next to the war memorial, open north of Clett 090°.

Several drying rocks lie south of Isay with a passage 2 cables wide south of them. A spit with a depth of 2·4 metres extending 1½ cables north of Groban na Sgeire at the south side of the entrance may cause momentary alarm.

If approaching Loch Bay by the south of Isay, keep Dunvegan Head bearing 280° astern and follow the south shore of the passage until the west side of Ardmore Point is open east of Mingay 338°. Sgeir nam Biast, a reef 2 cables across, part of which is above water, lies ¾ mile east of the south end of Isay and ½ mile from the south shore.

Anchorages

Isay, between Isay and Mingay. From north approach with the east side of Rubha Maol showing between Mingay and Clett 128° to clear Sgeir a' Chuain, or Waternish Hall open of Clett 090° as above, and turn in to the channel between the islands when the big ruined house on Isay is visible. From south approach with the west side of Ardmore Point open east of Mingay 338° to clear the east side of rocks south of Isay. Anchor between Isay and the south end of Mingay. May be lumpy with wind from north or south.

Ardmore Bay, at the north end of Loch Bay is well sheltered from north, but the holding is said to be poor; the west side of the bay is shoal.

Stein, on the east shore of the southeast part of the loch, SSE of the pier. There are many local boats on moorings, as well as HIDB visitors' moorings. Apart from the obvious westerly exposure, there is sufficient fetch to make this a very uncomfortable anchorage in strong south winds.

Supplies at Stein

Pub, restaurant. Shop, post office, telephone ¾ mile up hill. Camus Lusta Marine in Portree has boats for hire at Stein and will deliver chandlery; ☎ Portree (0478) 2592. Diver ☎ Waternish (047 083) 219.

Loch Snizort

57°35′N 6°30′W

Chart

1795 (1:100,000), *2533* (1:25,000). OS map *23*.

Tides

Constant −0030 Ullapool (−0450 Dover)

Height in metres

MHWS	MHWN	MTL	MLWN	MLWS
5·3	3·5	3·1	1·9	0·7

Ascrib Islands

These islands, 1¼ miles from the west side of the loch, are generally clean, but drying and submerged rocks extend 1¾ cables northwest of the southwest point of South Ascrib. Very occasional anchorage may be found in the bight on the west side of Eilean Garave, where the bottom is sand outwith the 2-metre line. A shallow landlocked pool lies northwest of the house on South Ascrib, and a shoal-draught boat might lie there at neaps with lines ashore.

See also dangers in approach to individual anchorages.

Lights

Waternish Point Fl.20s21m8M
Uig Pier head Iso.WRG.4s9m7-4M

Anchorages

Aros Bay, 57°33′N 6°33′W, an open bay on the west side of the loch where car ferries used to shelter when the weather was too wild for them to approach Uig.

Loch Diubaig, 57°30′N 6°27′·5W, occasional anchorage in an open bay in the southwest corner of Loch Snizort.

Loch Greshornish, 57°30′N 6°26′W, gives the best shelter in Loch Snizort. Drying rocks lie 1 cable west of the south end of Eilean Mor at the entrance, and 1½ cables north of Greshornish Point, the west side of the entrance, and ½ cable off the east side of Greshornish Point. The clear passage west of Eilean Mor is ½ mile wide; the passage east of Eilean Mor is 3 cables wide with no hazards. Large unlit fish cages lie at the mouth of the loch.

Submerged and drying rocks lie ¾ cable from the east shore 2 miles south of Greshornish Point. The east tangent of Greshornish Point in line with the west side of Eilean Mor 018° leads west of these rocks.

Shop, pub at Edinbane on the east shore.

Loch Snizort Beag, 57°29′N 6°20′W, gives some shelter 3 miles from the mouth, just within the middle arm, the head of which dries off for 1 mile. A submerged rock, Beatson, at a depth of 1·2 metres lies near the east shore of the loch 1½ miles from the mouth. Hotel at the head of the middle arm. Loch Treaslane, the western arm, is also sheltered although the head also dries off for 4 cables, and both these branches have good holding on mud. Loch Eyre, the eastern arm, dries off completely.

Christie Rocks which dry 2·2 metres lie 1½ cables offshore, about a mile south of the south point of Uig Bay. Stack of Skudiburgh, ¾ mile north of Uig Bay, open of the land 360° leads clear of these rocks.

Poll na h-Ealaidh, a small inlet southeast of Christie Rocks, provides some shelter in offshore winds.

Uig Bay

57°34′·5N 6°23′W

The terminal for the ferry to Harris and North Uist. A long pier provides some shelter, but most of the bay inshore of it dries. The pier is used by fishing boats morning and evening and it is not recommended for yachts to lie there overnight, although they can go alongside during the day.

At night approach in the white sector of the light at the pier and keep a good lookout for fishing boats.

Supplies

Petrol and diesel from garage at pier. Small shop at pier, larger shop with post office at head of the loch. Telephone at pier.

Other anchorages

Camas Beag on the south side of Uig Bay is an alternative anchorage in southerly winds but is deep until close to the head.

Duntulm (Tulm) Bay

57°41′N 6°21′W

Charts

1795 (1:100,000), also on *2210* (1:50,000). OS map *23*.

Tides

Off Rubha Hunish the spring rate is 3 knots. The northeast-going stream begins −0405 Ullapool (+0400 Dover). The southwest-going stream begins +0220 Ullapool (−0200 Dover).

Constant −0030 Ullapool (−0450 Dover)

Height in metres

MHWS	MHWN	MTL	MLWN	MLWS
5·3	3·5	3·1	1·9	0·7

Marks

A lattice communications tower stands on Cnoc Roll southeast of the bay.

An t-Iasgair, 22 metres high, lies 1½ miles offshore NNW of Ru Bornesketaig.

Tulm Island lies in the middle of the bay and the ruins of Duntulm Castle stand on Ru Meanish at the south point of the bay.

Dangers

A drying reef extends about ½ cable southeast from the south end of the island and drying reefs extend ½ cable west and northwest from Ru Meanish on Skye.

At the north end of Eilean Tulm a reef partly drying and partly submerged extends 1¾ cables NNW. Sgeir nan Sgarbh which dries 4·6 metres lies near the Skye shore, with a narrow channel on either side of it.

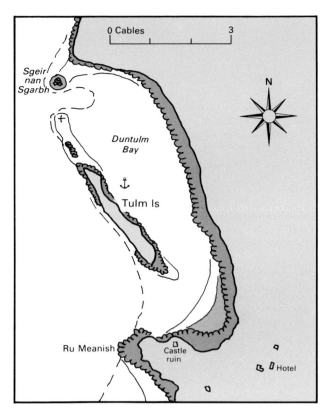

Duntulm Bay

Directions

Approach by the south entrance keeping midway between Tulm Island and Skye, or if Sgeir nan Sgarbh is visible either midway between the rock and the Skye shore, or ¼–½ cable south of the rock. Anchor close to the northeast side of Tulm Island, north of the mid-point of the island.

Services

There is a hotel at Duntulm.

IV. Sound of Sleat and Loch Alsh

Chart

2208 (1:50,000). OS map *33*.

Tides

The northeast-going stream begins +0550 Ullapool (+0130 Dover). The southwest-going stream begins −0010 Ullapool (−0430 Dover).

Dangers

On the Skye side of the sound, rocks above water and drying lie up to 2 cables offshore southeast and south of Armadale. Tartar Rock, 4 miles NNE of Armadale with a depth of 1·5 metres, lies 2 cables offshore.

Off the mainland shore submerged and drying rocks lie up to 2 cables NNE of Airor Island, and at the mouth of Glen Ghuserein, 1½ miles northwest of Airor, a bank dries off ¼ mile from the shore.

Conspicuous marks

Mallaig village at the southeast point of the entrance to the sound.

Armadale Pier, with a white building on its head.

Isle Ornsay light tower, white, 18 metres high.

Sandaig Island light beacon (north of Loch Hourn entrance) 12 metres high.

Lights

Sgeir Dhearg, Mallaig Fl(2)WG.8s6m5M

Mallaig Steamer Pier Iso.WRG.4s6m9-6M

Armadale Pier Oc.R.6s6m6M (not easily seen among shore lights)

Isle Ornsay Oc.8s18m15M 157°-vis-030°

Isle Ornsay north Fl.R.6s8m4M

Sandaig Island light beacon Fl.6s12m8M

At night to clear dangers off Armadale keep Isle Ornsay light in sight bearing not more than 030°; to clear Tartar Rock keep this light bearing not more than 025°. To clear the land north of Loch Nevis keep the white sector of Sgeir Dhearg light at Mallaig in sight.

Shelter

Glaschoille (Loch Nevis), Armadale, Isle Ornsay.

Loch Nevis

57°01′N 5°42′W

Chart

2541 (1:25,000), 1987 and later editions only. OS map *33*.

Tides

Streams in the entrance south of Rubha Raonuill run at ½ knot; elsewhere they are weak except at the narrows where they run at 3 knots.

The in-going stream begins +0530 Ullapool (+0110 Dover). The out-going stream begins −0050 Ullapool (−0510 Dover).

Constant −0040 Ullapool (−0500 Dover)

Height in metres

MHWS	MHWN	MTL	MLWN	MLWS
5·0	3·8	2·9	2·0	0·7

Dangers and marks

Rocks above water and drying lie on the N side of the entrance between Eilean Glas and Rubha Raonuill. Bogha cas Sruth which dries 1·8 metres 3½ cables WSW of Rubha Raonuill, is the most dangerous.

Inverie House just showing south of Rubha Raonuill 083° leads 1 cable south of Bogha cas Sruth. A submerged rock lies over a cable SSW of Rubha Raonuill at a depth of 1·2 metres; the beacon on Bogha Don in line with Inverie Church 075° leads close south of this rock.

On the south side of the loch Bo Ruag dries 3 metres, ¾ cable offshore and about 3 cables west of Rubha na Moine, the point where the shore turns sharply to the south.

Anchorages

Port Giubhais, 57°01′N 5°44′·3W, on the east side of Eilean Giubhais provides occasional anchorage for small boats under a steep hillside on the south side of the loch. Drying reefs extend northeast of Eilean Giubhais and a detached rock dries 1·2 metres northwest of Eilean Giubhais; Bo Ruag, described above, lies 1 cable ENE of the mouth of the inlet.

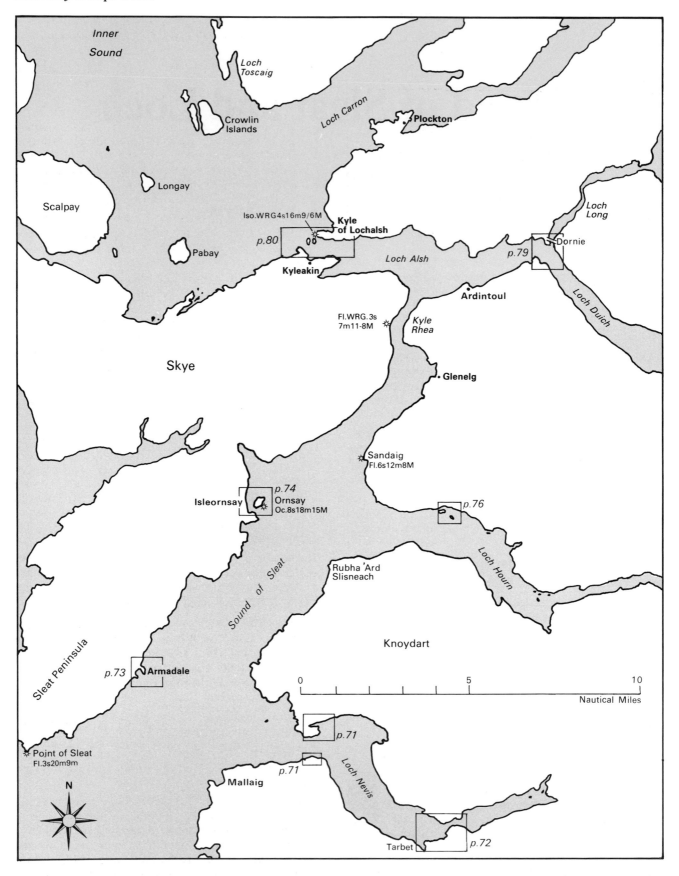

Inner
Sound

Loch
Toscaig

Crowlin
Islands

Loch Carron

•Plockton

Longay

Scalpay

Pabay

Iso.WRG4s16m9/6M

**Kyle
of Lochalsh**

p.80

Loch Long

p.79

•Dornie

Kyleakin

Loch Alsh

Loch Duich

Skye

Fl.WRG.3s
7m11-8M

*Kyle
Rhea*

•**Ardintoul**

•**Glenelg**

Sandaig
Fl.6s12m8M

p.74
Ornsay
Oc.8s18m15M

Isleornsay

p.76

Rubha 'Ard
Slisneach

Loch Hourn

Knoydart

0   5   10

Nautical Miles

Sleat Peninsula

p.73 •**Armadale**

Sound of Sleat

p.71

✷ Point of Sleat
Fl.3s20m9m

p.71

N

Mallaig

Loch Nevis

Tarbet

p.72

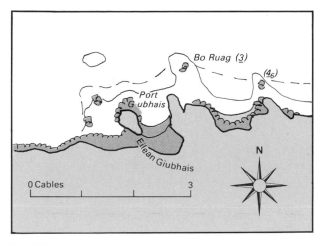

Port Giubhais

Glaschoille, 57°02'N 5°43'W, is particularly suitable in northerly winds to which Mallaig is exposed. Drying rocks in the approach are marked as follows: Bogha Don by a tapered stone beacon with a cross topmark, Sgeirean Glasa by a tripod beacon. Drying reefs extend about ¼ cable northwest and southeast of Sgeirean Glasa beacon and other rocks lie further inshore. A white monumental statue stands near the southeast point of Rubha Raonuill.

The bay south of Glaschoille House and east of Eilean na Glaschoille is occupied by workboats on moorings, but space can usually be found to anchor among them. The bottom falls away steeply ½ cable from the low water line. Holding is said to be good, even in easterly winds.

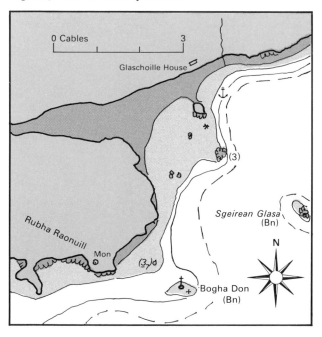

Glaschoille

Inverie, 57°02'N 5°41'W, is in the northeast corner of the outer loch. Anchor clear of moorings and the approach to the pier, but the holding is poor. The pier is constructed of concrete piles, with steps at its east side.

Shop, post office, telephone, hotel, ferry to Mallaig. Meals available at The Pier House if booked in advance.

Tarbet Bay, 56°58'·3N 5°38'W, on the south shore near the west end of the narrows. Green huts belonging to an adventure centre stand on the shore of a bay west of Ardintigh Point, ½ mile west of Tarbet Bay, and a wooden house stands on Torr an Albannaich, the east point of the bay, with a flagstaff on an islet off the point; a drying rock lies ¼ cable west of the islet. Lobster creels with floating lines are often moored in the bay; it is liable to be very squally, especially in southerly winds.

Loch Nevis Narrows, 56°59'N 5°37'W, is entered eastward of Torr an Albannaich (see above). Roinn a' Chaolais, a long shoal spit, extends southwest from the north point of the entrance to the narrows and there are various drying rocks in and beyond the narrows. Tidal streams run at 3 knots, turning as above.

Steer for the north side of Torr an Albannaich and when ½ cable from the shore steer for a white cottage on the south shore beyond Kylesmorar 065°. Alter course again to keep in mid-channel at the beginning of the narrows, closing the north shore beyond the white cottage to avoid Sgeir an t-Sruith and a drying spit at the east end of the south side of the channel.

A shoal rock on the north side, 3 cables beyond the east end of the narrows is avoided by keeping Kylesknoydart cottage open south of the north point at the east end of the narrows 257°. Drying rocks lie up to a cable off either shore. At the head of the loch anchor either north or southeast of Eilean Maol as convenient clear of any moorings; the head of the loch dries for ½ mile. A new jetty was being built in the bay ½ mile west of Eilean Maol in 1989.

Occasional anchorages in Sound of Sleat

Sandaig Bay, 57°02'·5N 5°46'W, is an attractive daytime stop, but if coming from Loch Nevis the rocks on the east side should be carefully studied. At the head of the bay a rock dries at half tide about a cable southeast of the islet.

Dun Ban, 57°04'N 5°47'·3W.

Airor, 57°05'N 5°46'W, is best visited at neaps or with a very shallow-draught boat; the entrance between the island and a reef off the south point is only ½ cable wide and submerged rocks extend ½ cable southwest from the island.

Camas Daraich, 57°01'N 6°00'W, lies immediately east of Point of Sleat with a beach at its head; a rock more than a cable from the west side of the bay dries at about half tide with a drying reef north of it and other drying rocks southwest. Cables which formerly obstructed the west side of the bay are not shown on current charts.

Port na Long is a more open bay a mile east of Camas Daraich.

Inverie   Inverie House

Loch Nevis entrance.

Rubh Raonuill

Tarbet Bay and the Narrows

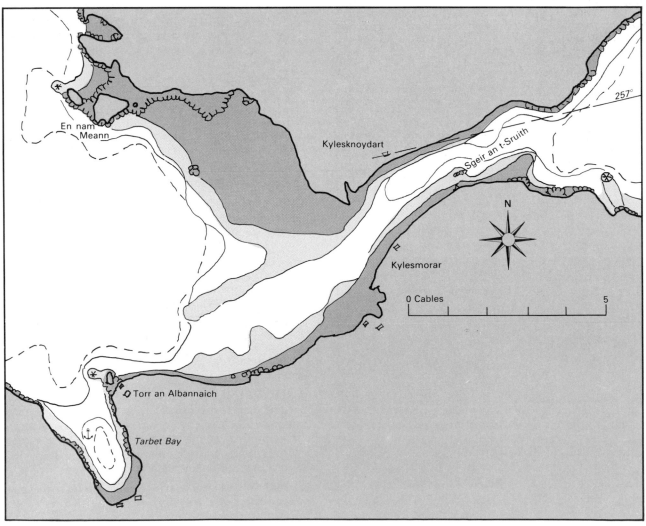

En nam Meann

Kylesknoydart

Sgeir an t-Sruith

257°

N

Kylesmorar

0 Cables   5

Torr an Albannaich

Tarbet Bay

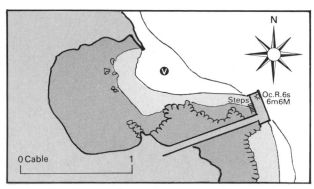

Armadale.

Eilean Giubhais, Loch Nevis. Rubha Raonuill beyond with Glaschoille House to the right.

Acairseid an Rudha on the west side of the Sleat peninsula 7 cables north of the light beacon has a jetty and leading beacons, originally for servicing the light, but is probably best visited from the land.

Armadale

57°04'N 5°53'·5W

Tides

As at Mallaig (interpolated, as Mallaig tides are related to Oban in Admiralty *Tide Tables*).

Constant −0040 Ullapool (−0500 Dover)

Height in metres

MHWS	MHWN	MTL	MLWN	MLWS
5·0	3·8	2·9	2·0	0·7

Dangers and marks

Eilean Maol, 3 metres high, is the outermost of a group of rocks east of Ardvasar Promontory (Rubha Phoil), SSE of Armadale Pier. A white building on the head of the pier is conspicuous. A detached rock dries ½ cable NNE of Eilean Maol; the NNE face of the pier open leads clear of the detached rock.

Anchorage

HIDB visitors' moorings are laid in the bay. Together with Sleat Marine Services' moorings these leave little room for anchoring, but the bottom is firm sand. The bay is exposed to seas from northeast and in these conditions Knock Bay (see below) may be more comfortable.

Lights

Armadale pier head shows Oc.R.6s6m6M, but is not easily picked out among the shore lights.

At night, when approaching from southwest keep Isle Ornsay light in sight to clear Eilean Maol.

Services and supplies

Shop, hotel, water at pier (concrete steps on the north side are very abrasive). Diesel, emergency repairs to hull, engine and sails, and some chandlery, from Sleat Marine Services (☎ 047 14 216). Doctor and district nurse.

Other anchorages

Knock Bay, 3 miles NNE of Armadale; the holding is said to be bad and the west side of the bay foul; the depth decreases suddenly from 18 to 1 metre.

Camas Croise, 57°08'N 5°48'W, has a bottom of stiff clay.

Armadale   *Photo:* Mike Balmforth

Isleornsay Harbour

57°08′·8N 5°47′·7W

Tides

Constant −0050 Ullapool (−0510 Dover)

Height in metres

MHWS	MHWN	MTL	MLWN	MLWS
4·8	3·7	2·7	1·6	0·7

Dangers and marks

A white lighthouse 19 metres high stands on Eilean Sionnach, a tidal islet southeast of Ornsay. A grey stone light beacon stands on the northeast side of a reef off the north end of Ornsay, but part of the reef extends northwest of the beacon – give the north shore of Ornsay a berth of well over a cable. The bay shoals gradually towards its head and dries about a cable short of the pier.

Lights

Ornsay lighthouse Oc.8s18m15M
Ornsay Island light beacon Fl.R.6s8m4M
Pier head 2F.R(vert) and floodlights

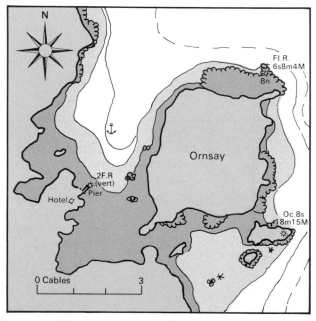

Isleornsay Harbour

Anchorages

Fishing boats use the pier and moorings in this anchorage and enter and leave at night, including, contrary to custom in Scotland, on Sunday; a good anchor light must be shown. Salmon nets may be encountered on the west side of the bay. Anchorage off Duisdale Hotel at the west side of the entrance is

Ornsay lighthouse

more out of the way and said to be more sheltered, as well as being a shorter distance to row ashore. Visitors' moorings had been laid some years ago but it is thought that they are not currently maintained.

Supplies

Small shop at hotel by the pier. Post office, petrol, water tap.

Other anchorages

Loch na Dal, 57°10′N 5°47′W, is a better anchorage in northerly winds.

Sgeir Ghobhlach

Stands above water on a coastal reef ¾ cable offshore on the north side of the entrance to Loch na Dal and detached rocks, both drying and submerged, lie more than a cable from the shore in places up to 2 miles northeast of Sgeir Ghobhlach.

Loch Hourn

57°08′N 5°40′W

One of the most spectacular lochs in Scotland but subject to very high rainfall and severe squalls.

Chart

2541 (1:25,000). OS map *33*.

Tides

The in-going stream begins −0610 Ullapool (+0155 Dover). The out-going stream begins +0005 Ullapool (−0415 Dover). Streams run at 3 knots in narrows east of Corr Eileanan, with an eddy on the flood on the south side of the inner loch, but they are weak in the outer loch.

Constant −0110 Ullapool (−0530 Dover)

Height in metres

MHWS	MHWN	MTL	MLWN	MLWS
5·0	3·8	2·9	2·0	0·8

Dangers and marks

Sgeir Ulibhe, in the entrance of the loch about one third of the width from the north side, dries 2·1 metres, with the remains of a metal beacon on it. A rock just submerged lies a cable west of Sgeir Ulibhe, and Clansman Rock, halfway between Sgeir Ulibhe and the north shore, has a depth of only 2·1 metres over it.

Eilean Rarsaidh, Loch Hourn, from north.

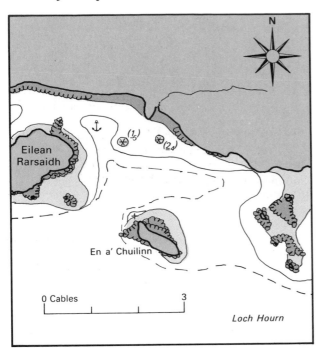

Eilean Rarsaidh

Anchorages

Eilean Rarsaidh, 57°09′N 5°37′W, on the north shore of the outer loch has several drying rocks as on the plan which are not correctly shown on older copies of chart *2541*. Anchor north or east of Eilean Rar-saidh. Shelter is said to be better than would appear from the chart and it is often preferred to Isleornsay.

Camas Ban, 57°08′N 5°34′W, Arnisdale. Anchor on the west side of the bay close northeast of Eilean Tioram.

Eilean a' Phiobaire (57°07′N 5°35′W) – The Piper's Island – has a navigable passage between the island and the south shore. Anchor south of the island. Sgeir Leathan, 2·7 metres high, lies ¼ mile from the east shore east of Piper's Island.

Poll a' Mhuineil, 57°06′N 5°34′W, is deep until close to the head of the pool and subject to severe squalls from south.

Loch Hourn Beag

57°06′·6N 5°24′W

Directions

The upper part of Loch Hourn is reached through a sequence of narrow passages east of Corr Eileanan. The head of Barrisdale Bay, south of Corr Eileanan, dries up to half a mile. Ellice Shoal lies 4 cables west of the two southern Corr Eileanan, and Duncan Shoal lies 2 cables west of the north Corr Eilean. The tide runs at 3 knots through the narrows east of Corr Eileanan.

Upper Loch Hourn from the north shore. Eilean a' Gharb-Iain is right of centre and Caolas Mor at upper left.

The main passage is south of Corr Eileanan, and the southwest shore should be kept between ¼–½ mile until the south point of the first narrows is open south of the south Corr Eilean. Pass within 2 cables south of the south island and then steer to pass within a cable south of Eilean a' Gharb-Iain to avoid an extensive bank which dries off the south shore.

The passage between the north and middle Corr Eileanan is clean but the south side of Eilean a' Gharb-Iain must be kept in sight in the passage 085° to avoid Duncan and Ellice Shoals.

At Caolas Mor, 1¼ miles east of Corr Eileanan, the south shore should be kept ½ cable off to avoid an extensive bank which dries southwest of the promontory on the north side of the narrows.

At Eilean Mousker (Mhogh-sgeir), just over a mile ENE of Caolas Mor, the passage is south of the island, keeping closer to the island to avoid a drying bank off the south shore. Island Rock, ½ cable east of the island, covers at half tide.

Caolas an Loch Bhig, 1¼ miles further east, lead to Loch Beag. The channel winds around and is only 0·6 metre deep, but if the passage is taken on the last two hours of the flood it should present little problem. When you can see clear water through the middle of the entrance there is 2·4 metres in the channel. At this time Island Rock, east of Eilean Mhogh-sgeir, is just covered, around half tide.

After passing the cottage at Skiary on the south shore outside the narrows, close the south shore when a ruined shed is abeam. Keep about 20 metres from the south shore until you come to a weed-covered spit with two rocks on the shore above it; follow closely the edge of the spit until on a line between the two rocks and the west end of the beach on the north shore.

Follow close to the north shore and then along the edge of the shingle spit which extends from the north shore, until more than midway across the channel again and then make for the middle of Loch Beag. The tidal stream runs at about 2 knots and tends to set a yacht off course.

Holding in Loch Beag is poor and the head of the loch dries out to a line from the steps on the south side to the ruins of a boathouse on the north side. In a westerly gale the best shelter is in a bight of the north shore north of Eilean Mhogh-sgeir.

Sandaig Bay
57°10′N 5°41′·5W

Lies 1½ miles north of the entrance to Loch Hourn (not to be confused with the bay of the same name north of the entrance to Loch Nevis) southeast of Sandaig Islands, on the northwest point of which is a light beacon. Rocks submerged and drying lie up to 1½ cables southeast of the islands, and off Sgeir nan Eun the most southerly above-water rock. A drying reef extends about a cable from Rubha Mor at the southeast point of the bay. Good shelter in winds with any northerly component.

The tortuous channel leading to Loch Hourn Beag, from the south shore at low water springs.

Glenelg

57°12′·5N 5°38′W

On the east shore of Sound of Sleat a mile southeast of the entrance to Kyle Rhea. A wooden jetty lies a cable south of the promontory Rubha Mhic Cuinn on which stands a monument. A submerged rock lies a cable west of Rubha Mhic Cuinn. Anchor southwest of the jetty (the head of which covers at HW) clear of moorings, but the holding is poor. A small pool where local boats are moored, the entrance to which dries, lies north of the promontory.

Supplies at Glenelg

½ mile from the jetty: shop, post office, *Calor Gas*, petrol, hotel.

Kyle Rhea and Loch Alsh

Chart

2540 (1:20,000). OS map *33*.

Tides

Tidal streams in Kyle Rhea run at up to 8 knots and possibly more on occasions, with eddies along both sides; during the second half of the flood (north-going) tide the stream sets onto rocks on the west side of the channel.

At the south entrance to the kyle a southerly wind and ebb tide set up dangerous overfalls. An eddy forms in Bernera Bay southeast of the south entrance on the south-going tide. The stream runs at its fastest in the south entrance to the kyle.

The north-going stream begins +0600 Ullapool (−0140 Dover). The south-going stream begins at HW Ullapool (−0420 Dover).

Dangers and marks

Drying rocks extend up to ¾ cable off both shores of Kyle Rhea.

During the second half of the flood the stream sets across rocks on the west shore which are covered.

A light beacon stands on the west shore of the kyle.

Sgeir na Caillich, nearly 2 cables north of the west point of the north entrance, is marked by a concrete pillar 2 metres in height.

Directions

Keep in mid-channel. If tacking beware eddies inshore. Coming south if the wind is southerly beware overfalls ½ mile south of the entrance near the west shore. The worst can be avoided by steering for the southeast shore until clear south of a line between Dunan Ruadh and Glenelg village.

Anchorages

To wait for the tide at the south end anchor off the jetty at Glenelg (see above) or south of the mouth of

Kylerhea River on the west shore, north of a cable beacon standing 3½ cables south of the river. A drying bank extends nearly 2 cables from the river mouth.

At the north end anchor at least 1½ cable WNW of Sgeir na Caillich beacon to avoid submerged rocks (although with the large-scale chart space can be found closer to the shore).

Lights

Kyle Rhea light beacon Fl.WRG.3s7m11-8M
Sgeir na Caillich light beacon Fl(2)R.6s3m4M

At night the white sectors of Kyle Rhea light beacon lead through the entrances to the kyle.

Supplies

Glenelg, see above.

East Loch Alsh and Loch Duich

Chart

2541 (1:25,000 and 1:12,500). OS map *33*.

Tides in East Loch Alsh

The in-going stream begins −0610 Ullapool (+0155 Dover). The out-going stream begins −0005 Ullapool (−0425 Dover).

Constant −0025 Ullapool (−0445 Dover)

Height in metres

MHWS	MHWN	MTL	MLWN	MLWS
5·3	3·8	3·0	2·1	0·7

Dangers and marks

Glas Eilean, 6 metres high with extensive drying banks all round it, lies in the middle of the entrance to the east part of Loch Alsh. In the channel to the north of Glas Eilean, Racoon Rock, at a depth of 1·8 metres, is marked by a green conical buoy on its northwest side. Rocks awash and drying extend over ½ cable from the shore northwest of Racoon Rock leaving less than a cable between them and the buoy. A drying bank on the north side of Glas Eilean encroaches on a direct line between the buoy and Eilean Aoinidh, a promontory on the south shore 1½ miles east of Glas Eilean, and a detached drying reef lies 4 cables east of the north part of Glas Eilean.

The channel south of Glas Eilean has drying banks on both sides extending up to 1½ cables in places. In the approach from west a drying bank extends a cable north of Ardintoul Point. A submerged rock lies over a cable east of Glas Eilean on the north side of the channel. Do not approach Ardintoul Point to a depth of less than 10 metres and thereafter keep equidistant between visible shorelines. The low water lines of Glas Eilean and Ardintoul Point in line lead south of the rock east of Glas Eilean.

Anchorages

Avernish Bay, north of Glas Eilean, although obstructed by underwater cables, is useful for shelter in strong east or northeast winds.

Ardintoul Bay, southwest of Glas Eilean, is occupied by fish cages, but there may be space to anchor inshore of them.

Loch Duich is entered between Eilean Aoinidh, a rocky wooded point on the south shore, and Eilean Tioram, which is low and grassy, on the north side. The foreshore of Eilean Tioram dries off 2 cables on the west side and ¾ cable on other sides. Aile More Bank at a depth of 1·8 metres lies in the middle of the loch 3 cables east of Eilean Aoinidh. Eilean Donnan Castle is conspicuous on the northeast shore at the east side of the entrance to Loch Long. Many fish cages are moored off the southwest shore of the loch.

Ob Aoinidh (Totaig), 57°16′N 5°31′·5W, is a small bay on the east side of Eilean Aoinidh. It is surrounded by trees and an extensive reef partly above water lies in the middle of the bay. The bottom is rather hard so that an anchor does not dig in easily and the tide runs strongly round the bay, apparently clockwise on the flood and anticlockwise with the ebb. Several moorings restrict anchoring space.

A rocky shelf extends east of the north point of Eilean Aoinidh but further south the west shore of the bay is steep-to and a line can be taken ashore to restrict swinging and hold a yacht out of the worst of the tide. A rock awash lies less than ¼ cable off the old ferry cottage at the east point of the bay.

Water can be had from a tap at the ferry cottage.

Dornie, 57°17′N 5°31′W, at the mouth of Loch Long northeast of Eilean Aoinidh is an occasional anchorage for buying stores or visiting the castle, but the tide runs strongly into and out from Loch Long. A new bridge is being built across the mouth of Loch Long with restricted headroom. Anchor off a slip on the northwest side of the castle.

Shops, hotels, post office, telephone, petrol, gas.

Ratagan Bay, 57°13′·2N 5°26′·5W, southeast of a promontory which lies southeast of Ratagan youth hostel, a prominent white building. The head of the bay dries out 4 cables, but on the southwest side a depth of 5 metres can be found a cable from the shore, and good shelter has been found there.

Invershiel Anchor off a concrete slip by the hotel on the east side of Bay of Invershiel.

Post office, telephone, hotel, petrol and diesel. Baths at hotel. Shop at Shiel Bridge, ¾ mile.

Loch Alsh, west part

Chart

2540 (1:20,000).

Dangers and marks

A submerged wreck, 2 cables off the south shore of Loch Alsh between Kyle Rhea and Kyle Akin, is marked by an east cardinal buoy.

In Scalpaidh Bay, ½ mile ENE of Eileanan Dubha a rock which dries 0·8 metre lies over a cable offshore.

Anchorages

The following bays on the north side of Loch Alsh have been used for anchoring under appropriate conditions:

Aird a Mhill Bay, 57°16′·5N 5°36′W, provides some shelter in easterly winds but the head of the bay dries off 1 cable and the bottom drops rapidly to over 30 metres. Anchor in 5 metres just east of the mouth of the burn.

Balmacara Bay, 57°17′N 5°39′W; anchor towards the west side of the bay east of a jetty below trees. The rest of the bay dries off for 1 cable.

Scalpaidh Bay, 57°17′N 5°41′·5W; a long rock dries over a cable south of an islet on a drying reef in the middle of the bay. Anchor WSW of the islet.

Loch na Beiste, 57°16′N 5°43′W, south of the east entrance to Kyle Akin is deep, and foul with old moorings, but a narrow shelf on the northwest side has suitable depths for anchoring and it is sheltered from all but easterly winds.

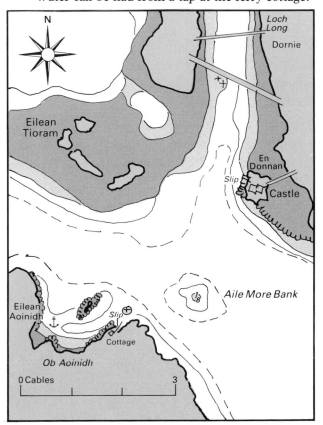

Dornie and Ob Aoinidh

String Rock Buoy   Fishery Pier   Ferry slip

Approach to Kyleakin.

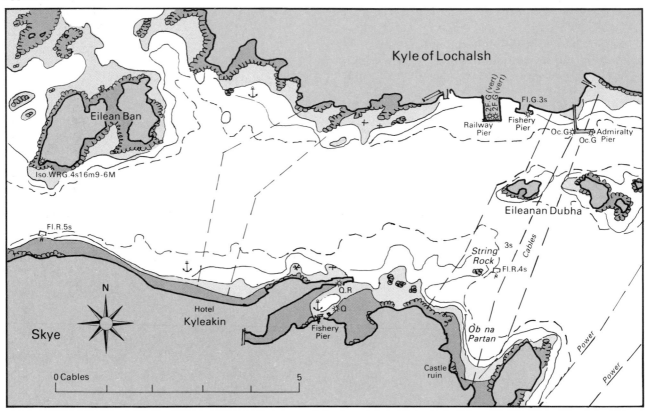

Kyle Akin

Kyle Akin

57°16′·5N 5°43′W

A narrow passage, in places only 1½ cables wide, linking Loch Alsh with the Inner Sound. Plans are being prepared for building a bridge across the west end of the kyle.

Charts

2540 (1:20,000 and 1:12,500), *2209* (1:50,000). OS map *33*.

Tides

Tidal streams in Kyle Akin vary widely between springs and neaps, and are affected by barometric pressure, wind direction, rain, and melting snow. At neaps the wind, in particular, may reverse the direction of flow, a southerly or southwest wind tending towards a west-going stream, and a northerly wind tending towards an east-going stream.

To present the information as simply as possible, perhaps over-simplifying it, the east-going stream begins −0300 Ullapool (+0050 Dover) at springs, and +0100 Ullapool (−0320 Dover) at neaps; the west-going stream begins +0330 Ullapool (−0050 Dover) at springs and −0600 Ullapool (+0110 Dover) at neaps. The west-going stream is usually the stronger, running at up to 4 knots at an extra spring tide. For more detail see the Admiralty *Pilot*.

Constant −0030 Ullapool (−0450 Dover)

Height in metres

MHWS	MHWN	MTL	MLWN	MLWS
5·3	3·9	3·0	2·2	0·8

Dangers and marks

Eileanan Dubha are a group of islands at the east end of the kyle, north of mid-channel. Off Rubha Ard Tresnish, the point of Skye south of Eileanan Dubha, a drying reef extends ½ cable. String Rock which dries, 1½ cables off the south shore 1¾ cables southwest of Eileanan Dubha, is marked by a red can light buoy. Drying rocks lie to the west of String Rock, up to 1½ cables from the shore.

North of Eileanan Dubha at Kyle of Lochalsh several jetties and piers project from the shore but the passage between the islands and the north shore is a cable wide. Rocks drying and submerged lie up to ¾ cable from the shore west of Kyle of Lochalsh.

Kyle Akin lighthouse stands at the west end of the passage at the southwest point of Eilean Ban on the north side of the channel; drying rocks extend ¼ cable south of the lighthouse and a shoal spit ½ cable southeast of it. A red can light buoy lies on the edge of a drying shingle bank on the south side of the channel south of the lighthouse.

Black Eye Rock red can light buoy, 2 cables north of the head of a jetty at a quarry on Skye, west of the west entrance to the kyle, marks the most northeasterly of a patch of submerged rocks; Bogha Beag, a reef which dries 0·6 metre lies 3 cables WSW of the light buoy. An unlit red can buoy lies 3½ cables west of the light buoy. A green conical light buoy 7 cables northwest of the lighthouse marks the outer limit of submerged rocks on the east side of the passage.

Lights

String Rock light buoy Fl.R.4s
Jetties and piers at Kyle of Lochalsh from east to
    west:
    Admiralty Oc.G.6s at each end of its head
    Fishery Pier Fl.G.3s
    Railway Pier 2F.G(vert) at each end of the head
Kyleakin Ferry Slipway Q.R
Eilean Ban lighthouse Iso.WRG.4s16m9-6M
Light buoy south of lighthouse Fl.R.5s
Blackeye Rock light buoy Fl(2)R.10s
Quarry jetty 2F.R(vert)
Light buoy northwest of lighthouse Q.G

At night from either direction the white sector of the lighthouse leads to the entrance to the kyle. Approaching the lighthouse steer towards the red light buoy south of it to clear the reefs off the lighthouse.

Anchorages

Kyleakin, 57°16′·4N 5°43′·5W; a small pool on the south side of Kyle Akin entered through a dredged channel between the ferry slip and a half-tide rock a cable east of it. Most of the inner part of the inlet dries, as well as the bay on its southeast side. A fishery pier with two dolphins stands on the south side of the pool and a mooring lies in the middle of the pool. A yacht should be able to anchor clear of the mooring or lie alongside other boats at the fishery pier or, at three-quarters flood, lie temporarily alongside the quay on the north side of the pool.

Shops, post office, telephone, garage, gas, hotel. A wider selection of shops across the ferry at Kyle of Lochalsh. For water by hose ask at CalMac office on the north quay.

North of Kyleakin, off the King's Arms Hotel; do not anchor to the east of the hotel as cables cross the kyle there. Disturbed by passing traffic and swell in northerly wind. The bottom is blue clay.

Ob na Partan, south of String Rock buoy, has cables running from the head of the bay to the mainland, but ½ cable from the west side there is a depth of 7 metres clear of the cables.

Kyle of Lochalsh

57°16′·8N 5°42′·7W

Berth at the east side of the Railway Pier where dues are charged, or at the Fishery Pier, which is of open-pile construction and subject to disturbance from fishing boats, to go ashore for stores.

Supplies

Shops (including butcher, baker, hardware which stocks some chandlery and paint), post office, bank, telephone, garage, gas, hotel. Diesel from garage (may deliver). Water at Railway Pier. Tourist information office. Doctor, dentist, chemist. Electronic repairs. Showers at car park.

Anchorage

The bay ½ mile west of Railway Pier is clear north of the cable area, with moderate depth for anchoring.

V. The Inner Sound

The Inner Sound, which extends some 20 miles from Broadford Bay to the north end of Rona, together with the Sound of Raasay and Loch Carron, provide an area of sheltered water with spectacular scenery and a wide variety of anchorages; Lochs Torridon and Gairloch may be reached without rounding a major headland.

Cloud caps blowing off the Skye hills are taken to be an indication of imminent squalls.

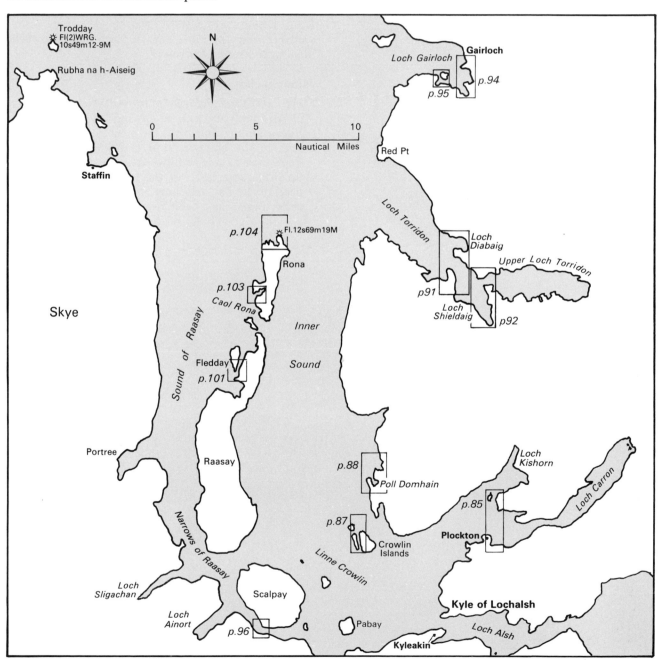

The sound cannot be covered in a simple linear sequence; it will therefore be described in the following order.

- Loch Carron
- The passage and anchorages northeast of Crowlin Islands
- The main fairway
- Loch Torridon and Loch Gairloch
- Broadford and Caolas Scalpay
- Caol Mor and Sound of Raasay
- Caol Rona, Rona and the passage north of Rona
- North and northeast Skye

Charts

2209, 2210 (1:50,000).

Loch Carron (outer part) and Loch Kishorn

57°21′N 5°42′W

Charts

2498 (1:25,000), *2528* (1:15,000). OS map *24*.

Tides

Tidal streams are negligible.

Constant −0010 Ullapool (−0430 Dover)

Height in metres

MHWS	MHWN	MTL	MLWN	MLWS
5·1	3·8	2·9	2·0	0·7

Dangers and marks

The northwest side of the loch is clean and steep-to, but the southeast side is indented with many bays (some of which are suitable for occasional anchorage), with offlying islands and drying rocks. A course from the green light buoy, northwest of Kyle Akin lighthouse, towards An Dubh-aird, a promontory 4 miles northeast, keeping two cables off each island and point passes clear of all hidden dangers, although a drying reef southwest of Black Islands, ¾ mile NNE of the light buoy, is close to this line.

In Loch Kishorn an oil platform construction site on the north shore has ceased working. For the inner part of Loch Carron see page 86.

Lights

A directional light on the south side of Rubha na h-Airde, the promontory dividing Loch Carron from Loch Kishorn, Fl(3)WRG.10s8m6-4M, gives some guidance, and the inner part of Loch Carron is well lit as far as Strome Narrows.

Minor anchorages

Camas an t-Strathaidh, 57°20′N 5°41′W, ¾ mile south of An Dubh-aird can be entered by either side of Eilean Dubh Dhurinish, the most northwesterly island in the entrance, but a drying reef extends more than a cable southwest, and a submerged reef up to a cable ESE, of the island. The sides and head of the bay are shoal and drying, with drying rocks more than a cable from the shore.

Loch Carron approach.

Kishorn Island, 57°22'·5N 5°39'W; the anchorage is between the island and Rubha na h-Airde, the promontory on the south side of Loch Kishorn. Drying rocks extend more than a cable SSW of the island, leaving a passage less than a cable wide between Kishorn Island and Garbh Eilean (Garra Islands). If approaching from seaward, make for the middle of Garbh Eilean and keep less than ½ cable from that island; the approach by the north side of the island is safer.

Head of Loch Kishorn A reef which dry 3·6 metres lies 4 cables from the east shore northwest of Achintraid village, and most of the area between the reef and the shore dries. Anchor between the reef and a promontory 3 cables south of it. Alternatively, west of Ardarroch on the north side of the head of the loch, off boat houses northeast of an islet on the east side of the mouth of River Kishorn.

Shop, post office, garage (petrol and diesel) on main road about ¼ mile from Ardarroch.

Plockton

57°20'·5N 5°38'·5W

Tides

Tidal streams are negligible.

Constant −0020 Ullapool (−0440 Dover)

Height in metres

MHWS	MHWN	MTL	MLWN	MLWS
5·5	4·1	3·1	2·2	0·8

Chart

2528 (1:15,000). OS maps *24, 25*.

Buoys and beacons

These have been changed frequently over the past ten years, partly to meet the needs of the construction yard at Loch Kishorn, the materials for which were transported by barge from the railway at Strome Ferry, and it is essential to have up-to-date information. The buoys have in the past been removed when work ceases at the construction yard and replaced when a new contract begins; however they were re-established in 1987.

Dangers and marks

Dangers and marks in the approach to Plockton are described below; those for the passage further up Loch Carron are described in later pages.

Eilean a' Chait (Cat Island) is a tidal islet with a disused lighthouse north of Rubha Mor, the promontory north of Plockton. Between An Dubh-aird 1¼ miles WSW, and Cat Island, drying rocks extend more than a cable northwest of above-water rocks and islets. The south tangent of Eilean an t-Sratha, the largest of Strome Islands (or alternatively the summit of Creag Mhaol, east of Strome Islands) open north of Cat Island 092° leads clear of the most northerly of these drying rocks.

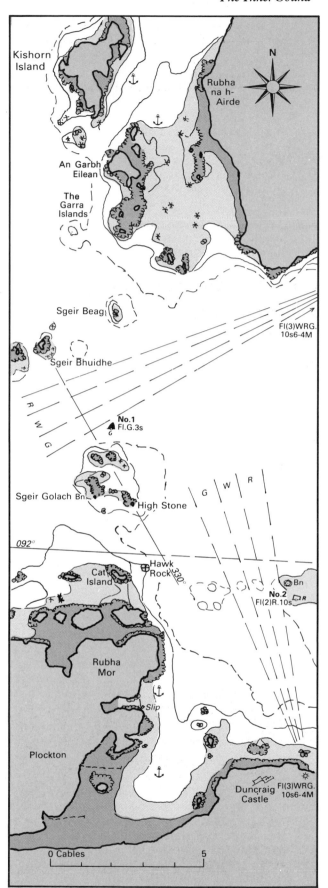

Plockton

Plockton from south; Loch Kishorn upper right.

Sgeir Golach, an area of drying rocks about ¼ mile across, lies ¼ mile north of Cat Island. The southeast point of these rocks is High Stone, 1 metre high, and an iron tripod beacon with a basket topmark stands on the southwest point. A drying rock lies nearly ½ cable south of the line between the beacon and High Stone. A green conical light buoy (*No. 1*) lies off the north side of Sgeir Golach.

Sgeir Bhuidhe, 4 metres high, and Sgeir a' Chinn 1 metre high, lie 3 cables northwest of *No. 1* light buoy; Sgeir Beag, ¼ mile ENE of Sgeir Bhuidhe, dries 1·5 metres and is very dangerous if passing direct between Loch Kishorn and Plockton.

Hawk Rock, almost awash at LW lies ¾ cable ENE of Cat Island. High Stone in line with Sgeir Bhuidhe 330° leads east of Hawk Rock.

Bogha Dubh Sgeir, on which is a beacon similar to that on Sgeir Golach, lies ½ mile east of Cat Island, with *No. 2* red can light buoy south of it.

Plockton Rocks dry at half tide ¾ cable northwest and 1¼ cable NNW of Sgeir Bhuidhe, an islet (different from the one of the same name above) off the southeast shore. *No. 1* buoy or High Stone in line with the east tangent of Rubha Mor leads west of these rocks. A reef dries nearly ½ cable off Roinn an Fhaing at Plockton village.

Directions

After passing An Dubh-aird steer for *No. 1* buoy about 060° until Eilean an t-Sratha is clear open north of Cat Island; steer to pass between Cat Island and High Stone until High Stone is in line with Sgeir Bhuidhe 330°. Steer to keep this line astern until Rubha Mor is abeam and steer for Plockton village.

Lights

Directional light on south side of Rubha na h-Airde Fl(3)WRG.10s6-4M

No. 1 light buoy Fl.G.3s
Duncraig directional light on south shore Fl(3)WRG. 10s6-4M
No. 2 light buoy Fl(2)R.10s

At night approach in the white sector of the first light; after passing *No. 1* buoy alter course to steer for *No. 2* buoy, and after another ½ mile steer for the lights of Plockton village.

Anchorage

Anchor off the slip at the north end of the village or between the village and Duncraig Castle; Rubha Mor in line with the west side of Kishorn Island 350° leads ¾ cable west of Plockton Rocks.

Supplies

Shop, hotels, post office, telephone, *Calor Gas* from caravan site (¼ mile north of village). Water from tap (hidden in old rusty pump beside the track across the village green); use of a hose may also be offered from house by the slip at the north end of the village. Showers in post office building (ask at house on south side of post office). Laundry at caravan site. Diesel from Calum Mackenzie (Leisure Marine ☎ 059 984 306). Sailing Club.

Strome Narrows and Inner Loch Carron

Chart

2528 (1:15,000) only as far east as Strome Narrows; for the inner loch use *2209*. OS maps *24, 25*.

Tides

In Strome Narrows tidal streams run at up to 3 knots but are negligible elsewhere. The in-going stream begins +0605 Ullapool (+0145 Dover). The out-going stream begins +0005 Ullapool (−0415 Dover).

Constant −0010 Ullapool (−0430 Dover)

Height in metres

MHWS	MHWN	MTL	MLWN	MLWS
5·1	3·8	2·9	2·0	0·7

Directions

From the approach to Plockton pass south of *No. 2* light buoy, north of *No. 3* green conical light buoy and Ulluva island on which stands a rough stone beacon, and south of two further red can light buoys. If the buoys are not in place, Bogha Dubh Sgeir beacon and Ulluva are sufficient guide. The bay to starboard dries off 2 cables, and at the narrows green conical buoy *No. 6* marks a shoal area on the south side. Buoy *No. 7* (red can) is of no significance to yachts.

Loch Carron

Loch Carron is an extensive village on the northwest shore of the loch; Slumbay Island, a peninsula at the south end of the village partly shelters a bay known as Slumbay Harbour the shores of which dry off more than a cable. Two rocks on drying reefs, Sgeir Chreagach and Sgeir Fhada, stand ½ mile offshore; Red Rocks some of which are submerged and some awash at LWS lie in the gap between Slumbay Island and Sgeir Chreagach. Take this passage above half tide and anchor 2 cables offshore in Slumbay Harbour, or at the northeast end of the village closer inshore; the foreshore in front of the village dries off ¼ mile, there is a drying area ¼ mile northeast of Sgeir Fhada, and the head of the loch dries off for 1 mile.

Supplies

Shops, post office, telephone, hotel, petrol and diesel at garages, *Calor Gas* at West End Garage. Bicycle hire.

Caolas Mor

57°21'N 5°49'W

Chart

2480, 2498 (1:25,000).

Dangers and marks

In the passage northeast of Crowlin Islands rocks submerged and drying on the northeast side of the passage extend 3½ cables south of Aird Mhor on the west side of Loch Toscaig. The northeast tangent of Eilean na Ba open of a 5-metre rock off the southwest side of Aird Mhor 334° leads close southwest of the outermost rock.

A rock which dries 1·1 metres lies 2 cables north of Eilean Beag, the most northwesterly of the Crowlin Islands, with other rocks between the drying rock and the island.

Light

A light beacon, Fl.6s32m6M, stands on the west side of Eilean Beag.

Tides

In Caolas Mor tidal streams run at 1 knot at springs. The southeast-going stream begins +0605 Ullapool (+0145 Dover). The northwest-going stream begins +0005 Ullapool (−0415 Dover).

Anchorages

Loch Toscaig, 57°22'N 5°48'·5W. An occasional anchorage east or southeast of the pier. In approach note the rocks described above; coming from west there is a clear passage 2 cables wide north of Bo Du, the most northerly rock, which dries 1·5 metres. Shellfish farming equipment on both sides of the loch are marked by orange buoys. Camas na Ba on the west side of the loch is occupied by moorings.

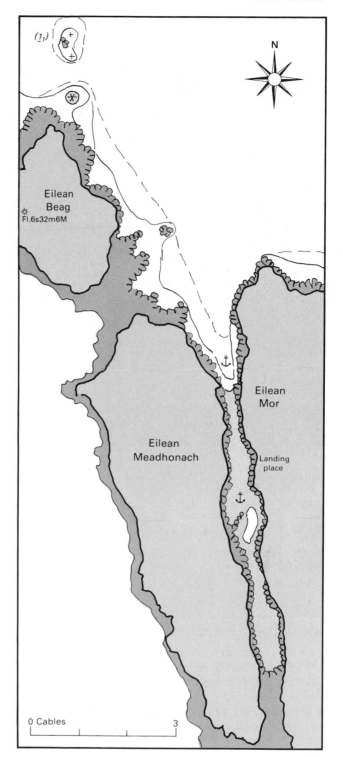

Crowlin Islands

Crowlin Harbour, 57°21'N 5°50'·6W, between Eilean Mor and Eilean Meadhonach provides an occasional anchorage in its entrance. Above half tide the creek can be entered, but most of it is shallow and the flood tide runs strongly in the entrance. Approaching from west keep at least ¼ mile north of Eilean Beag to avoid the drying rock described above.

87

Anchorage at the entrance to Crowlin Harbour

Poll Domhain and Poll Creadha

57°24′N 5°49′W

Chart

2480 (1:25,000). OS map *24*.

Tides

Constant −0015 Ullapool (−0435 Dover)

Height in metres

MHWS	MHWN	MTL	MLWN	MLWS
5·3	4·0	3·1	2·2	0·7

Poll Domhain

Poll Domhain is entered by the north side of Ard Ban which is identified by a conspicuous white beach on its west side. Sgeir Mhor, which dries 3·2 metres 2 cables west of Ard Ban, is marked by a thin steel perch which is almost covered at HW, but this is not at the outer edge of the rock, and like all the perches described below may be missing. The high water line of the east side of Eilean na Ba in line with the east side of Eilean Mor (Crowlin Islands) 168° leads west of Sgeir Mhor. Drying reefs extend a cable north of

Ard Ban. From northwest pass south of An Ruadh Eilean. The head of the pool is narrowed by drying reefs on either side.

Extensive reefs lie on the west side of the inlet. The best landing place is on the west side of the more southerly reef.

Poll Creadha

Poll Creadha is obstructed by drying reefs and safe access depends on the perches shown on the plan being in place. It should not be attempted if any swell is running. Some of the perches have been altered in the last few years and may be altered again, so that even more caution than usual should be exercised. A pair of white posts on shore used to mark the passage south of the central reef. The rear post has been destroyed, but the remaining post just to the right of the right-hand corner of the second cottage from the left, see photo page 90, leads through the passage on approximately 123°. Several poles which carry overhead cables might be confused with the post.

Supplies

Post office, basic stores, petrol at Camusterrach.

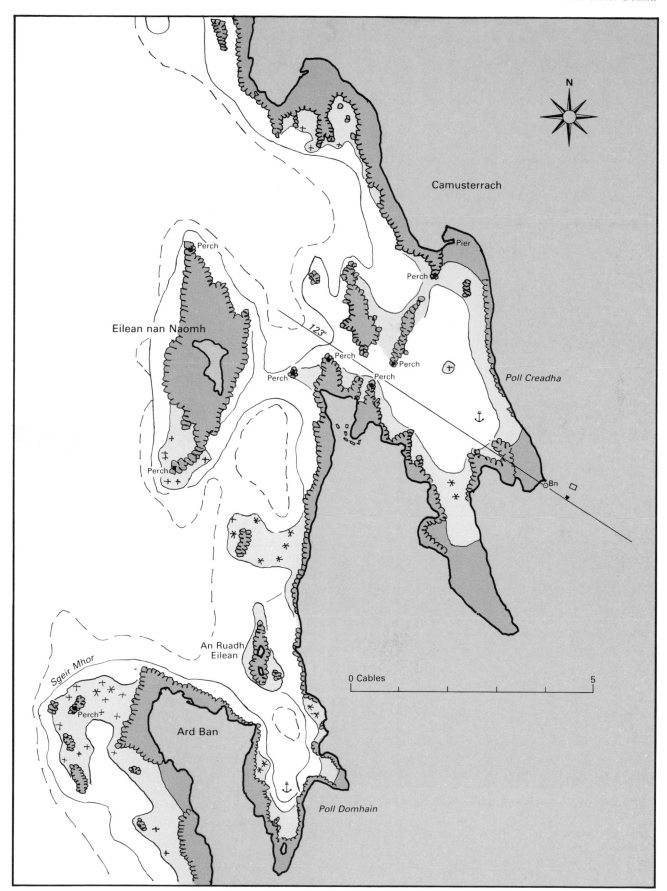

Poll Domhain and Poll Creadha

Poll Domhain

Poll Creadha at low water springs. The perch off the end of the reef shows how difficult it would be to identify at high water.

Inner Sound

The direction of buoyage throughout the Inner Sound and Sound of Raasay is northward although the flood tide runs southward.

Charts

2209, 2210 (1:50,000). OS map *24*.

Tides

In the Inner Sound the flood stream runs south, and spring rates are no more than 1 knot off headlands. The south going stream begins +0605 Ullapool (+0145 Dover). The north-going stream begins −0005 Ullapool (−0415 Dover).

Dangers and marks

The fairway of Inner Sound is clean, but both in Caolas Mor, northeast of Crowlin Islands (above, page 87), and on a passage to Caol Mor between Scalpay and Raasay (below, page 98), there are specific dangers.

The Crowlin Islands, and Dun Caan on Raasay, the conspicuous plug of a former volcano, are useful reference marks.

An oil platform construction site south of Crowlin Islands, formerly marked by yellow buoys, has been discontinued.

Drying rocks lie up to 2 cables from the shore between ¾ and 1 mile south of the Range Control building (see below).

Underwater weapons testing is carried out in a restricted area between Raasay and the mainland marked by yellow pillar light buoys. Operations are controlled from the Range Control building at Ru na Lachan on the east shore 7 miles north of Crowlin Beag. The buoys are as follows:

C in mid-sound 3½ miles northwest of Crowlin Beag.
D 5 cables off Raasay, 2¾ miles west of *C*.
B about 1 mile NNW of the Range Control building.
4 special yellow buoys near the Range Control building mark a cable area.

When underwater testing is being carried out a red flag is shown at the Range Control building (or, by night, a red light). A vessel approaching the restricted area will be contacted by VHF or by a patrol boat, usually a naval MFV. It is helpful for yachts approaching this area to call *Range Control* on VHF and to listen to traffic on Ch 13. Yachts will be directed to pass clear of the restricted area to one side, usually to the west. Information about each day's testing programme is broadcast on Ch 8 at 0800.

Lights

Eilean Ban (Kyle Akin) lighthouse Iso.WRG.4s16m 9-6M
Crowlin Islands light beacon Fl.6s32m6M
Eyre Point, Caol Mor Fl.WR.3s5m9/6M
Ru na Lachan Oc.WR.8s21m10M (note, the light beacon was moved to a point 6 cables north of the Range Control building in 1988)
Restricted area buoys:
  C Fl.Y.5s
  D Fl.Y.10s
  B Fl.Y.10s
Cable area buoys off Range Control building Fl.Y.5s
Garbh Eilean (south end of Rona) Fl.3s
Various other light beacons on the east side of Rona have no navigational significance.
Rona lighthouse Fl.12s69m19M is obscured from 358°-050°

Loch Torridon

57°35′N 5°45′W

An impressive loch in three parts joined by passages 4 and 2 cables wide, surrounded by spectacular mountains in its upper part.

Charts

2210 (1:50,000), obsolete chart *2638* (1:25,000) with depths in fathoms. OS *Outdoor Leisure Map of Cuillin and Torridon Hills* (1:25,000) shows useful detail in Upper Loch Torridon. OS map *24*.

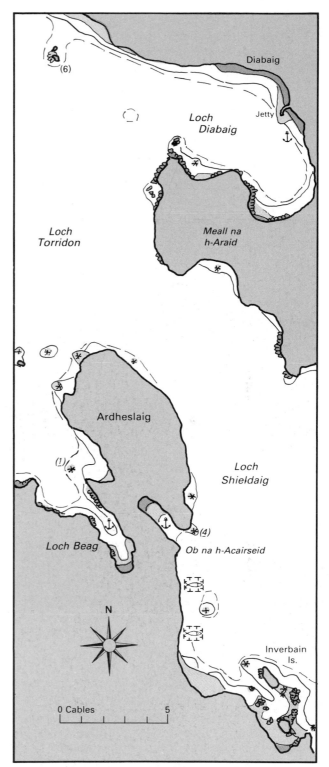

Loch Torridon

Tides

The in-going stream begins −0605 Ullapool (+0200 Dover). The out-going stream begins −0005 Ullapool (−0425 Dover).

Constant −0020 Ullapool (−0440 Dover)

Height in metres

MHWS	MHWN	MTL	MLWN	MLWS
5·6	4·2	3·2	2·2	0·7

Ob Gorm Mor, Upper Loch Torridon   *Photo:* Wallace Clark

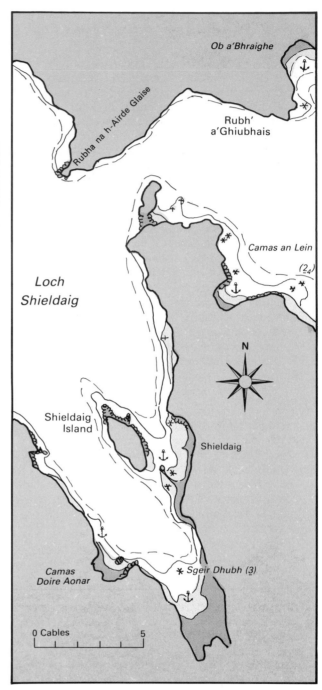

Loch Torridon

Dangers and marks in the outer loch

The entrance is 3 miles wide between Rubha na Fearn on the south side and Red Point on the north. Murchadh Breac 3 cables offshore a mile west of Rubha na Fearn dries 1·5 metres and is a danger to yachts coming from south. Sgeir a' Ghair, 1¼ cables northeast of Rubha na Fearn, is 0·5 metre high.

Murchadh Breac is cleared on its west side by keeping Ard na Claise Moire, a point 5 miles south, open west of Eilean Chuaig 187°. The school house at Diabaig in Loch Torridon (the most southerly house there) open of Rubha na Fearn 098° leads north of Murchadh Breac.

Towards the north side of the entrance Sgeir na Trian, 2 metres high, lies 1¼ miles SSE of Red Point and is in the way when coming from, or going, north. Sgeir Ghlas, 1 metre high lies outside the mouth of a bay, 3 cables offshore 4 cables ESE of Red Point.

The southwest shore between Rubha na Fearn and Ardheslaig, the promontory on the south side of the first narrows, is very broken with bays between rocky points and rocks which dry more than a cable from the shore.

The northeast shore is almost featureless as far as Rubha na h-Airde on the north side of the narrows. Sgeir Dughall, 6 metres high, lies ¼ mile offshore 7 cables northwest of Rubha na h-Airde.

Minor anchorages in the outer loch

Camas Eilean, 1¼ miles west of Ardheslaig. Occasional anchorage on the west or south side of the bay south of Eilean Mor. A fish cage is moored southeast of Eilean Mor; the passage between Eilean Mor and the mainland is constricted by drying reefs.

Loch a' Chracaich, 57°33'N 5°44'W, a mile southwest of Ardheslaig. Rocks ½ cable east of Sgeir Glas off the north point of the bay dry 3 metres, and submerged rocks lie about a cable from the south shore east of the mouth of a burn. Fish cages are moored south of the north point and on the southeast side of the bay. Anchor in the northwest corner, or at the south end of the southwest side of the bay; weed may be a problem. Telephone. No stores.

Loch Beag, 57°33'N 5°43'W, a narrow inlet ¾ mile south of Ardheslaig is occupied by fishing-boat moorings. Dubh Sgeir, 2 metres high, lies ¼ mile west of Ardheslaig, northwest of the approach to the inlet. A drying reef lies 1¼ cables ENE of Dubh Sgeir, and a submerged rock ½ cable NNW. Other drying rocks lie near the shore further east. A rock 1 cable northwest of the north point of Loch Beag dries 1 metre. Rocks drying and submerged extend ¼ cable from either shore in places. Several inshore fishing boats are moored in Loch Beag, but it is a useful alternative anchorage to Ob na h-Acairseid (see below) in easterly winds.

Red Bay, 57°38'N 5°48'W, immediately east of Red Point gives good shelter from northerly winds off a sandy beach. A submerged rock lies ½ cable west of Sgeir Ghlas, 1 metre high, which lies 3 cables south of the middle of the head of the bay, and salmon nets and fishing floats lie in the bay. Telephone 1½ miles along track.

Loch Diabaig, 57°34'·5N 5°42'W, on the northeast side of the outer loch northeast of Rubha na h-Airde. Sgeir Dughall, 6 metres high, stands 2 cables offshore ¾ mile northwest of Rubha na h-Airde. Anchor either side of the jetty, the head of which covers at high water; the bay on the south side of the head of the loch is full of fish cages.

Loch Shieldaig

57°32'N 5°40'W

This is the middle part of Loch Torridon, with a good anchorage between Shieldaig village on the east side of the loch and Shieldaig Island, which is 41 metres high and thickly wooded. Drying rocks extend a cable from the northwest point of the island and ½ cable north from its northeast side. A rock ½ cable south of the point below the church at the north end of the village dries 2 metres. The south end of the passage is blocked by drying and above-water rocks.

Supplies

Shops, post office, telephone, hotel. *Calor Gas* at Camas Doire Aonar on the west side of Loch Shieldaig.

Anchorages

The head of Loch Shieldaig dries for 2 cables and Sgeir Dhubh, in the middle of the loch 3½ cables from its head, dries 3 metres. Holding is said to be poor. Camas Doire Aonar on the southwest shore is full of small-boat moorings, but good shelter and holding are found off the entrance in a strong southwest wind.

Inverbain Islands, 1 mile west of Shieldaig Island, have a basin on their south side which might be worth investigating. A rock which dries 1·2 metres lies ½ cable west of the northwest island, and drying rocks lie in the middle of the passage south of that island but an apparently clear channel lies between the rocks and the island.

Ob na h-Acairseid, 57°32'·5N 5°42'W, on the east side of Ardheslaig is a clean inlet but very narrow. Clach na Be off the north point of the entrance dries 4 metres. Many fish cages are anchored off the east side of Ardheslaig, and the inlet may now be used by work boats. Steel stakes, dangerous to inflatable dinghies, were found at the north end of the beach some years ago.

Upper Loch Torridon

A clean passage 2 cables wide leads from the northeast side of Loch Shieldaig to Upper Loch Torridon which is generally free from dangers apart from detached drying rocks in two places 1¼ cables off the south shore. Occasional anchorages may be found in most of the inlets around the shore depending on wind direction, but some are occupied by fish cages. The upper loch is very squally if there is any wind.

Anchorages

Camas an Lein, on the east side of the peninsula which separates Loch Shieldaig from the upper loch, provides good shelter in westerly winds. A rock dries 2·4 metres 1 cable off the south point of the bay.

Ob a' Bhraighe on the north shore NNE of Rubh' a' Ghiubhais, ¾ mile ENE of the narrows, has a rock which dries 1·5 metres ½ cable off the west side of the entrance.

Ob Gorm Beag has 3 rows of floats across it with a gap at alternate ends of each row, and a mooring for a fishing boat at the head.

Ob Gorm Mor has only two rows of floats, and there is more space to anchor.

At the head of the loch, the best anchorage is on the south side close to the southwest shore, between a jetty at Eilean Chasgaig ¼ mile northwest of the hotel and Rubha an t-Salainn, a wooded rocky promontory 3 cables northeast of it. Hotel nearby.

Torridon village on the north side of the head of the loch has a shop and a post office. Anchor in quiet weather northwest of the head of a promontory which extends from the east shore.

Loch Gairloch

57°43 ′N 5°47′W

Charts

2528 (1:15,000), *2210* (1:50,000). OS map *19*.

Tides

Constant −0020 Ullapool (−0440 Dover)

Height in metres

MHWS	MHWN	MTL	MLWN	MLWS
5·2	4·0	3·0	1·8	0·6

Dangers and marks

The loch is clean except within the inlets of the south shore and between Eilean Horrisdale and Loch Shieldaig. Glas Eilean towards the head of the loch has a light beacon at its centre. Longa Island lies ½ mile from the north point of the entrance; in Caolas Beag, the channel between Longa and the mainland, the shore dries for 2 cables.

Lights

Glas Eilean Fl.WRG.6s9m6-4M
Gairloch Pier head Q.R.9m

Glas Eilean light beacon shows white towards the entrance clear of danger and towards Loch Shieldaig and the approach to Gairloch Pier.

Badachro (Caolas Bad a' Chrotha)

57°42′N 5°43′W

A well sheltered inlet easy to approach but quite fully occupied by fishing boats and local yachts. A rock above water stands at the east end of a drying reef on the west side of the channel leaving a passage ½ cable wide between the rock and Eilean Horrisdale; a submerged rock lies ½ cable SSE of the above-water rock at a depth of 0·9 metre. A rock which dries 3·7 metres on the southeast side of the fairway south of two tidal islets is marked by a perch. The head of the inlet dries off ¼ mile. The fairway is lined with moorings on either side. The hotel has two visitors' moorings.

A stone jetty and slipway stand on the west side of the mouth of a river which runs out on the south shore. The bed of the river effectively dries and the current is strong, especially after rain, but with care a yacht can go alongside after half flood to take on water from a hose. A post stands on the west side of the slip and when the foot of the post is covered there is 2·4 metres depth at the east side of the slip.

The passage south of Eilean Horrisdale although tortuous can be negotiated with care. If Badachro is too crowded, space can be found to anchor SSE of Eilean Horrisdale, or east of the island, inshore of Sgeir Dubh Bheag.

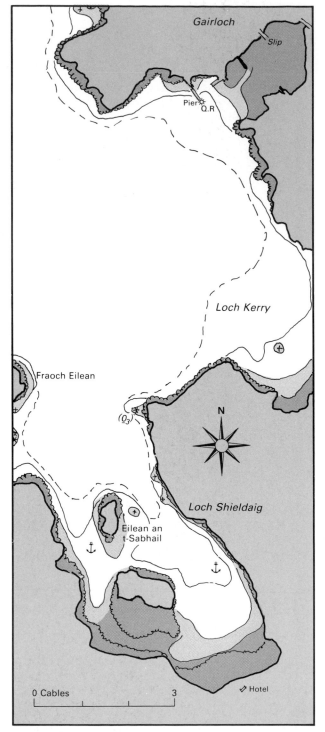

Gairloch Pier and Loch Shieldaig

Supplies

Shop, post office, telephone, hotel, baths at hotel, diesel from the hotel, water at slip, *Calor Gas*. Badachro chandlery ☎ 291.

Anchorages

Loch Shieldaig, 57°41′·5N 5°41′W, in the southeast corner of Loch Gairloch, is occupied by moorings, many of them belonging to east coast fishing boats and often not used during the summer. If there is

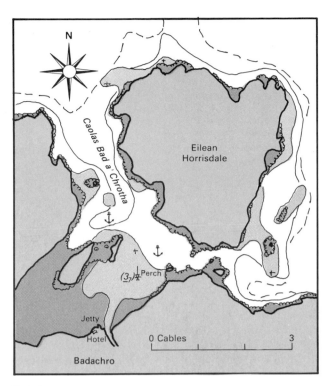

Badachro

Badachro from the head of the slip.

no space in the main part of the loch, anchor SSW of Eilean an t-Sabhail or in Camas na h-Airighe, southwest of Fraoch Eilean.

A rock which dries 0·3 metre lies ¼ cable off the east point of the entrance to Loch Shieldaig. Submerged rocks lie up to ¾ cable southwest of Fraoch Eilean, and a rock 1 cable south of the island dries 1·1 metres.

Loch Shieldaig, Gairloch.

Loch Kerry is partly occupied by fish cages and a submerged rock lies in the middle of the bay 1 cable from the southwest shore.

Gairloch Pier, 57°42′·6N 5°41′W, is used by fishing boats, and dues are charged even to go alongside for water. The river mouth dries off 2 cables and yachts should go no further in than a line joining the head of the east pier and the promontory on the south side of the river.

Supplies

Shop, post office, telephone, hotel, bank, petrol and diesel at garage which may deliver (☎ 2255). Water at pier, *Calor Gas* and mechanical repairs – ask at garage. Launching slip, sailing club.

Skye and Raasay

Charts

2498, 2534 (1:25,000), *2209* (1:50,000). OS maps *24, 32*. OS *Outdoor Leisure Map – The Cuillin and Torridon Hills* (1:25,000) provides more detail of the southwest side of the Inner Sound.

Broadford Bay

Tides

In Caolas Pabay the northeast-going stream begins +0550 Ullapool (+0130 Dover). The southwest-going stream begins −0010 Ullapool (−0430 Dover), at a spring rate of 1 knot.

Dangers and marks

The Skye shore is fringed with drying reefs and rocks, in places extending 3½ cables from the shore; the most extensive are south of Pabay. Drying rocks extend ½ mile SSW of Pabay to Sgeir Ghobhlach on which stands an iron beacon 9 metres high with a cage topmark. Submerged rocks lie 1½ cables southwest of the beacon.

Directions

From Kyle Akin pass north of both of the red buoys west of the lighthouse and from the second buoy steer for Sgeir Ghobhlach; when the east side of Pabay is abeam steer for the southwest corner of Broadford Bay.

Anchorages

In Broadford Bay a convenient anchorage is off Corry Pier on the west side of the bay but a drying rock lies about ½ cable south of the head of the pier. It is usually possible to lie alongside the south side of the pier to go ashore for stores, but all space may be taken by fishing boats and some crew should stay aboard in case it is necessary to move.

Supplies at Broadford

Shops, post office, telephone, hotel, petrol and diesel at garage.

Caolas Scalpay

Tides

The east-going stream begins +0550 Ullapool (+0130 Dover). The west-going stream begins −0010 Ullapool (−0430 Dover), at a spring rate of 1 knot.

Directions

From Kyle Akin approach as for Broadford and continue on that course until ¼ mile beyond a point where the beacon is abeam. An alternative course to Caolas Scalpay is by the north side of Pabay, but note that reefs dry 3 cables north and northwest of the island.

The channel is only 0·1 metre deep at its narrowest part between drying reefs extending 1 cable from Scalpay and a shingle bank which extends north from Skye. A beacon which marked the southwest end of the reef on the north side of the passage has collapsed, but the north side of the passage was defined in May 1989 by two small white buoys, of which the more easterly was half submerged; the west buoy lay close east of the southwest end of the reef.

A leading line to help in finding the buoys is the school house at Dunan, a white building on the Skye shore west of the narrows, under the peak of An Coileach which is beyond, and to the right of, the summit of Am Meall 291° as shown in the photo.

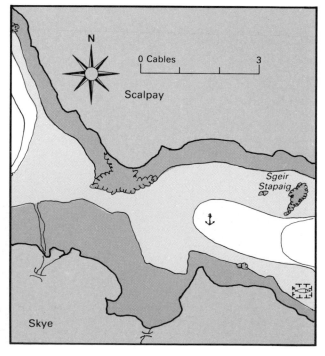

Caolas Scalpay

Caolas Scalpay from southeast.

Caolas Scalpay leading line.

Anchorage

Anchor as convenient either east or west of the narrows. Either may be squally. Note Sgeir Stapaig which dries, a cable off the Scalpay shore east of the narrows. Fish cages are moored off both shores.

At night the cages off the south shore are marked by Q.Y light buoys.

Loch Ainort

57°17′N 6°02′W

A wild and rather featureless loch surrounded by high hills. Anchor either at Luib in a slight indentation off the mouth of a valley on the southeast side, or in the south or west corners of the head of the loch.

Caol Mor and Sound of Raasay

57°20 ′N 5°05′W

Charts

2534, 2498 (1:25,000) for approach, *2209* (1:50,000). OS map *24*.

Tides

In Caol Mor, the spring rate is 1 knot; in Linne Crowlin, southwest of Crowlin Islands it is ½ knot, and between Scalpay and Longay 2 knots. The southeast and east-going stream begins +0605 Ullapool (+0145 Dover). The northwest and west-going stream begins +0005 Ullapool (−0415 Dover).

Constant −0025 Ullapool (−0445 Dover)

Height in metres

MHWS	MHWN	MTL	MLWN	MLWS
5·3	3·7	2·9	1·9	0·7

Dangers and marks in the approach to Caol Mor from southeast

Longay, ENE of Scalpay, has drying reefs ¾ cable southwest and 1½ cables northwest of it. Sgeir Dhearg, an islet 8 metres high surrounded by reefs lies ¾ mile northwest of Scalpay; Gulnare Rock which dries, halfway between Sgeir Dhearg and Scalpay, is marked on its south side by a green conical buoy. Sgeir Thraid, a reef drying 4 metres 6 cables WNW of Sgeir Dhearg, is marked by a red iron beacon with a cage topmark.

Pass either southwest or northeast of these rocks as convenient.

Light

A light beacon Fl.WR.3s5m9/6M stands at Eyre Point on the northeast side of Caol Mor showing red over the dangers described above, and white elsewhere.

Loch Sligachan

57°19′N 6°07′W

Tides

The spring rate in the entrance is 1½ knots. The in-going stream begins +0605 Ullapool (+0145 Dover). The out-going stream begins −0015 Ullapool (−0435 Dover).

Dangers and marks

Like Loch Ainort a wild and mountainous loch subject to squalls, but convenient for an expedition to the Red Cuillins. The entrance is partly blocked by An Corran, a drying spit on the north side. A ferry to Raasay operates from a slip on the south shore of the loch.

A shoal extends 4 cables from the south shore outside the entrance to Bo Sligachan over which the depth is 0·4 metre. Sconser Lodge, a stone house on the shore east of the entrance with a few trees around it, in line with the summit of Sgurr Mhairi, the highest hill on the south side of the loch, 215° leads WNW of the shoals to the entrance. 1 cable from the shore turn west and then WNW to pass south of An Corran which shows pale below the water.

Anchorages

Peinchorran, within the entrance on the north side. Sgeir Dhubh 0·6 metre high lies a cable off the northeast side of the bay and underwater cables (marked by rusty red cable beacons, and probably disused) cross the loch ½ cable further west from a ruined slip on the north shore. Anchor to the west of the ruined slip.

The head of the loch dries for more than ½ mile and banks on either side dry for more than a cable in places. Anchor towards the head of the loch, in a depth of not less than 5 metres as the bottom rises abruptly.

Raasay Narrows

57°20′·5N 6°05′W

Tides

The south-going stream begins −0605 Ullapool (+0200 Dover). The north-going stream begins −0040 Ullapool (−0500 Dover).

Constant −0025 Ullapool (−0445 Dover)

Height in metres

MHWS	MHWN	MTL	MLWN	MLWS
5·3	3·7	2·9	1·9	0·7

Dangers and marks in sequence from south to north

The passage is ½ mile wide between An Aird on Skye and Eilean Aird nan Gobhar, southwest of Ardhuish on Raasay, northeast of An Aird. Suisnish Pier stands at the southwest point of Raasay.

Loch Sligachan approach.

Photo: Jean Lawrence

Rainy Rocks dry 1·1 metres a cable east of the east point of An Aird. Penfold Rock red can buoy 2 cables northeast of An Aird, and Jackal Rock green conical buoy 6 cables east of An Aird, both mark rocks at a depth of 2·9 metres.

McMillan's Rock, 4 cables north of An Aird at a depth of 0·4 metre, is marked on its west side by a green conical light buoy.

A submerged rock lies a cable west of Eilean Aird nan Gobhar at a depth of 1·3 metres.

Sgeir Chnapach, 3 metres high, lies 1¼ miles north of Ardhuish, 3 cables from Raasay, with drying rocks inshore of it.

Directions

Pass northeast of Penfold Rock buoy to keep clear of Rainy Rocks. McMillan's Rock light buoy should be passed on its west side, or at least a cable to the east.

Lights

Eyre Point light beacon Fl.WR.3s5m6/9M shows red over dangers in approach from east.
Suisnish Point pier head 2F.G(vert)
McMillan's Rock light buoy Fl(2)G.12s

At night, from east keep north of the red sector of Eyre Point light. In Caol Mor this light is obscured north of 063° but a direct course between Suisnish Pier and the west side of McMillan's Rock buoy clears all dangers. There are no lights further north in the Sound of Raasay, but a mid-channel course can be estimated until Portree Harbour opens up. Look out for Sgeir Chnapach, described above.

Minor anchorages

Balmeanach Bay, 57°20′N 6°06′W, southwest of An Aird; two underwater power cables cross to Raasay from a point marked by a pole 2 cables west of the southwest point of An Aird, and part of the bay is taken up by fish cages. Holding has been found to be good.

Camas a' Mhor-bheoil, 57°20′·5N 6°06′·5W, lies west of the north point of An Aird. Sgeir Dhubh, 3 metres high, lies 3½ cables northwest of the north point of An Aird, and a rock at the 2-metre contour ¼ mile from the head of the bay dries 0·8 metre. Northerly swell sets into the bay.

Churchton Bay, Raasay, 57°21′N 6°05′W, southeast of Ardhuish. Perch Rocks, more than a cable southwest from a promontory in front of Raasay House, dry 2·9 metres; the outer rock is marked by an iron perch and the inner by a pole supported by wire stays. Anchor either side of the rocks. The southeast side of the bay is foul with submerged rocks more than a cable offshore.

Portree

57°25′N 6°11′W

Tides

Constant −0025 Ullapool (−0445 Dover)

Height in metres

MHWS	MHWN	MTL	MLWN	MLWS
5·3	3·7	2·9	1·9	0·7

Portree from northeast   *Photo:* Mike Balmforth

Dangers and marks

Westerly winds funnel fiercely out of Portree Harbour and down the sides of the hills making it difficult for a sailing boat to approach in these conditions.

Sgeir Mhor, a reef part of which is above water extends a cable from a promontory on the north shore, ½ mile east of Portree Pier, and needs to be given a good berth if approaching from north, or tacking.

Lights

A light at the pier head, 2F.R(vert)6m4M, is only shown occasionally, but the town lights should be enough at night.

Anchorages

Much of the area northeast of the pier dries, and a large area is occupied by moorings. There are HIDB visitors' moorings off the north shore but these may be found untenable in a southerly wind owing to the fetch from Loch Portree, the drying bay on the south side of the harbour. The anchorage northeast of the pier in 7–10 metres is soft mud with not very good holding.

The north side of the pier and stone slip dries almost completely at springs but a yacht may be able to go alongside temporarily at a suitable rise of tide; the sea level may be raised deceptively by the wind and there are small underwater obstructions at the slip. Dues are charged, but not for a brief visit, and crew should remain on board at all times to shift berth if necessary.

Camas Ban An alternative anchorage is in Camas Ban, east of Vriskaig Point but it is subject to severe downdraughts in southerly winds. These downdraughts are known locally as 'whirlies', and anywhere along the east side of Trotternish in strong southerlies they can be seen spinning over the surface sucking up a rotating cloud of spray. Admiralty vessels sometimes use this anchorage, but are unlikely to be as far inshore as a yacht would anchor.

Supplies

Shops, post office, telephone, hotels, swimming pool (limited opening to public), petrol and diesel at West End Garage (½ mile on Dunvegan Road). Diesel also in multiples of 10 gallons from BP depot on the pier, water from hose at pier, *Calor Gas* at West End Garage (Dunvegan Road, ½ mile).

Chandlery and hardware: North Skye Fishermen's Association on the pier, Camas Lusta Marine and JansVans, both at Dunvegan Road. Mechanical repairs, West End Garage.

Fladday Harbour

57°28'·5N 6°01'·3W

Southeast of Fladday Island on the west side of the north end of Raasay.

Chart

2209 (2210), (1:50,000). OS map *24*.

Tides

Constant −0025 Ullapool (−0445 Dover)

Height in metres

MHWS	MHWN	MTL	MLWN	MLWS
5·3	3·7	2·9	1·9	0·7

Dangers and marks

Griana-sgeir, 7 metres high, and a line of rocks lie between ¼ and ½ mile west of Fladday.

Bo Leachan, south of Griana-sgeir, is cleared by keeping the west tangent of Rona open west of Griana-sgeir 018°.

Bo na Currachie, north of Griana-sgeir, is cleared by keeping the west tangent of Raasay open west of Griana-sgeir 201°.

At Manish Point, the south point of Loch Arnish, drying reefs extend more than a cable northwest.

The southwest side of the bay is enclosed by islets and drying rocks which, depending on the light, may be very difficult to distinguish; a few cottages on the shore of Loch Arnish may help to identify the way in.

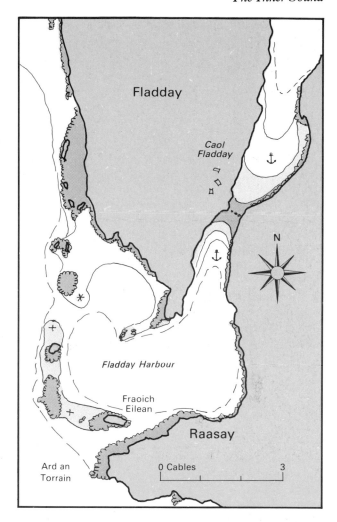

Fladday Harbour.

Two cottages on Fladday show up well if there is any afternoon sunshine.

Directions

The entrance is about 60 metres wide between Ard an Torrain on Raasay and Fraoich Eilean ½ cable northwest of it, which must be identified before proceeding. Reefs dry part of the way across the passage from Ard an Torrain, but the depth in the northwest half of the passage is at least 6 metres. After passing Fraoich Eilean head for the inlet between Fladday and Raasay. The inlet is blocked ¼ mile from its mouth by boulders and a stone causeway which dry at low water; take care not to go too far in. The bottom appears to be stony with weed, but there is some clear sand under the cliffs of Fladday.

Anchorages

Caol Fladda (Fladday North Harbour) is the north part of the inlet between Fladday and Raasay. Bo na Faochag lies 3½ cables north of Fladday at a depth of 1·8 metres, and the summit of Beinn na h-Iolaire open east of Fladday 156° leads 1½ cables east of Bo na Faochag. Caol Fladda is full of kelp and the holding is poor.

Caol Rona

57°31′N 5°59′W

Chart

2479 (1:18,000). OS map *24*.

Tides

The southeast-going stream begins +0505 Ullapool (+0045 Dover). The northwest-going stream begins −0055 Ullapool (−0515 Dover). The spring rate is at least 2 knots. The northwest-going stream sets towards Eilean Seamraig.

Dangers and marks

Eilean an Fhraoich stands in the middle of the channel with a beacon *No. 4* on its southwest side. Eilean Seamraig on the northeast side of the channel is separated from Garbh Eilean by a channel obstructed by rocks. Garbh Eilean is a tidal islet joined to Rona by a stony isthmus.

A submerged rock lies ½ cable southwest of Eilean an Fhraoich at a depth of 0·4 metre and a drying reef extends ½ cable northwest.

No. 5 beacon stands on Rubha Ard Ghlaisen on Raasay, nearly a mile SSE of Eilean an Fhraoich. A light beacon, *No .8*, an orange and white triangle, stands on the southeast point of Garbh Eilean.

Eilean an Fhraoich can be passed on either side.

Lights

Rona lighthouse Fl.12s69m19M is obscured from 358°-050°

Fladday Harbour approach, from northeast. A yacht is in the passage between Ard an Torrain, on the extreme left, and Fraoich Eilean. The south point of Fladday is at the right.

Ru na Lachan light beacon Oc.WR.8s21m10M, ¾ mile north of the Range Control building, shows red towards Caol Rona.
Light beacon *No. 8* Fl.3s8m5M

Acairseid Mhor, Rona

57°32′N 5°59′W

A popular anchorage on the west side of Rona, difficult to identify, as Eilean Garbh in the entrance merges with the background, and a white arrow is painted on the south side of the island to help identification! Drying heights of rocks shown on the plan are only approximate.

Chart

2479 (1:18,000). OS map *24*.

Tides

Constant −0025 Ullapool (−0445 Dover)

Height in metres

MHWS	MHWN	MTL	MLWN	MLWS
5·3	3·7	2·9	1·9	0·7

Directions

Approach southeast of Eilean Garbh and pass between the rock which dries 5·3 metres and the promontory close southeast of it. If the rock is covered pass the promontory about 10 metres off on a line with the southeast tangent of Eilean Garbh astern; the rock shows pale below the water. Steer for the islet and when within about a cable of it alter course towards the cottage to pass west of the islet. A rock at a depth of 1·2 metres was discovered some years ago the hard way, ½ cable NNW of the islet.

The passage north of Eilean Garbh has fewer reference points than the south passage; swell usually breaks on rocks on either side of the passage.

Acairseid Mhor, Rona from the head of the inlet.

Acairseid Mhor, Rona

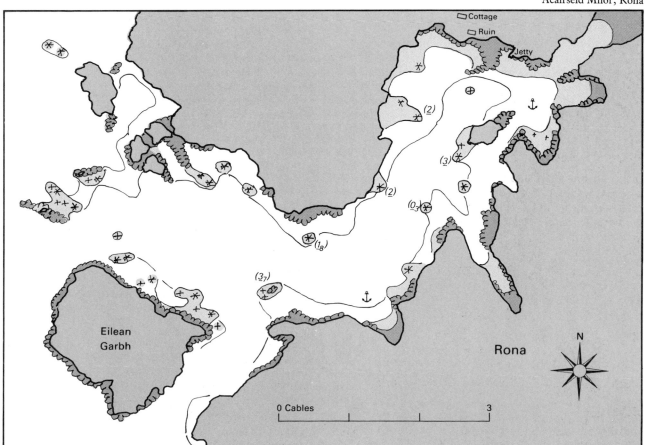

Anchorage

Anchor northwest or northeast of the islet clear of drying reefs as shown. Holding is poor in places, consisting of soft black mud well ploughed by yachts' anchors. There is said to be space to anchor west of the reef west of the jetty. Alternatively anchor off the south shore, east of the rock in the entrance.

The jetty is not convenient for landing at low tide. There are cleared landing places in most of the bays round the shore.

Loch a' Bhraige

57°34'·5N 5°58'W

Chart

2534 (1:7,500).

This inlet is used by the Admiralty and is elaborately marked and lit, providing a harbour if needed when coming from the north of Skye after dark but it has little other attraction for a yacht.

Directions

Sgeir Shuas is a group of islets on the north side of the entrance, on one of which is a light beacon. A drying rock lies ¾ cable southwest of the north point of the loch, otherwise it is clean to near the head where a reef partly above water, with light beacon *No. 9* on it, extends 1½ cables northwest. An inlet in the northeast corner where there is a piled quay with rubber fendering gives good shelter. Admiralty vessels often lie at the quay overnight.

Pass either side of the detached light beacon and anchor in the northeast inlet clear of the approach to the quay. Alternative anchorages are either side of the reef on which beacon *No. 9* stands; a mooring buoy is laid south of the reef.

Lights

Rona lighthouse Fl.12s69m19M 358°-obscd-050°
Sgeir Shuas light beacon Fl.R.2s6m3M
No. 9 light beacon Q.WRG.3m4-3M
No. 10 light beacon Iso.6s28m5M
Detached light beacon off NE inlet Fl.R.5s4m3M
Quay, southwest corner 2F.R(vert)
No. 1 light beacon Fl.G.3s91m3M

At night, light beacons *No. 9* and *No. 10* in line lead into the loch 136·5°.

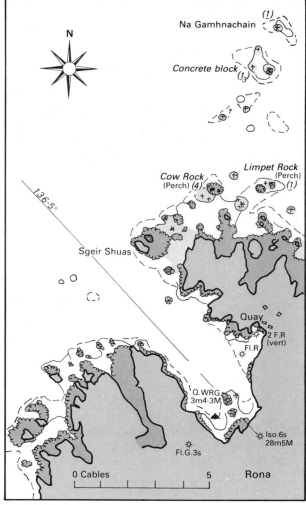

Loch a' Bhraige

Passage at the North end of Rona

Dangers and marks

Rocks submerged and drying extend 8 cables north of Rona to Na Gamhnachain which dries 1 metre.

A rock 1½ cables south of Na Gamhnachain has a concrete block built up on it which dries 1·3 metres.

Several submerged rocks lie between Na Gamhnachain and Rona.

Cow Rock, 4 metres high, 2 cables north of the northwest point of Rona, and Limpet Rock, 1 metre high and 2 cables further east, both have perches on them.

A submerged rock at a depth of 1·8 metres lies ½ cable north of a direct line between these two rocks, apart from which the nearest charted hazard is a submerged rock 2 cables north of Cow Rock, and an inshore passage north of these rocks may be taken in clear settled weather.

Unlit Admiralty buoys have formerly been laid northeast of Rona.

Northeast Skye

Rubha na h-Aiseig is the northeast point, and Rubha Hunish the northwest point of Trotternish, the north peninsula of Skye. Eilean Trodday, a grassy flat-topped island with a light beacon on its centre, lies nearly a mile north of Rubha na h-Aiseig. Islands and rocks more than two miles northwest of Rubha Hunish are described in Chapter VII, together with the passage to Harris and Lewis. The west side of Skye is described in Chapter III.

Kilmaluag Bay, Skye.

Chart

2210 (1:50,000). OS map *23*.

Tides

Tidal streams round the north end of Skye follow the coast with eddies in the bays between headlands. Heavy overfalls occur between Rubha na h-Aiseig and Staffin Bay.

In the passage between Rubha na h-Aiseig on Skye and Eilean Trodday the spring rate is 2½ knots. The east-going stream begins −0350 Ullapool (+0415 Dover). The west-going stream begins +0235 Ullapool (−0145 Dover).

Off Rubha Hunish the spring rate is 2½ knots. The northeast-going stream begins −0405 Ullapool (+0400 Dover). The southwest-going stream begins +0220 Ullapool (−0200 Dover).

Lights

Eilean Trodday Fl(2)WRG.10s49m12-9M
Rona Fl.12s69m19M 358°-obscd-050°

Minor anchorages

Staffin Bay, 57°38′·5N 6°13′W, is a clean open bay exposed northeast and subject to squalls in westerly winds. Anchor either on the east side of the bay or in its southwest corner. There is no passage between Staffin Island and Skye.

A shop and restaurant stand on the main road ½ mile from Quiraing Lodge, the large house at the mouth of a burn on the south side of the bay.

Clach nan Ramh, 2 cables off Skye 7 cables NNW of Eilean Flodigarry, north of Staffin Bay, dries 3·8 metres. If approaching or leaving by the passage between Skye and Eilean Flodigarry, when beyond the north end of Flodigarry keep Staffin Island hidden behind Eilean Flodigarry 153° to clear this rock.

Kilmaluag Bay, 57°41′·5N 6°18′W, a small inlet ¾ mile south of Rubha na h-Aiseig, is convenient for waiting for suitable conditions for a passage beyond the north end of Skye or as an overnight anchorage in settled weather, although the bottom is stony in places and the anchor chain may grumble. A drying reef extends more than 1½ cables from the south point of the entrance. The bay is subject to fierce squalls in strong westerly winds.

VI. Northwest mainland

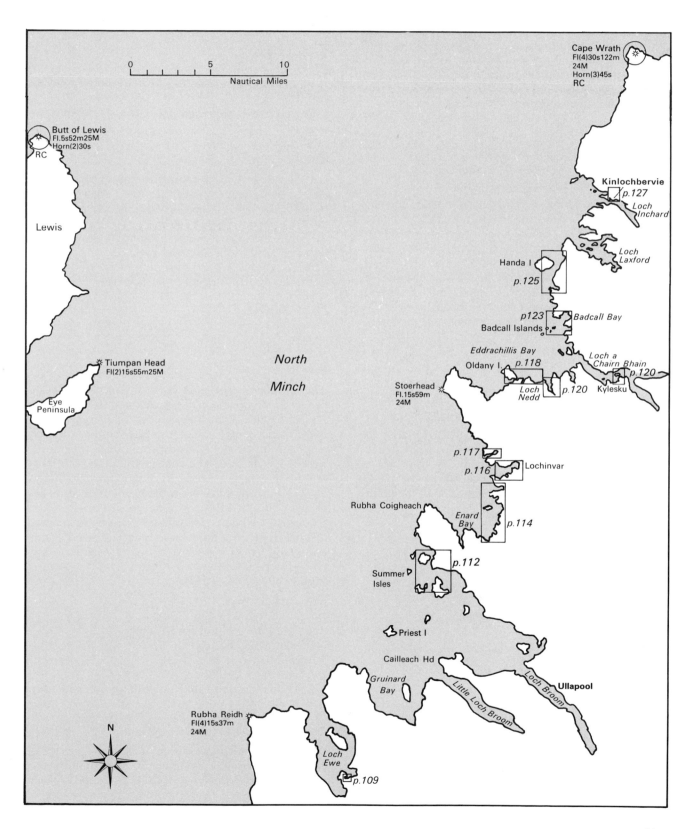

0   5   10
Nautical Miles

Cape Wrath
Fl(4)30s122m
24M
Horn(3)45s
RC

Butt of Lewis
Fl.5s52m25M
Horn(2)30s
RC

Lewis

Kinlochbervie
p.127
Loch
Inchard

Loch
Laxford

Handa I
p.125

p123
Badcall Islands
Badcall Bay

Eddrachillis Bay
Oldany I.   p.118
Loch a
Chairn Bhain
p.120
Kylesku

Tiumpan Head
Fl(2)15s55m25M

North

Minch

Stoerhead
Fl.15s59m
24M

Loch
Nedd
p.120

Eye
Peninsula

p.117
p.116   Lochinvar

Rubha Coigheach
Enard
Bay
p.114

p.112

Summer
Isles

Priest I

Cailleach Hd

Gruinard
Bay

Little Loch Broom

Loch Broom

Ullapool

Rubha Reidh
Fl(4)15s37m
24M

N

Loch
Ewe
p.109

Passage notes – Rubha Reidh to Loch Inchard

The 40 miles of coast from Rubha Reidh to Loch Inchard is deeply indented, consisting of great bays between impressive headlands, with almost no continuous length of coastline facing seaward. Two of the headlands, Rubha Reidh and Point of Stoer, are notorious for heavy seas, caused mainly by their exposure and the strength of the tidal streams around them. Seas around these headlands are particularly dangerous with wind against tide and they should be given a berth of several miles if it is necessary to pass them under such conditions.

Charts

1794, 1785 (1:100,000). OS maps *19, 15, 9.*

Tides at Rubha Reidh

The northeast-going stream begins −0335 Ullapool (+0430 Dover). The southwest-going stream begins +0305 Ullapool (−0115 Dover). The spring rate of these streams is 3 knots. There may be eddies inshore on the downstream side of the point.

At Rubha Coigeach and Point of Stoer the north-going stream begins −0250 Ullapool (+0515 Dover). The south-going stream begins +0420 Ullapool (HW Dover). The spring rate of these streams is 2½ knots.

Dangers and marks

Rubha Reidh (57°52′N 5°48′W) is marked by a white lighthouse 25 metres in height and a conspicuous radio mast stands on a hill 1½ miles southeast of the point.

Point of Stoer is a bold headland with a stack, the Old Man of Stoer, 56 metres in height, on its northwest side, which shows very distinctly from northeast. Stoerhead lighthouse, a white tower 14 metres in height stands on a cliff 1¾ miles SSW of the point.

Lights

Rubha Reidh Fl(4)15s37m24M
Soyea Island (Loch Inver) Fl(2)10s34m6M
Stoerhead Fl.15s59m24M
Rubha na Leacaig (Loch Inchard) Fl(2)10s30m8M
Tiumpan Head (Lewis) Fl(2)15s55m25M
Cape Wrath lighthouse Fl(4)30s122m24M is
   obscured east of 025°

At night in clear moderate weather these lights will be sufficient for a passage along the coast.

Radiobeacons

Eilean Glas 294·2 kHz LG (·−··/−−·) 50M Seq 6
   57°51′N 6°38′W
Stornoway Aero 669·5 kHz SWY (···/−−/·−−)
   60M 58°17′N 6°21′W (non-A2A)
Butt of Lewis 298·8 kHz BL (−···/·−··) 150M Seq 2,
   5 58°31′N 6°16′W

Cape Wrath 298·8 kHz CW (−·−·/·−−) 50M Seq 1
   58°37′·5N 5°00′W

Shelter

Loch Torridon, Gairloch, Isle of Ewe in Loch Ewe, Summer Isles, Loch Inver, various lochs on the south side of Eddrachillis Bay, Loch Laxford, Kinlochbervie; all provide some shelter during a passage along the coast.

Loch Ewe

Charts

2509 (1:25,000) approach only, *3146* (1:12,500). OS map *19.*

Tides

Off the entrance tidal streams run at up to 2½ knots. The NNE-going stream begins −0335 Ullapool (+0430 Dover). The SSW-going stream begins +0305 Ullapool (−0115 Dover).

Within the loch streams turn at HW and LW and may reach 1 knot in narrower passages.

Constant −0010 Ullapool (−0430 Dover)

Height in metres

MHWS	MHWN	MTL	MLWN	MLWS
5·1	3·8	2·9	2·0	0·7

Directions

The entrance lies 4 miles east of Rubha Reidh and has no hidden dangers. *Fairway* buoy (RW) and *No. 1* green conical light buoy are in the fairway. Isle of Ewe, 2 miles long, is near the east shore of the loch, and Sgeir an Araig, 12 metres high, is ½ mile northwest of Isle of Ewe. The passage round the south end of Isle of Ewe is marked by 3 red can light buoys. NATO Fuelling Jetty is on the mainland ESE of Isle of Ewe.

Greenstone Point, 3½ miles NNE of the entrance to Loch Ewe, produces heavy seas with wind against tide.

Lights

Fairway light buoy LFl.10s
No. 1 light buoy Fl(3)G.10s
Red light buoys east of Ewe Island:
   D (south) Fl(2)R.10s
   E (middle) Fl.R.2s
   F (north) Fl(4)R.10s
NATO fuelling jetty and dolphins north and south
   each Fl.G.4s

Anchorages

Several bays on the west side of the loch provide an occasional overnight anchorage to save going further up the loch; Acairseid nan Uamh, 1 mile SSW of the *Fairway* buoy, has been found satisfactory in settled weather.

Acairseid Mhor, 57°50'·6N 5°38'W, sometimes known as Camas Angus, on the east side of the north end of Isle of Ewe is clean apart from a drying reef on its south side, and found to give good shelter and holding in gales between south and northwest. A mooring and small fish cages lie in the mouth of the bay.

Aultbea, 57°50'·3N 5°35'·5W, on the east side of the sound is partly sheltered by Aird Point on which there is a stone pier which dries alongside, with a decaying timber-piled pier head. Much of the bay inshore of the pier dries or is shoal, with moorings for inshore fishing boats. Anchor off a hotel on the east shore, or close east of the pier for some protection from northwest. In west or southwest winds Acairseid Mhor gives better shelter.

Shop (Bridgend Stores chart agent and *Calor Gas*), butcher ¼ mile. Post office, telephone, hotels, water tap at pier. Petrol (but not diesel) at Forbes Garage, who can help with mechanical and electrical repairs in emergency.

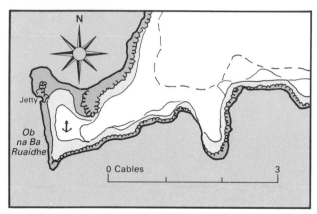

Loch Thurnaig

Loch Thurnaig, 57°47'·5N 5°35'W, 2 miles south of Isle of Ewe was formerly obstructed by rafts and buoys used for experiments in pollution control but these were not there in October 1989. The bottom is soft mud with some rock, but shelter may be found in Ob na Ba Ruaidhe in the southwest corner behind a drying reef which extends from the north side of the entrance to this bay. The bottom is partly rocky and partly very soft mud.

Camas Glas, 57°46'·7N 5°36'·5W, is an occasional anchorage from which to visit Inverewe Gardens. Anchor off a stone jetty on the north side of Creagan nan Cudaigean, a wooded rocky promontory on the east side of the head of the loch, ½ mile north of Poolewe and the trees mop up winds from most directions. Good holding is found south of the promontory at Port na Cloiche Gile well offshore, but the head of the bay dries off and the depth should be carefully checked.

Poolewe Southwest corner of the head of the loch provides fair shelter in southwesterly wind. Boor Rocks, 1 mile northwest of Poolewe, stand up to 3 metres above water with drying rocks more than a cable further northwest.

Shop, post office, telephone, hotel. Petrol, *Calor Gas* and diesel at garage (which will also help with small engineering repairs). Swimming pool.

Gruinard Bay has no regular anchorages, although there are moderate depths in places around its shore, and a jetty at Laide on the southwest side of the bay. Shop and post office. Rocks are adequately shown on chart *1794*.

Cailleach Head, at the east side of Gruinard Bay 15 miles ENE of Rubha Reidh, is marked by a 6-metre-high white light beacon at a height of 55 metres.

Little Loch Broom

57°54'N 5°22'W

Chart

2500 (1:25,000). OS map *19*.

South of Cailleach Head. Ardross Rock lies 4 cables ENE of the south point of the entrance in a depth of 0·6 metre; the loch is otherwise clean but provides little shelter and the head dries off for ½ mile. Anchor on the south side about 1½ miles from the head of the loch at Camusnagaul, east of a slight promontory about a mile ESE of a conspicuous fish farm.

Alternatively, in northerly winds, off the jetty at Scoraig, 1 mile within the north side of the entrance.

Supplies

Hotel, telephone at Dundonnell at head of the loch. Boatbuilder at Scoraig on the north side of the entrance: C. D. Dawson ☎ (085 483) 277.

Loch Broom

Tides

Streams are weak within the loch, but reach 1 knot in the narrows southeast of Ullapool. The in-going stream begins −0555 Ullapool (+0210 Dover). The out-going stream begins +0005 Ullapool (−0415 Dover).

Constant 0000 Ullapool (−0420 Dover)

Height in metres

MHWS	MHWN	MTL	MLWN	MLWS
5·2	3·9	3·0	2·1	0·7

Dangers and marks

A rock 1 metre high lies a cable off Leac Dhonn, 1½ miles ENE of Cailleach Head.

Rubha Cadail, 4½ miles further east, marked by a white light beacon 9 metres in height, is on the north side of the entrance to Loch Broom.

Ullapool Point (57°53'·6N 5°10'W) is on the northeast side of the loch, 2½ miles southeast of Rubha Cadail. A red can light buoy 4 cables northwest of Ullapool Point marks shoal water at the mouth of a river. Ullapool pier is 2 cables northeast of the point.

Ullapool

The only town on the northwest coast of Scotland, Ullapool was founded by the British Fisheries Society in 1788, and is able to provide or arrange for most services. A large car ferry runs from Ullapool to Stornoway on Lewis. In late summer (usually after the end of the sailing season) several dozen Russian and East European fish-carriers, 'klondikers', congregate in Loch Broom and the approaches to buy fish direct from the fishing boats, generating at times a lot of small-boat traffic.

Lights

Cailleach Head Fl(2)12s60m9M
Rubha Cadail light beacon Fl.WRG.6s11m9-6M
Light buoy northwest of Ullapool Point Q.R
Ullapool Point Iso.R.4s8m6M
Pier 2F.R(vert)

Moorings

Yachts can go alongside the east end, or inside the eastern arm of the pier for a short time but the depth there should be watched and some crew must stay on board at all times to move the boat if necessary to let fishing boats in or out.

Many moorings lie east of the piers; there is space to anchor among them but yachts must keep clear of the approach to the piers; there is a lot of rubbish on the bottom and a tripping line is essential. Some moorings are not maintained and some are in frequent use and local advice should be sought if using one.

Supplies

Shops (one usually open on Sunday), post office, telephone, banks, hotels, petrol and diesel at garage, water hoses at pier. *Calor Gas* at supermarket at West Argyll Street, one block back from the pier. Chandler and chart agent also in West Argyll Street: Ullasport ☎ (0854) 2621. Marine engineers and divers at the pier: Mackenzie Marine. For advice on all services, ask at Ullasport.

Harbourmaster ☎ (0854) 2091, VHF Ch 16, 12. Coastguard ☎ (0854) 2014.

Minor anchorages – Loch Broom and approaches

Loch Kanaird, 57°57′N 5°12′W. The basin east of Isle Martin, about a mile northeast of Rubha Cadail, is most easily entered by the north side of the island, as drying spits extend from both sides of the south entrance leaving a passage ½ cable wide with no satisfactory leading line except to keep the east tangent of Isle Martin bearing 358°. There are fish cages and moorings but space will usually be found either in the bight on the east shore of Isle Martin or off Ardmair on the southeast side of the bay. Drying rocks lie between Aird na h-Eighe, the southeast point of the bay, and Sgeir Mhor, a rock 1 metre high, about 2 cables north of the point.

Ullapool pier from northeast.

Annat Bay (Feith an Fheoir), 2 miles east of Cailleach Head. Anchor in the mouth of an inlet at the west end of the bay.

Altnaharrie, on the southwest side of the loch opposite Ullapool Point; moorings may be available overnight.

Loggie Bay, 57°52′N 5°07′W, on the southwest side of the loch immediately beyond the narrows 1½ miles southeast of Ullapool Point. Fish-farming rafts and moorings restrict the space.

Summer Isles

58°01′N 5°25′W

The name applies to the group of about 30 islands scattered over the approaches to Loch Broom, but only Tanera Mor and Tanera Beg on the north side have anchorages which are at all sheltered.

Priest Island, the most southwesterly of the group, has a bay on its northeast side only suitable as an occasional anchorage in settled weather. The bottom consists mainly of boulders.

Chart

2501 (1:26,000). OS map *15*.

Tides

Constant −0005 Ullapool (−0425 Dover)

Height in metres

MHWS	MHWN	MTL	MLWN	MLWS
5·1	4·0	3·0	2·1	0·8

Dangers and marks

Most rocks are above water but there are drying rocks in Dorney Sound north of Tanera Mor and Tanera Beg, in Horse Sound, and south of Horse Island.

In Dorney Sound north of Tanera Mor, Iolla a Mealan, which dries 0·8 metre, is avoided by keeping the south point of Eilean Mullagrach just open south of Isle Ristol 297°. On the south side of the sound, Sgeir Iasgaich, which dries 3·7 metres 3 cables east of Sgeir Dubh, is clear of the fairway but should be watched for. Sgeir a Chapuill, a cable north of Tanera Mor, dries 2·3 metres.

In Horse Sound Iolla Beg and Mary Rock, which dry ¼ mile off Rubha Dubh Ard at the southeast point of the sound, are cleared by keeping the northeast tangent of Meall nan Gabhar at the north end of Horse Island in line with Rubha Dunan, the point of the mainland to the north, and the summit of Meall an Fheadain 331°. The north end of Stac Mhic Aonghais open south of Horse Island 283° leads south of Iolla Beg.

Iolla Mhor, 2 cables south of Horse Island, dries 3·9 metres.

Anchorages

Achiltibuie Anchor ESE of pier on the northwest side of Badentarbat Bay, but not further inshore as it is shoal. Hotel and shops nearby; Polbain Stores (NW) and Sinclair Stores (SE), which also stocks *Calor Gas*, each about 10 minutes' walk in opposite directions. Post office at Achiltibuie.

The Anchorage, on the east side of Tanera Mor is generally deep and obstructed by fish cages. The Cabbage Patch, between Eilean Beag and Eilean Mor on the south side of the bay, is full of moorings, although a small boat might anchor inshore. There is a good modern pier where a boat might dry out for repairs. Water at the pier.

Acairseid Driseach at the northwest corner of Tanera Mor, on the east side of Eilean na Saile, is shoal and full of weed. A drying rock lies in the middle of the south end of the inlet. The approach from the south by Caolas Mhill Gharbh is straightforward.

Tanera Beg has several sheltered anchorages on its northeast side. Approach from north keeping ¼ cable off the west side of Eilean Fada Mor to avoid rocks submerged and awash on the west side of the channel. Floats and fishing nets are laid in this channel.

From south in quiet weather approach above half tide by the passage between the east end of Tanera Beg and Eilean Fada Mor, in which the least depth is charted as 0·8 metre with two rocks which dry 0·9 metre. The passage between the drying rock in the middle of the south entrance and reefs at the south end of Eilean Fada Mor is only ½ cable wide. Steer to pass ¼ cable from the east side of the passage heading 360° and as soon as the west end of the passage opens alter course to pass close northeast of the east point of Tanera Beg. A line astern for this passage, Cailleach Head lighthouse over the left tangent of Eilean Dubh 170°, has been found to lead between the rocks in this passage.

Caolas Eilean Ristol, 58°02′·5N 5°25′·5W. Anchor off the slip clear of moorings, and show an anchor light as fishing boats come in after dark. Light on end of the slip Fl.G.3s.

Shop at Polbain 2 miles.

Loch an Alltain Duibh provides occasional anchorage off the north shore of Eilean Ristol.

For passage notes see the beginning of this chapter.

Stac Mhic Aonghais

Horse Island

Stac Mhic Aonghais (Angus Stac) 283° open to the south of Horse Island clears Iolla Beg

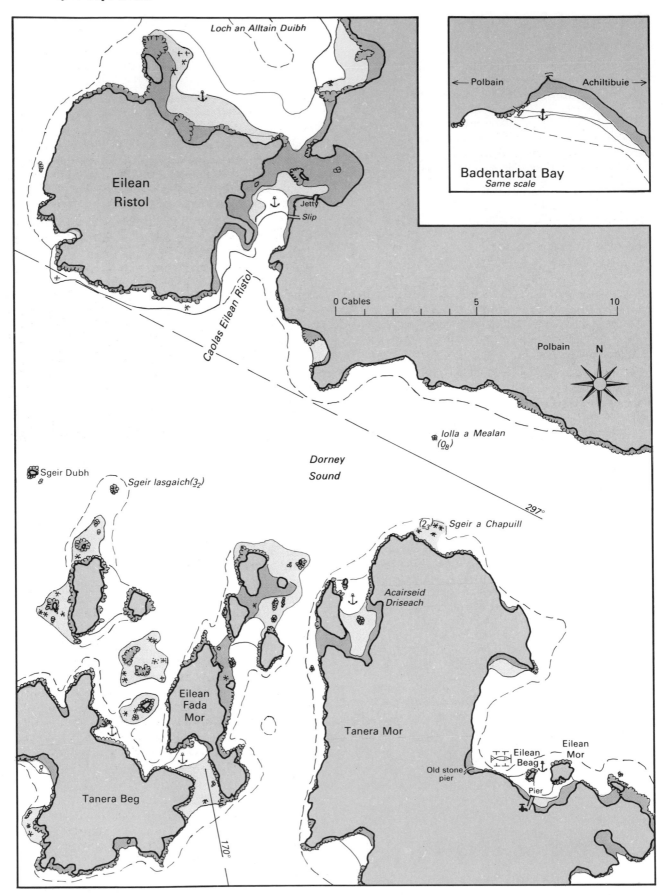

Loch an Alltain Duibh

Badentarbat Bay
Same scale

← Polbain   Achiltibuie →

Eilean
Ristol

Jetty
Slip

Caolas Eilean Ristol

0 Cables   5   10

Polbain

N

Iolla a Mealan
(0_8)

297°

Dorney
Sound

Sgeir Dubh

Sgeir Iasgaich(3_2)

(2_3) Sgeir a Chapuill

Acairseid
Driseach

Eilean
Fada
Mor

Tanera Mor

Tanera Beg

Eilean
Beag

Eilean
Mor

Old stone
pier

Pier

170°

Summer Isles

Acairseid Driseach from Tanera Mor.

Enard Bay

There are several moderately sheltered inlets on the east side of the bay with offshore islands which give some further shelter, but none can be particularly recommended.

Chart

2504 (1:25,000). OS map *15*.

Tides

Streams are insignificant in Enard Bay.

Constant −0005 Ullapool (−0425 Dover)

Height in metres

MHWS	MHWN	MTL	MLWN	MLWS
5·0	3·9	3·0	2·1	0·8

Dangers and marks

Detached drying rocks lie up to 2 cables off the shore, both of the mainland and of various islands. These are shown on chart *1794*, but for exploring inshore chart *2504* must be used. Eilean Mor, the highest island in Enard Bay, 4 miles east of Rubha Coigeach and ½ mile offshore, is a useful reference point.

Lights

Soyea Island (Loch Inver) Fl(2)10s34m6M
Stoerhead Fl.15s59m24M

Anchorages

Achnahaird Bay, 58°04′N 5°21′·5W, on the south side Enard Bay, has a fine sandy beach, but is too exposed for any but an occasional daytime anchorage.

Camas a' Bhothain, 58°05′N 5°21′W, immediately east of Achnahaird Bay, is named Sandy Bay on old charts, but fails to live up to this name as the bottom consists of boulders and the holding is poor. A drying reef extends north from Rubha Beag at the west side of the bay towards Black Rock which dries, 1 cable north of a rock which does not cover, on the reef. The entrance is between this reef and rocks which extend ½ cable west of Sgeir Bhuidhe in the middle of the bay.

Lochan Salainn, 58°05′N 5°17′W, is probably the best anchorage in Enard Bay. It is not named on some charts but lies about a mile southeast of Eilean Mor. Islets extend northwest from its entrance to Sgeir Ghlas Mhor and Bheag which have drying rocks up to 1 cable north of them and a submerged rock ½ cable southeast. A drying rock lies more than ½ cable from the northeast side of the inlet and there are some fish cages.

Loch an Eisg-Brachaidh from southeast.

Loch Inver from east. The pier is at the left foreground; Aird Ghlas is in the middle with Glas Leac beyond, and Soyea Island at upper right.

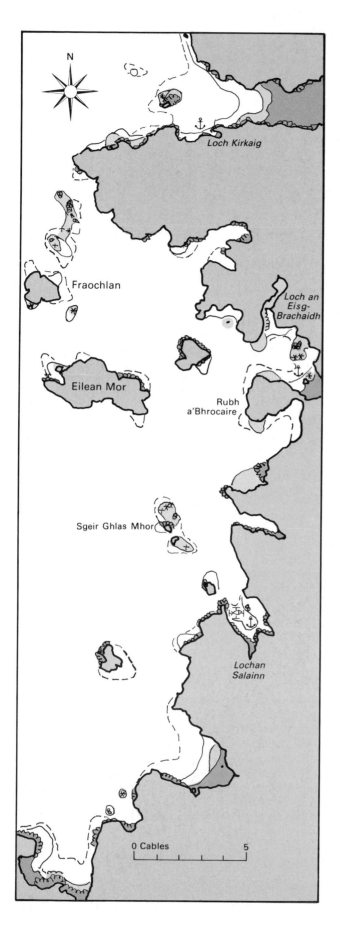

Enard Bay

Loch an Eisg-Brachaidh, 58°06′·3N 5°16′·5W, ¾ mile east of Eilean Mor, is sheltered by several islands and has several more rocks within than are shown on uncorrected copies of the current chart (see plan). A drying rock lies ¾ cable southeast of Fraochlan, the island north of Eilean Mor, and drying rocks lie in the middle of the passage north of Fraochlan.

Approach by either side of Eilean Mor, but if by the north side keep closer to Eilean Mor. Anchor close to the northeast side of Rubh a' Bhrocaire at the south side of the bay.

Loch Kirkaig, 58°07′·5N 5°17′W, ¾ mile southeast of Kirkaig Point at the entrance to Loch Inver, provides some shelter close to the south shore.

Loch Inver

58°09′N 5°15′W

Well marked and lit and easy to enter but a busy fishing harbour with little space to anchor clear of fishing boats.

Tides

Constant −0005 Ullapool (−0425 Dover)

Height in metres

MHWS	MHWN	MTL	MLWN	MLWS
5·0	3·9	3·0	2·1	0·8

Dangers and marks

Soyea Island, ½ mile off the entrance to the loch, has a submerged rock 2 cables north of its east end at a depth of 0·2 metre and drying reefs up to 2 cables northeast of its east point. Bo Caolas, which dries 3·2 metres, 3 cables northeast of the east point of the island, has a beacon with a cage topmark at its west end.

Glas Leac, 1¼ miles east of Soyea Island, is a small grass-topped islet 6 metres high with drying reefs and shoals up to ½ cable north of it.

Drying rocks lie more than a cable off the north shore north of Glas Leac, and off the east point of Camas na Frithearaich, ½ mile northwest of the islet.

Aird Ghlas, a promontory on the south shore 6 cables east of Glas Leac, has a black column with white bands marking a drying rock ½ cable off its north side. The pier lies ¼ mile further east.

Most of the bays on the south side of the loch are occupied by moorings and some have drying rocks in them.

Anchorage

Anchor between The Perch north of Aird Ghlas and the pier, clear of moorings and clear of the approach to the pier.

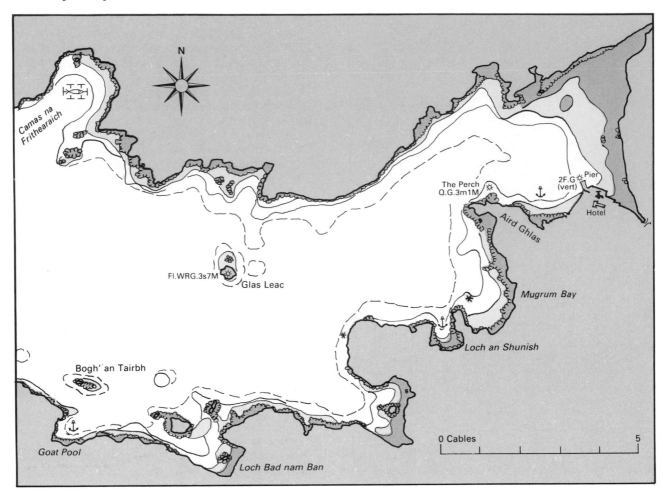

Loch Inver

Lights

Soyea Island Fl(2)10s34m6M
Glas Leac Fl.WRG.3s7m
Off Aird Ghlas Q.G.3m1M
The Perch, off Aird Ghlas Q.G.3m1M

At night Glas Leac light beacon shows white over the fairways both north and south of Soyea Island, but the south passage is cleaner; a white sector also shows eastward towards the harbour.

Minor anchorages

Goat Pool, 58°08'·3N 5°17'W, ½ mile east of Kirkaig Point, is deep and the bottom is rocky until close in. Pass either side of Bogh' an Tairbh which is only 0·3 metre high with drying reefs ½ cable east of it.

Loch Bad nam Ban, 58°08'·25N 5°16'·4W, has enough moorings to make it difficult to find space to anchor.

Supplies

Shops (shop at the pier open in evenings when fishing boats come in). Baker, post office, telephone, hotel. Petrol at garage, diesel and water at pier. Fishermen's chandlery; *Calor Gas* at chandlery. Harbourmaster has VHF.

Loch Roe

58°10'N 5°18'W

The entrance lies 1 mile north of Soyea Island. Bo Burrick, ½ cable NNW of Rubha Rodha, the south point of the entrance, dries 4·1 metres, and McAllister Rock ¼ cable off the north side of the entrance channel, dries 2·1 metres.

About 6 cables northeast of Rubha Rodha, two tidal islets about 4 metres high lie northeast of a promontory which extends northeast from the south shore, sheltering the anchorage at Pool Bay. Drying reefs extend 20–30 metres east of the islets, and Bo Pool which dries 1·7 metres lies less than ½ cable further east. Submerged rocks may lie at the sides of the channel. Approach either when Bo Pool is showing or when the tide has risen enough to pass safely over it and anchor in Pool Bay, south of the islets.

East of Bo Pool a sill with drying rocks on it lies across the loch, but it is possible with great care to pass further up the loch. Inshore fishing boats are moored in various inlets around the loch.

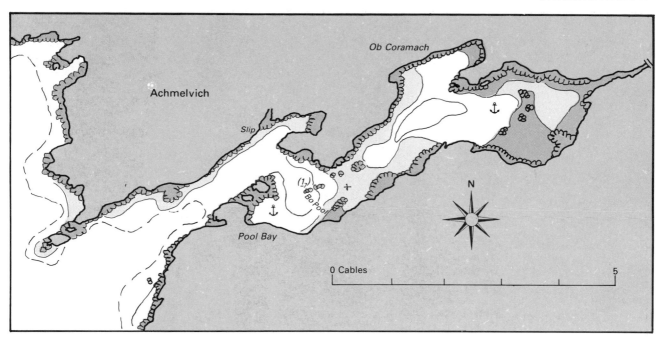

Loch Roe

Pool Bay, Loch Roe, from north.

Eddrachillis Bay

Between Point of Stoer and Handa Island is an entertaining collection of islands and lochs, well worth the effort of getting there. No general directions are necessary other than the passage notes at page 107 and a reminder of the heavy seas to be expected at Point of Stoer.

Chart

2502 (1:25,150) is essential for exploring the area in any detail. OS maps *15, 9*.

Tides

Except in Kylesku streams are insignificant in Eddrachillis Bay.

Constant 0000 Ullapool (−0420 Dover)

Height in metres

MHWS	MHWN	MTL	MLWN	MLWS
4·9	3·7	2·8	1·9	0·7

Anchorages

Clashnessie Bay, between Point of Stoer and Oldany Island, has no regular anchorage, but several bays and inlets might be rewarding to explore on a quiet day.

Culkein Drumbeg, 58°15′·2N 5°14′W, is a landlocked pool east of Oldany Island with rocks awash in the entrance which make the approach difficult, although they can often be seen breaking. Pass about a cable off Eilean nan Uan and steer 160° clear west of Eilean na Cille and when the north side of Eilean nam Boc comes abeam steer to starboard to pass ¼ cable off its east point and avoid the drying reef on the east side of the channel. Hold on toward the south side of the inlet before turning east to avoid a rock which dries 3 metres, and if going further east keep toward one side or the other to avoid a rock which dries 0·9 metre in mid-channel. The head of the jetty just dries. Water tap at jetty.

Loch Dhrombaig, 58°15′N 5°12′W, is straightforward to approach except for a submerged rock ½ cable west of the 15-metre islet north of the west entrance. Anchor off shingle beach at southeast side of the pool. In the east entrance to the loch the least depth is 1·8 metres. Submerged rocks lie 1 cable offshore ½ mile further east. Drying rocks lie

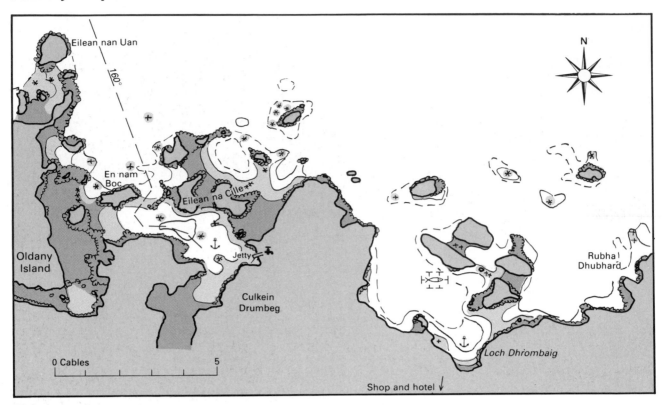

Drumbeg

Culkein Drumbeg from east.

Culkein Drumbeg entrance from southeast: a fishing boat is passing out through the entrance channel at the left of the photo, and a rock awash is showing off the north point of Eilean nam Boc.

Loch Dhrombaig from west.

west and southwest of Sgeir Liath, the outermost islet northeast of Loch Dhrombaig.

Shop, post office, telephone, hotel. Advice and assistance may be sought from Drumbeg Charters at the hotel, ☎ (05713) 236.

Loch Nedd, 58°15′N 5°10′W, can be safely approached in heavy northerly weather and provides good shelter. Drying reefs extend almost halfway across the entrance from the west side and up to a cable north of Rubha Dhubhard. Many moorings lie in the inner loch and the head dries off for ¼ mile.

Loch Ardbhair, 58°15′N 5°07′W. Even the outer part of this loch is occupied by fish cages and floats, but there is some space to anchor. Pass east of the reef in the mouth of the loch, which does not usually cover, and anchor in the southwest corner of the outer loch. 4 cables beyond the reef at the entrance the loch is almost completely blocked by drying rocks where the tide runs strongly, although a way through can be found. Further in there are more fish cages. South of an islet a reef occupies most of the middle of the loch and the head of the loch dries off ¼ mile, but anyone who has penetrated this far may find a clear anchorage under the west shore.

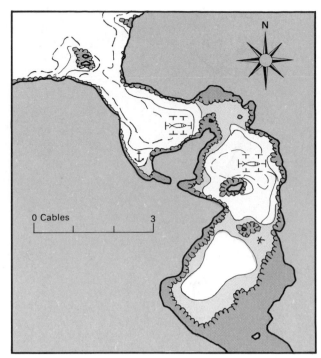

Loch Ardbhair

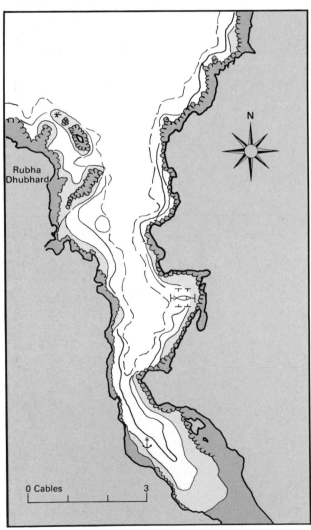

Loch Nedd

Loch a' Chairn Bhain

58°16′·5N 5°07′W

This loch is entered between Rubha nam Fias, 5 miles east of Oldany Island, and the Calbha islands. Ravens Rock, ¼ mile south of Calbha Beag, dries 1·8 metres and Lachen Shoal 4 cables WSW of Calbha Beag, at a depth of 2·1 metres, breaks heavily in gales. Several inlets on the north side of the entrance remain unexplored.

Loch Shark, 58°16′·8N 5°06′·3W, the most easterly of these, has a submerged rock in the middle of its entrance, which is only ¼ cable wide.

Kerrachar Bay, 4 cables SSE of Rubha na Fias, is an occasional anchorage, off a house on the shore. Reefs extend more than ½ cable from the north point of the bay, there are fish cages, and the bottom has been found to be thick with weed.

Loch a' Chairn Bhain runs in a southeasterly direction for 4 miles to Kylesku (Caolas Cumhann) a narrow passage where the tide runs strongly with eddies on each side. An elegant concrete bridge and power cables cross the narrows, both with 24 metres headroom.

Tides at Kylesku run at up to 2½ knots; the ingoing stream begins −0545 Ullapool (+0220 Dover). The out-going stream begins +0040 Ullapool (−0340 Dover).

Q.R.24m3M lights are shown from the north bridge supports on both sides, and Q.G.24m3M from the south bridge supports.

Loch Nedd

Poll a' Ghamhna, with Kylesku Bridge showing beyond Eilean a'
Ghamhna. The dark object at the right is a fish cage.

Poll a' Ghamhna, south of Eilean a' Ghamhna, 1 mile west of Kylesku is rather deep until close inshore, and the head of the bay dries off ½ cable. A shoal spit extends ½ cable south from the southeast point of the island.

Kylestrome A pool north of Garbh Eilean on the north side of Kylesku is entered by a narrow channel northeast of Garbh Eilean across which runs a power cable with headroom of 15 metres. Reefs extend more than halfway across the entrance channel from the north side leaving a passage perhaps no more than 20 metres wide; keep close to the southwest shore at the point where the channel narrows.

North Ferry Bay, north of Eilean na Rainich, is entered by the east and north sides of that island. Drying and submerged rocks extend 1 cable from the north shore of the inlet and there are some fishing boat moorings.

Camas na Cusgaig (South Ferry Bay), south of the east point of the narrows, has several moorings in it. A new fishing jetty stands at the northwest side of the head of the inlet. A drying rock lies ¼ cable offshore at the north side of the entrance and although this sounds close enough to the shore, it can catch a stranger coming round the corner.

2F.G(vert) lights are shown at the jetty in Camas na Cusgaig.

Shop, post office, telephone. Hotel, petrol and diesel at hotel by south ferry slip, water at jetty.

Lochs Glendhu and Glencoul Beyond Kylesku the loch divides into two parts, Loch Glendhu to the east and Loch Glencoul to the southeast. Loch Glendhu is clean with moderate depths at the head.

Loch Glencoul has several hazards. In its outer part the northeast shore is clean but on the southwest side a drying rock lies ¼ cable east of Eilean a Choin a' Chreige, the island furthest from the shore. Another rock which dries 0·3 metre lies 2 cables southeast of the same island.

A narrow passage leads southwest of a group of islands of which the largest is Eilean Ard, to Loch Beag. A drying reef extends northeast from Eilean an Tuim at the west side of the narrows; hold towards the island north of Eilean Ard and then keep midway between the next island and the south shore. An uncharted drying rock lies south of the east end of this island.

Calbha Bay (58°17′N 5°07′·5W), east of Calbha Mor, has fish cages along its west shore. Should these later be moved to the east side, care will be needed to avoid a reef extending about 1 cable from the west side which dries 3·1 metres.

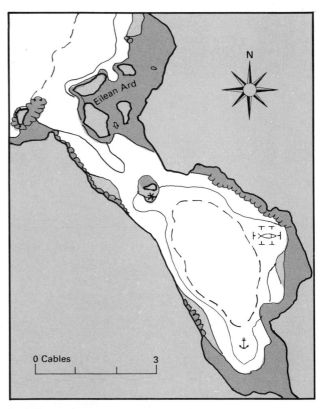

Loch Beag

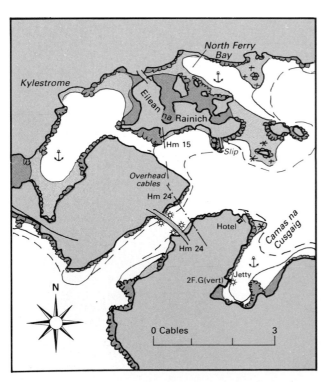

Kylesku

Badcall Bay

58°19′N 5°09′W

A well sheltered anchorage behind a dense group of islands on the east side of Eddrachillis Bay. A large group of fish cages lies on the southeast side of the bay.

Tides

Constant +0005 Ullapool (−0415 Dover)

Height in metres

MHWS	MHWN	MTL	MLWN	MLWS
4·5	3·4	2·6	1·6	0·9

Approach

From south, a possible hazard is a rock which dries 0·9 metre 1 cable south of Eilean na Bearachd. South Channel is east of Eilean na Bearachd, and west of Sgeir an Tairbh which is 1 metre high. At the northeast end of Eilean na Bearachd keep in mid-channel as reefs and drying rocks extend from either side. Continue north for 2 cables until past a rock 0·9 metre high to starboard, and then head northeast.

Main Channel leads north of Ceannamhor and Eilean na Bearachd. A submerged rock lies a cable north of Ceannamhor at a depth of 1·8 metres, and a rock which dries 0·3 metre lies ¼ cable south of Eilean Garbh.

From north, pass between Glas Leac and Eilean Garbh and enter by Main Channel.

Lochan Saile on the north side of Badcall Bay is sheltered by islands and drying reefs; to enter from Badcall Bay pass ¼–½ cable east of Eilean Dubh to avoid reefs which extend east from the island, and drying and submerged rocks on the east side of the passage. Pass east and north of the 9-metre islet north of Eilean Dubh and anchor in the western part of the bay.

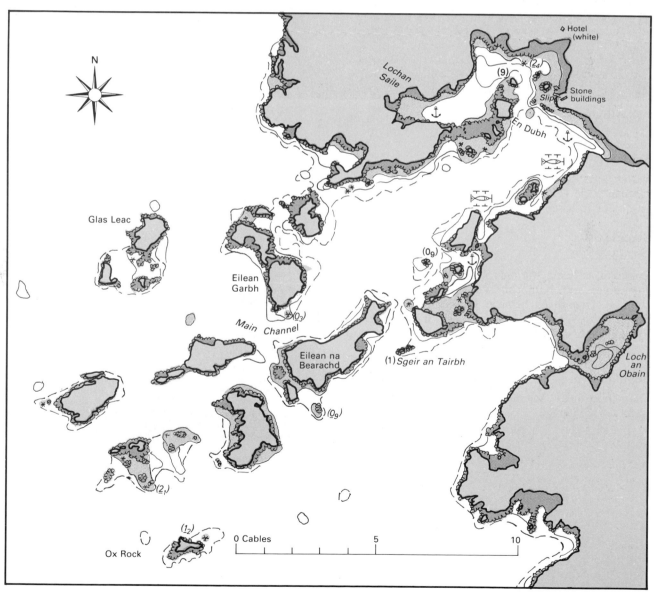

Badcall Islands

Badcall Bay from east; Lochan Saile is on the right.

Supplies

Water at slip on the east side of the passage to Lochan Saile. Hotel in the northeast corner, otherwise none (but see Scourie, below).

Scourie

58°21′N 5°10′W

Included as being the only source of stores between Lochinver and Kinlochbervie, apart from a small shop at Drumbeg. Scourie Bay is completely exposed, with several submerged and drying rocks in the entrance. If in doubt, do your shopping by land from Badcall.

Supplies

Shop, post office, telephone, hotel. Petrol, diesel and *Calor Gas* at garage.

The head of Scourie Bay from southwest.

Handa, Loch Laxford and Loch Inchard

Chart

2503 (1:25,000). OS map *9*.

Handa Sound

58°23′N 5°10′W

Handa Island is a RSPB bird reserve, with a resident warden.

Tides

Tidal streams in the sound run at up to 3 knots. The north-going stream begins −0405 Ullapool (+0400 Dover). The south-going stream begins +0220 Ullapool (−0200 Dover).

Dangers and marks

Bodha Morair, in mid-channel in Handa Sound at a depth of 1·8 metres, causes heavy overfalls. At the north end of the sound a drying reef extends 1 cable from Roinn Dubh on Handa, and Bodha Iasg lies in mid-channel at a depth of 1·6 metres. Sgeir Bellaire, 1 metre high, lies on the northeast side of the passage, 1 cable south of Eilean an Aigeich, the largest and highest island in the north channel.

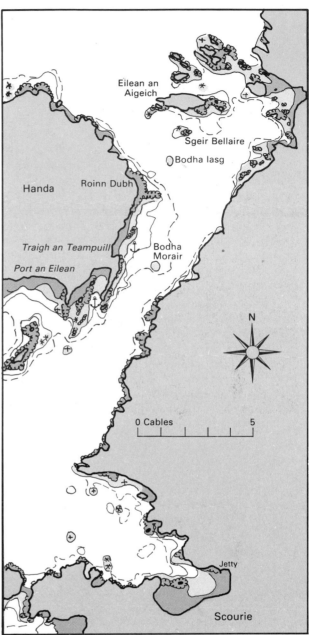

Handa Sound and Scourie Bay

Handa Sound from northeast. Traigh an Teampuill, Handa, is on the right, and Point of Stoer on the horizon with the Old Man of Stoer beside it.

Occasional anchorages

Traigh an Teampuill on the east side of Handa, as close inshore as depth allows.

Port an Eilean at the southeast of the island. Approach from SSW; there are no clearing marks for the rocks on either side of the entrance.

Loch Laxford

58°25′N 5°07′W

Much of the land round the loch is bare reddish-coloured rock, with a little heather growing on peat in the hollows. The shores are broken and indented to an extraordinary extent and many anchorages can be found with the large-scale chart, although several of them contain fish cages.

Tides

Streams in the loch are insignificant.

Constant +0015 Ullapool (−0405 Dover)

Height in metres

MHWS	MHWN	MTL	MLWN	MLWS
4·9	3·5	2·8	1·9	0·7

125

B.Spenue   Ru Ruag   Fonnbhein   Arkle   Stack of Laxford

Handa ESE 2 miles

Directions

The entrance, 2 miles northeast of Handa, is clean and straightforward, as is the fairway. There are no lights and no supplies are available nearer than Scourie, which is about 5 miles by road from Foindle.

Anchorages

Crow Harbour (Fanagmore), 58°24′N 5°07′W, is the first anchorage on the south side on entering the loch. Pass north and east of Eilean Ard ('69' on chart *1785*), the largest and highest island in the loch, although with only the small-scale chart it would be possible to cautiously thread a way through among the outer islands where the principal hazard is a drying rock 1 cable southwest of Sgeir Iosal which is 3½ cables WNW of Eilean

Ard. Although there is an extensive fish farm in the bay swinging room can still be found. Anchor on the west side, off the jetty.

Foindle Bay (58°23′·8N 5°05′W), Bagh na Fionndalach Moire on the chart, about a mile ESE of Crow Harbour, is rather deep and the sides shelve steeply. Enter by the north and east side of Eilean a Mhadaidh.

Weaver's Bay, 58°23′N 5°04′W, nearly a mile southeast of Foindle Bay, provides the best shelter in moderate depths of any bay on the south side of the loch.
    Nearest supplies are at Scourie.

Loch a' Chadh-fi, 58°24′·5N 5°04′W, on the northeast side of the loch is entered by the east side of Eilean an Eireannaich (61 metres). A rock which dries 2·8

Fanagmore Bay (Crow Harbour), Loch Laxford from southwest.

metres lies ½ cable from the southeast shore 3 cables within the loch. About ¾ mile inside the loch Eilean a' Chadh-fi lies in mid-channel. The deeper and broader channel is west and north of the island, but the west side of the loch is full of fish cages and moorings. Hazards north of the island are avoided by keeping ½ cable off its shore. Anchor north of the island, or anywhere in the upper part of the loch, but the head is shoal for about ¼ mile.

Several other anchorages may be found with the large-scale chart.

Loch Inchard

58°27'·5N 5°05'W

Tide

Constant +0020 Ullapool (−0400 Dover)

Height in metres

MHWS	MHWN	MTL	MLWN	MLWS
4·9	3·6	2·8	1·9	0·7

Dangers and marks

Dubh Sgeirean are a group of islands about a mile offshore between Loch Laxford and Loch Inchard with a channel ½ mile wide between them and Sgeirean Cruaidhe nearer the shore. Whale Back, which dries 3·8 metres southwest of Dubh Sgeirean is usually breaking; Sgeir Geinn, 1½ cables west of the most southerly of Sgeirean Cruaidhe is awash at HW. The most northerly of Sgeirean Cruaidhe is 8 metres high, which is not clear from chart *1785*, and Sgeir an Daimh, 3 metres high, lies 3 cables northwest of it. The passage inshore of Dubh Sgeirean and east of Sgeir an Daimh can usually be taken.

Glas Leac, two islets at the south side of the entrance to Loch Inchard joined at low water, have a clear deep passage more than ½ cable wide inshore of them, but 3-metre patches 1½ cables southwest of them might cause a bad breaking sea if much swell is running.

Eilean an Roin Beag, 2 miles northwest of the mouth of Loch Inchard, is the most southwesterly point of land northwest of the approach to the loch. Bodha Roin, nearly a cable southwest of the island, dries 0·7 metre.

Kinsale Rock (Bodha Ceann na Saile), 4 cables within the entrance just south of mid-channel at a depth of 3 metres, breaks if a swell is running. The southern extremity of the north shore of the loch in line with the south shore of Loch Sheigra ahead 098° leads north of Kinsale Rock.

Lights

Rubha na Leacaig on the north side of the entrance Fl(2)10s30m8M

Cape Wrath lighthouse, Fl(4)30s122m24M, is obscured east of about 025°, or the line of the coast north of Eilean an Roin Beag.

Loch Bervie (Kinlochbervie)

58°27'·5N 5°03'W

The third largest fishing harbour in Scotland by volume of fish landed, and is often too busy for a visiting yacht to find space although a pontoon has been provided for small craft in the NNE corner. Yachts should make a brief visit for supplies (dues are charged for even a brief stay) and anchor overnight elsewhere.

Leading beacons at the head of the harbour, framework towers with topmarks consisting of orange triangles on white squares, bearing 327° lead into the harbour. Two red columns to port and one green column to starboard mark shoal water on either side of the entrance.

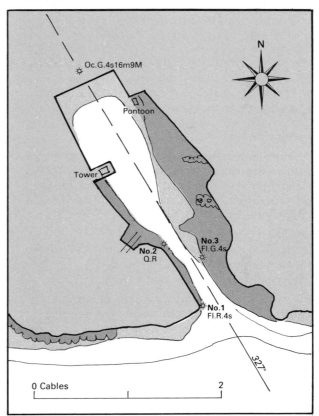

Kinlochbervie

Lights

Leading lights Oc.G.8s16/26m9M
No. 1 beacon Fl.R.4s
No. 2 beacon Q.R
No. 3 beacon Fl.G.4s

Radio

VHF Ch 12, 16.

Services and supplies

Shop (up hill from harbour), post office, telephone, hotel. Showers may be available at the Royal Nation-

Loch Bervie from the northeast shore. The small-boat pontoon is at the bottom right.

al Mission to Deep Sea Fishermen (not weekends). Petrol at garage. Diesel and water at quay, *Calor Gas*. Fishermen's chandlery, mechanical, electronic, hull repairs.

Minor anchorages

Mol Bhain (Camas Blair) on the south shore ½ mile southwest of the entrance to Loch Bervie. Anchor ½ cable off the southwest shore; subject to swell, and wash from passing traffic, and a fish farm is being established.

Loch Sheigra, 58°27′N 5°01′W, 1 mile east of Loch Bervie, is mostly shoal and drying, but has a depth of 2 metres 1 cable within the entrance.
　　Stores at Badcall on the north shore.

Achriesgill Bay, 1 mile further southeast, dries at the head and the bottom drops steeply to more than 15 metres.

Rhiconich, 58°26′N 5°00′W, at the head of the loch. The water in the middle is shoal for about ½ mile from the head of the loch, but deeper on either side. Hotel, post office, telephone, garage.

Loch Clash, 58°27′·7N 5°04′W, is open to the west and used by fishing boats for landing, but in quiet weather is an alternative to entering Loch Bervie for stores.

Coastal passage to Cape Wrath

Cape Wrath is 10 miles from Eilean an Roin Beag and there is no secure shelter eastward nearer than Loch Eriboll, a further 14 miles.

Dangers and marks

Dubh Sgeir, 10 metres high, lies ½ mile north of Eilean an Roin Beag and rocks above water and drying lie between Dubh Sgeir and the coast ½ mile NNE. Am Balg, 44 metres high, lies a mile offshore 4 miles north of Eilean an Roin Beag with drying rocks up to 2 cables from it.

Duslic Rock which dries 3·4 metres lies 7 cables NNE of Cape Wrath. Am Balg just open northwest of Cape Wrath 215° leads west of Duslic Rock.

Tides

Tidal streams reach 1¾ knots at springs. The north-going stream begins −0110 Ullapool (−0530 Dover). The south-going stream begins +0505 Ullapool (+0045 Dover).

VII. East coast of Harris and Lewis

Crossing the Minch from Skye and the mainland

Crossing to the Hebrides from Gunna Sound, Sound of Mull, and from Canna to Barra and the Uists is described in Chapter I. Crossing from Dunvegan or Uig presents no particular problem, nor, except for exposure, does a crossing from Gairloch or Loch Broom or the northern part of the mainland. Throughout the Minch the bottom is uneven and the sea may be very rough.

For details of the north of Skye see Chapter IV.

Charts

1794 or *1795* (1:100,000). *2210* (1:50,000) shows the north end of Skye in greater detail. OS map *14*.

Tides

Off Rubha Hunish the northeast-going stream begins −0405 Ullapool (+0400 Dover). The southwest-going stream begins +0220 Ullapool (−0200 Dover).

Off Scalpay, Harris, the northeast-going stream begins −0305 Ullapool (+0500 Dover) at springs and −0505 Ullapool (+0300 Dover) at neaps, beginning at NNE and gradually turning to east. The southwest-going stream begins +0320 Ullapool (−0100 Dover) at both springs and neaps. This has the effect that at neaps the NNE-going tide runs for 8½ hours and the southwest-going tide for 4 hours.

Northeast-going streams run at 2½ knots at springs, but both streams vary according to the wind direction and strength.

Dangers and marks

Described in sequence from Skye towards Harris.

A group of islets of which the largest is Fladda-chuain lies between 2½ and 3½ miles northwest of Rubha Hunish.

Sgeir nam Maol beacon, 12 metres high, with six legs and a cylindrical cage with a cross on top, is at the centre of a patch of rocks 2½ miles NNW of Rubha Hunish. *Comet Rock* red can light buoy is over a mile east of these rocks. (One of the ships used for the hydrographic surveys of the Hebrides in the 1850s was H.M.S. *Comet*).

Sgeir Graidach beacon, of a similar shape to that on Sgeir nam Maol but painted red, is 2¾ miles NNW of Fladda-chuain. Eugenie Rock lies ½ mile SSE of this beacon at a depth of 0·9 metre.

Sgeir Inoe, 3 miles ESE of Eilean Glas lighthouse dries 2·3 metres, and is marked by a green conical light buoy nearly a mile NNW of it.

Apart from these dangers the bottom of the Little Minch is very uneven and the strong wind and tide, together with any swell, create very heavy seas.

Large commercial vessels pass through the Little Minch and are recommended to pass between Trodday and Comet Rock buoy in a northeasterly direction, and through Sound of Shiant and northwest of Sgeir Inoe light buoy in a southwesterly direction, but this is not a mandatory separation scheme. A good lookout needs to be kept for vessels following these tracks – as well as for those which ignore the recommendations.

Directions

The shortest crossing from the north of Skye is to East Loch Tarbert, Harris and the direct line passes between Comet Rock and Fladda-chuain, but it may be preferable to keep down-wind or down-tide from the dangers described above and with a southwest wind and/or a northeast-going tide it may be better to pass east of Troddday and northeast of all the rocks and enter East Loch Tarbert by Sound of Scalpay.

On a passage to the Sound of Harris from north Skye there are no hidden dangers. An t-Iasgair, 21 metres high, lies about 3 miles WSW of Rubha Hunish.

A course from north Skye to the north part of Lewis passes close to the Shiant Islands which lie between 10 and 12 miles north of Rubha Hunish. If making for Loch Shell heavy seas in the Sound of Shiant are avoided by passing east of the Shiant Islands. The east end of Eilean Mhuire, the most easterly island, is clean, but rocks above water and drying extend 1¼ miles west of Garbh Eilean, the most westerly island; for details of the Shiants see page 149 below.

For the passage beyond Gob na Milaid see page 150 below.

From Gairloch or Loch Broom the shortest crossing is to Tob Limervay in Loch Shell; a passage to East Loch Tarbert, Harris passes close south of the Shiant Islands.

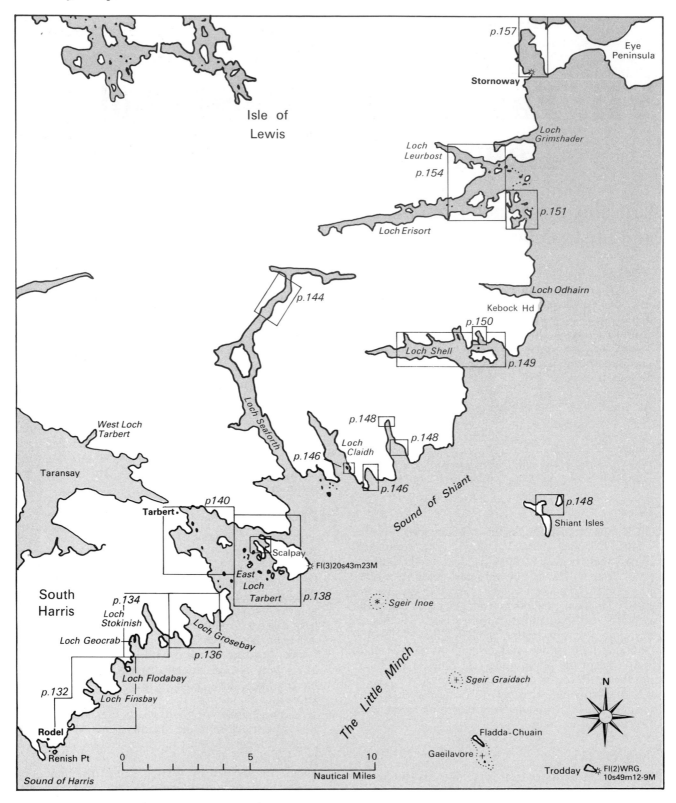

Isle of
Lewis

p.157

Eye
Peninsula

Stornoway

*Loch
Grimshader*

*Loch
Leurbost*

p.154

p.151

Loch Erisort

Loch Odhairn

p.144

Kebock Hd

p.150

Loch Shell

p.149

*West Loch
Tarbert*

p.148

p.148

Loch
Seaforth

p.146

*Loch
Claidh*

p.146

Taransay

p.148

Shiant Isles

p140

Tarbert

Scalpay

☀ Fl(3)20s43m23M

*East
Loch
Tarbert*

p.138

Sound of Shiant

South
Harris

p.134

*Loch
Stokinish*

Loch Geocrab

Loch Grosebay

p.136

⊙ *Sgeir Inoe*

Loch Flodabay

p.132

Loch Finsbay

⊕ *Sgeir Graidach*

N

Rodel

The Little Minch

Renish Pt

Fladda-Chuain

Sound of Harris

Gaeilavore ⊕

| 0 | | | 5 | | 10 |

Nautical Miles

Troday ◁☀ Fl(2)WRG.
10s49m12-9M

Tides around the Shiant Islands

Tides run strongly as follows: the north-going stream begins −0320 Ullapool (+0445 Dover). The south-going stream begins +0305 Ullapool (−0115 Dover). The spring rate of the south-going stream is 2 knots, but the streams bend south of the Shiant Islands to run WSW and ENE. 1 mile southeast of the islands the rate in both directions is 3 knots with heavy overfalls during the east-going stream.

Around Shiant South Rock, 2½ miles southwest of the Shiant Islands the streams are rotatory but follow the same pattern.

Radiobeacons

Eilean Glas 294·2 kHz LG (·—··/——·) 50M Seq 6 57°51′N 6°38′W
Stornoway Aero 669·5 kHz SWY (···/——/·——) 60M 58°17′N 6°21′W (non-A2A)
Butt of Lewis 298·8 kHz BL (—···/·—··) 150M Seq 2, 5 58°31′N 6°16′W
Cape Wrath 298·8 kHz CW (—·—·/·——) 50M Seq 1 58°37′·5N 5°00′W

Lights

Eilean Troddon Fl(2)WRG.10s49m12-9M
Comet Rock light buoy Fl.R.6s
Sgeir Inoe light buoy Fl.G.6s
Eilean Glas lighthouse Fl(3)20s43m23M
Shiants light buoy Q.G
Rubh' Uisenis light beacon Fl.5s24m11M
Gob na Milaid light beacon Fl.15s14m10M

At night look out for large commercial vessels. Crossing from Skye to East Loch Tarbert keep in the white sector of Eilean Troddon light beacon and pass northeast of Sgeir Inoe light buoy; in spite of the lack of lights Sound of Scalpay is probably easier for a stranger at night than the passage south of Scalpay, but approaching East Loch Tarbert in the dark is best avoided.

A night passage to or from Stornoway in the absence of electronic devices depends on bearings of Eilean Troddon, Gob na Milaid and Arnish Point light beacons, but their nominal range is such that at their furthest range, east of Shiant Islands, each would only be faintly visible for part of the passage.

Shelter

Some shelter in Duntulm Bay (see page 67) south of Rubha Hunish and Kilmaluag Bay (see page 105) on the east side of Skye. Good shelter in East Loch Tarbert, Loch Claidh, Loch Shell, Loch Erisort and Stornoway.

Coastal passage from Renish Point to East Loch Tarbert

The coast is very deeply indented, with few features to assist identification and several dangerous rocks up to 2 cables from the shore, although none affect a direct passage from Renish Point to East Loch Tarbert outwith this distance from the shore.

Charts

1795 (1:100,000). There are no larger-scale charts, and the plans in this book are based on Admiralty surveys from about 1860 at a scale of 1:10,560, supplemented by individual observations. OS maps *18* and *14* include valuable detail.

Tides

Interpolated between Leverburgh and Tarbert.

Constant −0035 Ullapool (−0455 Dover)

Height in metres

MHWS	MHWN	MTL	MLWN	MLWS
4·8	3·8	2·8	2·0	0·7

Dangers and marks

Roneval (Roinebhal), behind Rodel, is 458 metres high but further northeast the hills stand back from the coast and are not so high. A lattice radio mast stands about a mile north of Rodel.

Rubha Quidnish, 4 miles from Renish Point, has the appearance of being split into blocks; drying rocks lie 1½ cables outside the islands southwest of Rubha Quidnish.

Ard Manish (Aird Mhanais), on which a small triangulation pillar stands, has drying rocks up to 1½ cables south and east of it.

Rubha Cluer (Chluar), 3 miles northeast of Rubha Quidnish, is steep-sided with a grassy top and a small stone cairn on its summit. A rock which dries 2·9 metres lies a cable southeast of the point.

Lights

There are none southwest of the entrance to East Loch Tarbert, but the following will be some help:
Eilean Glas, Scalpay, East Loch Tarbert Fl(3)20s43m 23M
Neist Point, Skye Fl.5s43m16M
Waternish Point, Skye Fl.20s21m8M

Rodel is included in Chapter II as it appears on the chart of the Sound of Harris.

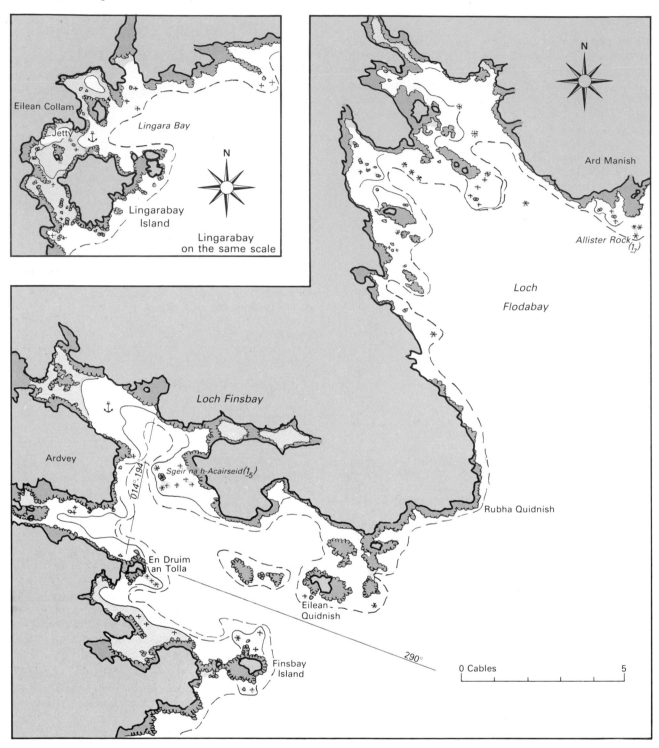

Lochs Finsbay and Flodabay

Anchorages

Lingarabay, 57°45′N 6°56′W, provides some shelter in westerly winds, but the west end of the inlet is too much obstructed by rocks for a yacht to go much further in than abreast of Eilean Collam and there is a loading jetty for a quarry in the inlet. Submerged rocks lie over a cable from the shore 4 cables east of the entrance.

Loch Finsbay

57°46′N 6°54′W

The entrance lies ¾ mile southwest of Rubha Quidnish, between Finsbay Island, which is 17 metres high, steep-sided with grass on top, on the south side, and Eilean Quidnish which is 13 metres high with a sharper peak. Drying and submerged rocks lie up to a cable north of Finsbay Island, and drying reefs and submerged rocks lie up to 2 cables ESE and northeast of Eilean Quidnish.

Directions

From south, do not turn in to the loch until about midway between the two islands.

From northeast keep Ard Manish open east of Rubha Quidnish 032° astern to clear the rocks east of Eilean Quidnish.

Inside the loch, keep Eilean Druim an Tolla, which is at the tip of a promontory on the south side, bearing 290° to avoid drying rocks on the north side of the channel, then pass a cable north of Eilean Druim an Tolla. Turn to starboard and steer with the promontory off which Eilean Druim an Tolla lies bearing 194° astern, and the conspicuous bluff on the east side of an inlet ahead bearing 014° (not the inlet further east), passing about ¾ cable east of Ardvey, between Sgeir na h-Acairseid which dries 1·5 metres and drying reefs off Ardvey. Fish cages occupy part of the anchorage.

Anchorages

Ardvey Anchor north of Ardvey in 4 metres, mud. Post office, telephone and small shop west of Ardvey.

Loch Flodabay, 57°47′N 6°52′W, is not particularly recommended, but the original Admiralty survey shows a passage about ¾ cable wide northeast of several drying and submerged rocks all 1 cable off the northeast shore.

Loch Gheocrab and Loch Beacravik

57°48′N 6°51′W

Ard Manish, described above, has detached drying rocks off its south and east sides; Allister Rock which dries 1·7 metres lies 1½ cables south of the point,

and Earr Manish which dries 2·3 metres lies over 2 cables east of the point. A large shed (salmon hatchery), with a stone gable facing seaward and red sides, stands at the head of Loch Beacravik. This building kept in sight at the west side of the entrance about 330° leads east of Earr Manish.

Directions

From north head for Ard Manish then Eilean Mhanais and when the salmon hatchery has been identified approach with it bearing 330° as above to clear rocks south and west of Aird Mhor. Sgeir Dubh, an above-water rock off the southwest point of Stockinish Island in line with the HW line of the tidal islet at the southeast point of Stockinish Island 073° leads close south of a rock which dries 3·0 metres, south of the southern entrance to Loch Stockinish.

In the entrance to Loch Beacravik rocks dry more than half of its width from the east side; keep a quarter of the width from the west side. Within the loch there are shoal rocky patches which give poor holding so that the anchor needs to be placed with care. Some fish cages are laid on the east side of the loch.

Loch Gheocrab provides little shelter, apart from a pool at the head of the loch behind a drying reef, and is also obstructed by fish cages.

Loch Stockinish

57°49′N 6°50′W

Directions

Caolas Mor, the main entrance to the loch, is littered with rocks, most of which cover and Caolas Beag, described below, is more straightforward. Du Sgeir Mor stands above water on a reef in the middle of the entrance and a rock which dries about 1 metre lies nearly a cable southeast of it. There is a clean passage 2 cables wide between this rock and islets and drying rocks off the west side of Stockinish Island. A drying rock lies ¾ cable off the west side of Eilean Leasait, the largest island off the west side of Stockinish Island, and a rock which dries 2 metres lies a little west of mid-channel 3 cables northwest of Eilean Leasait. These are not the only rocks in Caolas Mor, but are the ones which affect the fairway (if it can be so described).

Loch Stockinish itself is entered between Reef Rock which rarely covers, over a cable northwest of Stockinish Island and Am Maoladh, a tidal islet on the northwest side of the passage. A submerged rock known as Bo of the Den lies at a depth of 1·8 metres nearly a cable east of Am Maoladh.

Approach midway between Du Sgeir Mor and Eilean Leasait heading NNW; when the north end of Eilean Leasait is abeam steer towards the north end of Stockinish Island for about ¼ mile, then NNW towards the west side of Am Maoladh and pass midway between Reef Rock and Am Maoladh.

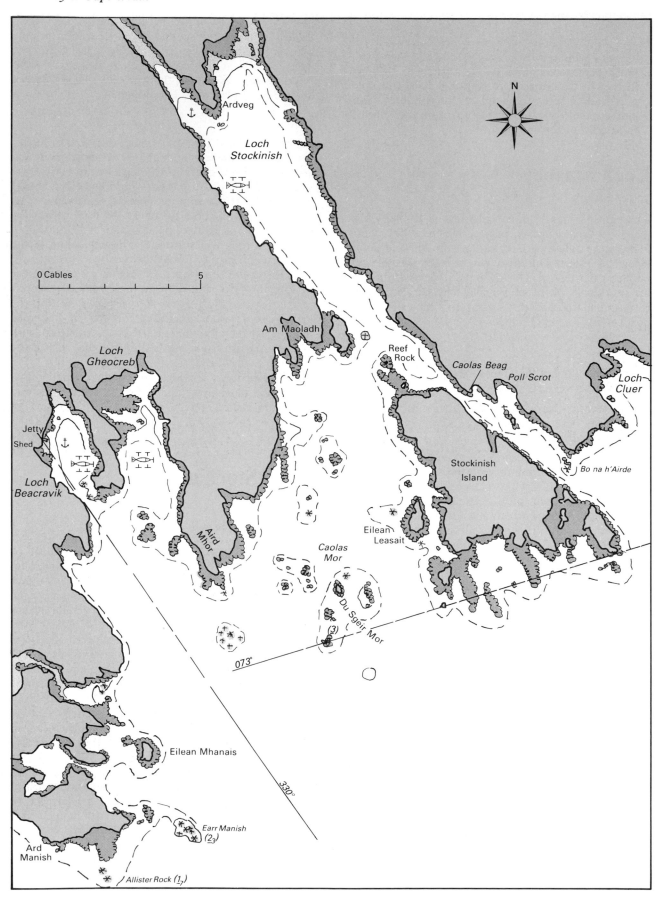

Loch Beacravik and Stockinish

Loch Beacravik from northwest. The salmon hatchery is left of centre.

Caolas Beag, on the northeast side of Stockinish Island, is less than 30 metres wide at one point but apart from Bo na h' Airde which covers at about half tide on the east side of the entrance, it is clean. A rock above water stands on a reef off the mouth of Poll Scrot on the north side of the channel with submerged rocks between the rock and the promontory northwest of it. A rough concrete quay stands on the east side of Poll Scrot and several inshore fishing boats lie at moorings there. The northeast side of the narrowest part of the channel dries off, leaving a channel 27 metres wide.

Rocks north and northwest of Stockinish Island have already been described; drying rocks extend up to ½ cable from the northeast shore opposite Reef Rock; to avoid Bo of the Den keep northeast of mid-channel. There are some fish cages in the main part of the loch. Drying rocks extend ¾ cable SSE from Ardvey, the promontory dividing the two arms of the head of the loch; anchor in the mouth of the more westerly arm. The only facility is a post office half-way along the east side of the loch.

Loch Beacravik entrance from northwest, showing how far the rocks extend from the east side.

Loch Grosebay

57°49′N 6°46′W

This loch has several islets and drying rocks in it and the shelter at the head is not good, but a very small inlet on the north side, Loch Scadabay, gives excellent shelter. Approaching from southwest the drying rock off Rubha Cluer described above must be avoided, and coming from the east Nun Rock, which is described below, is a hazard.

Cairam, an islet 22 metres high stands in the middle of the entrance and Glas Sgeir stands on a drying reef a cable north of Cairam. Sgeir na h' Iolla dries nearly a cable off the northeast shore, southeast of the entrance to Loch Scadabay. Rubha Reibinish open south of Aird Bheag 083° leads south of Sgeir na h' Iolla.

Patrick's Bo, which dries 1·5 metres, lies about 3 cables NNW of Glas Sgeir; the northeast sides of both Glas Sgeir and Cairam in line 153° astern lead close east of Patrick's Bo. John Rock which dries 3 metres lies ¼ mile NNW of Patrick's Bo near the northeast shore, and a rock which dries 1·5 metres lies ½ cable south of Sgeir a' Chais, which is marked by a cairn near the head of the loch. Pass northeast of Patrick's Bo and then keep to the southwest side of the loch and anchor north of Sgeir a' Chais.

Loch Scadabay may be found, if it is not otherwise apparent, by lining up the west side of Cairam with Rubha Cluer 206°. The passage west of Eilean an Duine is only 30 metres wide; after passing the island keep to starboard to avoid a rock-fall at the base of a cliff on the west side. A rough concrete jetty stands on the east side of the channel, and the head of the loch opens up to a basin with a depth of less than 2 metres of very soft mud in which a yacht's keel will come to no harm. Drying rocks in the middle of the entrance to this pool can be avoided by keeping to the southeast side.

Nun Rock lies 2 cables offshore at a depth of 0·6 metre, ¼ mile south of Rubha Bocaig at the south entrance to East Loch Tarbert. There is no clearing mark for the south side of Nun Rock.

Loch Grosebay

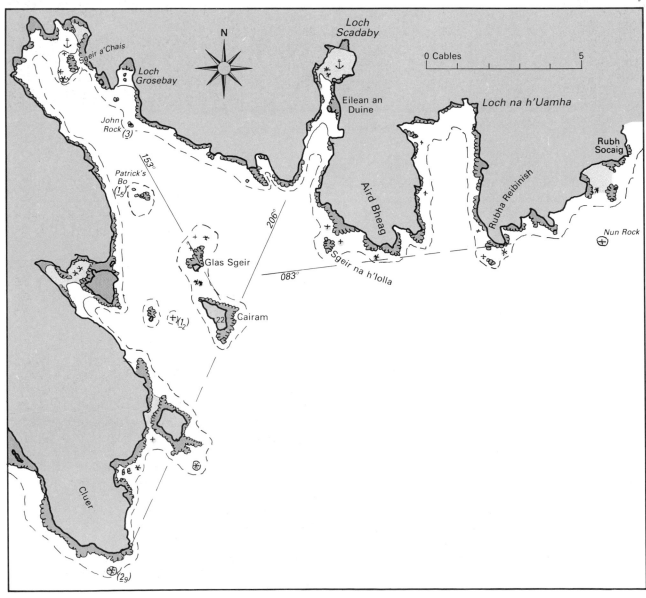

Loch Scadabay from its head; the rocks are not quite covered.

East Loch Tarbert

57°51′N 6°45′W

A broad loch with many bays providing a choice of anchorages. Braigh Mor, the main fairway, has various rocks and islets on either side. Scalpay, a substantial island 2½ miles long, lies on the north side of the entrance, separated from Harris by the Sound of Scalpay, which is only a cable wide at one point. Sound of Scalpay is much the most straightforward approach, particularly from east or northeast.

Scotasay stands in the middle of the loch, 8 cables west of Scalpay, and Tarbert village and ferry terminal are 2 miles further northwest.

Chart

2905 (1:10,000). OS map *14*.

Tides

The northwest-going stream in Braigh Mor flows round Scalpay to run east in Sound of Scalpay and begins −0520 Ullapool (+0245 Dover). The southeast-going stream (west-going in Sound of Scalpay) begins +0105 Ullapool (−0315 Dover).

Constant −0026 Ullapool (−0446 Dover)

Height in metres

MHWS	MHWN	MTL	MLWN	MLWS
5·0	3·7	2·9	2·1	0·8

Dangers and marks in Braigh Mor

Eilean Glas lighthouse at the most easterly point of Scalpay is a white tower with red bands, 30 metres in height.

Skerries and islets, of which the main group is the Gloraigs, extend up to 7 cables from the southwest shore of the loch. The most northeasterly of the Gloraigs is Dun Corr Mor on which is an inconspicuous light beacon.

When approaching from south Nun Rock, described above, is just cleared on its east side by keeping Eilean na Sgaite, 8 cables south of Dun Corr Mor, open of Sgeir Bhocaig, a rock 3 metres high close to Rubha Bhocaig, the southwest point of the entrance, bearing 008°.

Bogha Bhocaig, over which the depth is 1·4 metres, lies 4 cables east of Rubha Bhocaig and may be dangerous in a swell. Dun Corr Mor, the most northeasterly of the Gloraigs, under the summit of Scotasay 342° leads 2 cables east of Bogha Bhocaig. Sgeir an Leum Bhig, the most southeasterly of the Gloraigs, touching Stiughay, east of Scalpay 004°, leads clear west of Bogha Bhocaig.

In the approach from east, Bogha Lag na Laire, a group of rocks which just dries, lies 3 cables south of Meall Chalibost, the southern extremity of Scalpay.

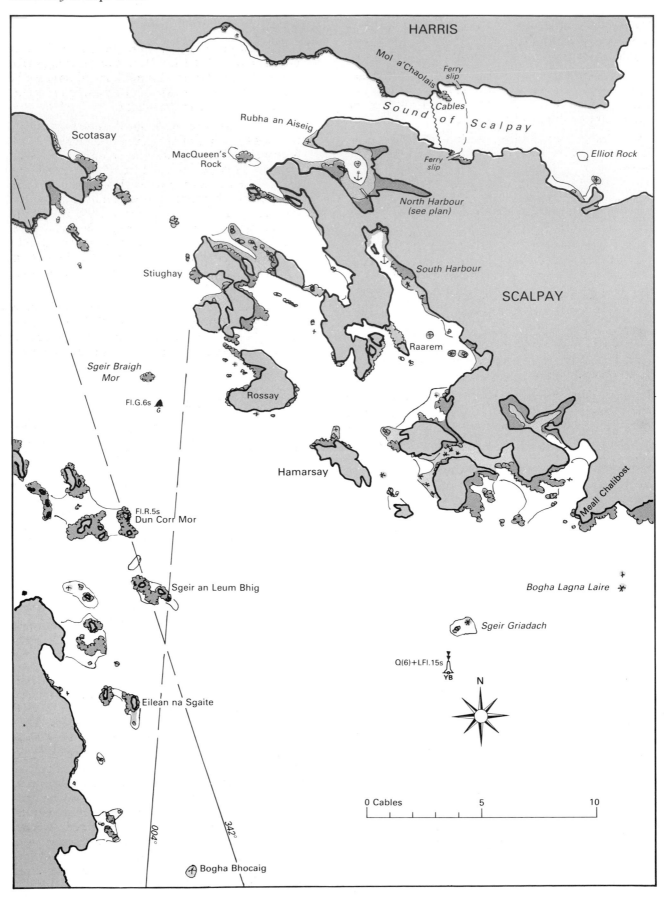

HARRIS

Mol a'Chaolais

Ferry slip

Sound of Scalpay

Cables

Ferry slip

Elliot Rock

Rubha an Aiseig

Scotasay

MacQueen's Rock

North Harbour (see plan)

Stiughay

South Harbour

SCALPAY

Sgeir Braigh Mor

Raarem

Fl.G.6s
G

Rossay

Hamarsay

Meall Chalibost

Fl.R.5s
Dun Corr Mor

Sgeir an Leum Bhig

Bogha Lagna Laire

Sgeir Griadach

Q(6)+LFl.15s
YB

N

Eilean na Sgaite

0 Cables   5   10

004°   342°

Bogha Bhocaig

Outer part of East Loch Tarbert, Braigh Mor and Sound of Scalpay

Sgeir Griadach, a patch of rocks part of which dries 1·5 metres 4 cables south of Scalpay, is marked on its south side by a south cardinal light buoy.

Approaching from east or northeast, Sgeir Griadach light buoy must be identified and approached on a bearing of not less than 260°; keep outwith the 40-metre contour until south of this line.

Sgeir Braigh Mor, 6 cables north of Dun Corr Mor, is marked on its south side by a green conical light buoy.

Bogha Ruadh, on the southwest side of the fairway a mile northwest of Dun Corr Mor, dries 0·5 metre. A pair of islands, Eileanan a' Ghille-bheid, lies ½ mile beyond Bogha Ruadh and a further ½ mile northwest is a larger island, Eilean Arderanish. Eilean Arderanish open northwest of Eileanan a' Ghille-bheid 305° clears the northeast side of Bogha Ruadh.

A light beacon 5 metres high stands on Sgeir Ghlas, on the southwest side of Scotasay.

Loch Ceann Dibig on the west side of the loch west of Scotasay has several bays around its shores, and drying rocks lie over 2 cables from its north side and up to 1½ cables from its south side.

Eileanan Diraclett extend up to 3 cables east of the north point of Loch Ceann Dibig, and a group of rocks lies 3 cables further east. Cuidsgeir, the most southerly rock, is 2 metres high; the others, extending ¼ mile north, cover. The main fairway is to the east of these rocks, and Dun Corr Mor touching Sgeir Ghlas 153° leads 1 cable ENE of them. The passage west of them is lined with rocks for which there is no good clearing mark. Paterson's Rock, over a cable SSE of the southeast point of Eileanan Diraclett, dries 0·6 metre but is not in the way of a direct passage from the entrance to Tarbert.

Sgeir Bhuidhe, a reef extending ¾ cable from the southwest shore northwest of Eileanan Diraclett is marked by a perch. Oban Rocks which dry 2 metres, 1½ cables from the north shore, are not marked.

Sound of Scalpay is a clean but narrow passage north of Scalpay. Drying rocks extend up to a cable off the northeast shore of Scalpay outwith the entrance. Elliot Rock, at a depth of 2 metres, lies 1½ cable off the head of a bay on the south side of the channel, and a reef which extends more than ½ cable southeast of Mol a' Chaolais, at the west side of the bay at the north ferry slipway dries 1·4 metres (so don't tack close inshore there).

Lights

Eilean Glas lighthouse Fl(3)20s43m23M
Sgeir Griadach light buoy Q(6)+LFl.15s
Dun Corr Mor light beacon Fl.R.5s10m5M
Sgeir Braigh Mor light buoy Fl.G.6s
Sgeir Ghlas light beacon Iso.WRG.4s9m9-6M
Tarbert pier and dolphin each 2F.G(vert)5M

At night

From south keep ¾ mile offshore (Eilean Glas bearing not more than 048°) until Dun Corr Mor light is in line with Sgeir Ghlas light and turn to head to the east of Sgeir Braigh Mor light buoy until in the white sector of Sgeir Ghlas light.

From east or northeast, although there are no navigation lights Sound of Scalpay is the more straightforward approach. If using the south passage, Sgeir Griadach light buoy must be identified and approached on a bearing of not less than 260°; keep outwith the 40-metre contour until south of this line. Keep in the white sector of Sgeir Ghlas light beacon passing Dun Corr Mor light beacon to port, and Sgeir Braigh Mor light buoy to starboard. Pass south and west of Sgeir Ghlas light beacon until in its northwest white sector, and steer with that light astern to Tarbert.

North Harbour, Scalpay has a light Q.G on the buoy northeast of Coddem as well as 2F.G(vert) at the seaward end of the pier, and may be approached by way of Sound of Scalpay in less than total darkness.

Anchorages in the outer loch

Plocrapool, 57°50'·5N 6°45'W, is a snug but shallow anchorage on the southwest side of the entrance to Braigh Mor. Approach by south of Dun Corr Mor and pass northwest of Sgeir Bun a' Loch which is in the middle of the entrance, closer to that rock than to the islands on the west side to avoid drying reefs off them. At spring tides look out for rocks at a depth of less than 2 metres which are not likely to be a problem at other times. Head to the east of houses steering 210° and anchor as far in as the depth allows. (See plan of inner loch.)

South Harbour, Scalpay, 57°52'N 6°42'W. Identify Hamarsay and Rossay (the highest of the islands southwest of Scalpay), and pass between them and midway between Raarem and the southeast shore to avoid drying rocks SSE of Raarem. When Raarem is abaft the beam and the promontory on the west shore is well open north of Raarem turn to pass ½ cable from its east side to clear Boundary Rock over which the depth is 0·4 metre and then keep close to the west side at the narrows. Anchor southeast of the islet off the southwest side of the inner loch, clear of a drying rock 50 metres from the shore ½ cable southeast of the islet. There is deep water further in, but more rocks than water, and several moorings.

At Eilean Glas lighthouse the former keepers' cottages have been converted to a small holiday centre with a restaurant, laundrette, telephone and small shop. VHF watch is sometimes kept on Ch 16. There is a very occasional anchorage in an inlet ¾ cable west of the lighthouse; A rock which dries 0·1 metre lies ½ cable south of the east point of the entrance and an overhead cable crosses the head of the inlet from a point just north of the jetty on the east side.

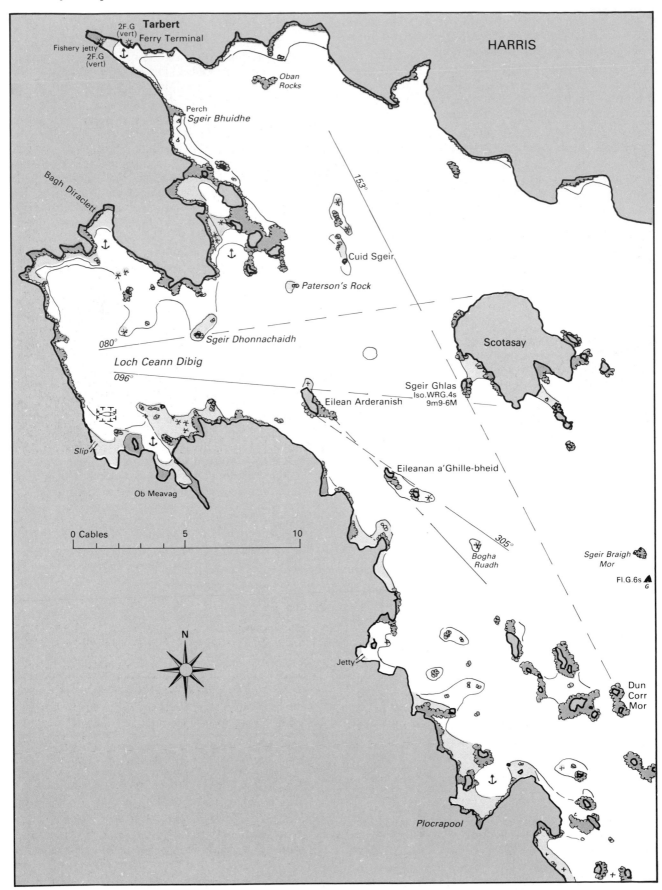

Inner part of East Loch Tarbert

Plocrapool from south with the Gloraigs and Scotasay beyond.

North Harbour, Scalpay

57°52'·5N 6°42'W

Dangers and marks

MacQueen's Rock, 1½ cables west of Rubha na Cud-aigean at the south side of the entrance, covers at high water (one of many changes recorded on the 1988 edition of the chart). Rocks extend a third of a cable west of Rubha an Aiseig on the north side of the entrance and a rocky shelf lies on the north side of the entrance channel. A drying wreck lies on the south side of the channel, northwest of Coddem, and a green conical light buoy lies northeast of Coddem.

Give Rubha an Aiseig a berth of at least ½ cable and keep in mid-channel in the entrance; pass north of the light buoy and anchor clear of the fairway to the pier, which is frequently used. Landing is most convenient at the slip ¼ cable east of the pier.

The stranded hulk (a ferrocement coaster from the first world war) lies in the northeast corner and fishing boats and the car ferry lie on its north side overnight.

A submerged rock at a depth of 1·1 metres is charted north of the middle of the harbour; an attempt was made to remove it with explosives but there is some doubt as to whether this was successful.

Supplies

Shops (including butcher), petrol, post office, telephone, water tap at pier. Harris wool and knitwear shop.

North Harbour, Scalpay

Rubha an Aiseig   *Light-buoy*   *Part of wreck*   *Coddem*

Approach to North Harbour, Scalpay.

North Harbour, Scalpay from south.

South Harbour, Scalpay, from the head of the inlet.

Anchorages in the northwest part of East Loch Tarbert

Loch Ceann Dibig, 57°52′·5N 6°48′W, on the west side of East Loch Tarbert is obstructed by rocks on all sides but has several sheltered anchorages. The north point of Eilean Arderanish touching the south end of Scotasay 096° leads clear of all dangers to the west shore.

Ob Meavag, on the south side of Loch Ceann Dibig is shoal and drying for 2 cables from its head and drying rocks lie 2 cables northwest of the entrance, with a rock 0·9 metre high over a cable to the east, which might be mistaken for the drying rocks. Sgeir Liath stands above water west of the entrance, with a conspicuous concrete slip beyond it, and a stone mill building south of the slip; the mill showing northwest of Sgeir Liath 210° leads close north of the drying rock. Approach from northwest with the head of the inlet bearing 138°.

Bagh Diraclett is a shallow bay on the north side of Loch Ceann Dibig with rocks above water and drying in the approach. Little Macnab's Rock which dries 0·8 metre, the furthest southwest of these, is cleared by keeping Sgeir Dhonnachaidh which is just above water, in line with the north side of Scotasay 080°.

Eileanan Diraclett, 57°53′N 6°47′W, are east of the north point of Loch Ceann Dibig with a sheltered anchorage on their west side. Fish cages and rocks obstruct the inner part of the inlet, but there are moderate depths to the south of them.

Tarbert village

The narrow inlet by the ferry terminal is mostly occupied by moorings and there is little space for visiting yachts. Keep clear of the approach to the ferry terminal; the piermaster will shout at you if you anchor to the south of the pier as the ferry needs space to turn when leaving.

Services and supplies

Shops (licensed stores at Harris Hotel only), butcher, post office, telephone, bank, hotel. Showers at Harris Hotel (beyond head of the inlet). Petrol and diesel at garage. Water at pier (not always available), also at the fishery jetty which dries on the south side of the head of the inlet. *Calor Gas* at Macleod Motel, beside pier. Doctor's surgery near Harris Hotel.

Tarbert, Harris. The inlet dries out beyond the fishery jetty in the foreground; the ferry terminal is on the left.

Southeast Lewis – East Loch Tarbert to Gob na Milaid

This section of coast is as bleak and remote as any in the Outer Hebrides. There are neither roads nor houses between Loch Seaforth and Loch Shell.

There are no hazards on a direct passage between Rubha Crago or Eilean Glas and Rubh' Uisenis except for the strength of the tide, with heavy and sometimes dangerous overfalls in the Sound of Shiant.

Charts

1794, 1795 (1:100,000). OS map *14* is also strongly recommended owing to the small scale of these charts.

Tides

In the Sound of Shiant between Rubh' Uisenis and Shiant Islands the northeast-going stream begins −0305 Ullapool (+0500 Dover). The southwest-going stream begins +0320 Ullapool (−0100 Dover). The spring rate in each direction is 3 or 4 knots.

Lights

Eilean Glas lighthouse Fl(3)20s43m23M
Sgeir Inoe light buoy Fl.G.6s
Rubh' Uisenis light beacon Fl.5s24m11M
Shiants light buoy Q.G
Gob na Milaid Fl.15s14m10M

Shelter

Eilean Hingerstay (Thinngarstaigh) in Loch Claidh and Tob Limervay in Loch Shell are easily approached in daylight.

Loch Seaforth

57°55′N 6°40′W

A long narrow loch with high hills crowding in on both sides and subject to dangerous squalls from unexpected directions. The loch within is clean but there are several dangers in the approach.

Tides

Tidal streams are generally weak but reach 1 knot in the channels either side of Seaforth Island, turning at local HW and LW. At the narrows to Upper Loch Seaforth which are impassable to yachts the streams reach 7 knots.

Constant −0016 Ullapool (−0436 Dover)

Height in metres

MHWS	MHWN	MTL	MLWN	MLWS
5·0	3·7	2·9	2·1	0·8

Dangers, marks and directions

Sgeir an Daimh, ½ mile from the shore 9 cables NNE of Rubha Crago, probably does not cover except at high spring tides although it is charted as drying 3·5 metres.

Sgeir Hal, in the entrance to Loch Seaforth 3 cables southwest of Rubha Bridog, the east point of the entrance, is charted as 2 metres above high water, but appears to be less, perhaps no more than 0·5 metre. Submerged reefs extend ¼ cable all round Sgeir Hal, and Sgeir Ruadh, over a cable south of Sgeir Hal, dries about 0·3 metre.

Iola Mhor, about ¼ mile SSE of Ard Caol at the west point of the entrance, dries about 0·5 metre. Sgeir Bhridag, about a cable SSE of Rubha Bridog, dries 2 metres.

Loch Seaforth entrance.

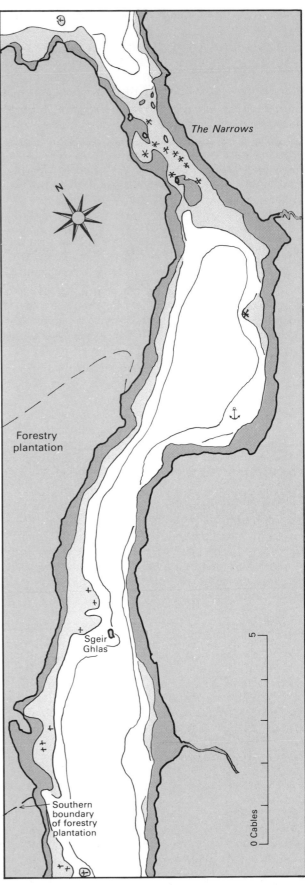

Loch Seaforth, northeast arm. Note this plan is not aligned on the meridian.

Kenmore, a conspicuous promontory on the east side of Loch Seaforth 3 miles from the entrance open of the west side of the loch 341° leads east of Iola Mhor, but Sgeir an Daimh is on this line and it should not be used until past that rock.

The south point of Loch Maaruig, on the west side of Loch Seaforth opposite Kenmore, open of the east side of the loch 322°, leads west of Sgeir Bhridag.

Sgeir nan Ron, which dries 2 metres, lies 75 metres from the west shore 3 cables north of Glas Sgeir, a green islet 1¼ miles NNW of Ard Caol, and about ½ cable from the north side of a slight indentation on the west shore.

Loch Maaruig lies on the west side of Loch Seaforth 2½ miles from the entrance. Its head dries 2 cables, and a rock awash lies off a bay on the south side of Goat Point, a promontory on the north side of the loch; this rock is cleared by keeping the east end of Goat Point open of the south point of the loch, although fish cages moored there make this of academic interest at present. A submerged rock lies about ¼ cable off the west end of Goat Point. Anchor west of Goat Point. Telephone box in the garden of a house on the north side of the loch, between the house and the loch.

Beyond Loch Maaruig the shores are less steep; Seaforth Island two miles further north can be passed on either side. The two bays on Harris west of the island are shoal and drying, but reasonable anchorage can be found off the jetty at Aline Lodge, northwest of Seaforth Island, or in the passage north of the island in about 7 metres, which may be more sheltered.

The loch extends a further 3 miles northeast of Seaforth Island to the narrows leading to Upper Loch Seaforth; the narrows are filled with drying rocks which form tidal rapids where the stream runs at up to 7 knots, with only about 5 minutes of slack water, and are not passable except in a kayak or an expendable dinghy.

Two miles beyond Seaforth Island Sgeir Ghlas stands southeast of the middle of the loch with rocks which dry extending north and west from it. There is a clear passage east of Sgeir Ghlas, and the depth is reasonable for anchoring ½ mile northeast of Sgeir Ghlas in a bay on the southeast shore; a drying rock lies a cable from the southeast shore 3½ cables beyond the south point of the bay. The plan is taken from an Admiralty survey of 1850.

Loch Maaruig from south; Goat Point is in the centre of the photo.

Photo: Jean Lawrence

Loch Claidh

57°55′N 6°36′W

The entrance lies between Eilean Mor a' Bhaigh a mile to the west, and Rubha Valamus Beag (Bhalamuis Bhig on the chart), a low rocky promontory, the most southerly point between Loch Seaforth and Rubh' Uisenis.

Tides

Constant −0026 Ullapool (−0446 Dover)

Height in metres

MHWS	MHWN	MTL	MLWN	MLWS
5·0	3·7	2·9	2·1	0·8

Dangers and marks

Pender Rock stands in a depth of 0·3 metre at the seaward end of a submerged reef which extends 4 cables SSE from Aird a' Bhaigh, the west point of the entrance; overfalls occur around Pender Rock. On the east side of the entrance, rocks ½ cable off Sgeir Niogag, a rock 5 metres high on a drying reef ½ mile WNW of Rubha Valamus Beag, dry up to 3·4 metres. A drying reef extends ½ cable southwest of Rubha Valamus Beag.

Directions

The south side of Eilean Mor a' Bhaigh in line with Uiseval, a hill 333 metres high on the north side of Sound of Scalpay, bearing 248°, leads close south of Pender Rock. Bring Loch Claidh well open before turning in to the entrance.

Anchorages

Eilean Hingerstay (Thinngarstaigh), 1¼ miles northwest of Rubha Valamus Beag, shelters a pool about ¾ cable across on the east side of the loch. The passage south of the island is beset by reefs, but the approach by the north of the island is straightforward. Holding and shelter have been found to be good in southerly and westerly gales, and even in northwesterly winds little sea comes in.

Tob Smuaisibhig, on the east side of Loch Claidh 1½ miles NNW of Eilean Hingerstay, provides some shelter.

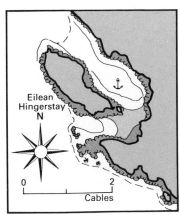

Eilean Hingerstay, Loch Claidh

Loch Valamus (Bhalamuis)

57°55′N 6°34′W

A narrow loch, shallow at the head, east of Rubha Valamus Beag, entered between that point and Sgeir Mhor Bhalamuis, a detached rock off the east point of the loch. Several drying rocks lie off the east side of the loch, and if approaching from east keep 3 cables offshore until the loch is well open. About ½ mile from the entrance a pool opens up on the east side with rocks awash and drying in it. Anchor ½ cable north of Transit Point if sufficient depth is found.

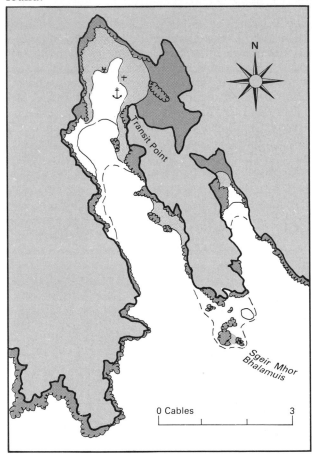

Loch Valamus

Loch Bhrollum

57°56′N 6°32′W

About two miles southwest of Rubh' Uisenis Loch Bhrollum is entered between steep points off both of which drying rocks extend over ½ cable. Aird Dubh, a grassy peninsula 15 metres high on the east side of the loch, is difficult to distinguish from the background; Meall Mor, ½ mile NNW is conspicuous. Bogha Dubh, a group of rocks which dry 0·3 metre, lies two thirds of a cable WNW of Aird Dubh.

Anchorages

Tob Bhrollum is an occasional anchorage in the bay northeast of Aird Dubh. On approaching keep 30 metres off Aird Dubh to avoid Bogha Dubh and a

Loch Valamus entrance from northwest.

Mol Mor, Shiant Isles.

Tob Bhrollum from southeast.

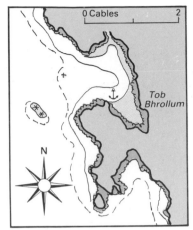

Tob Bhrollum

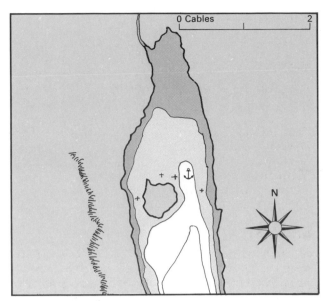

Head of Loch Bhrollum

reef which dries off the northwest point of Aird Dubh. A submerged rock at a depth of 0·3 metre lies nearly a cable NNW of Aird Dubh; when the west point of the entrance to Loch Bhrollum is shut in behind Aird Dubh this rock is cleared. Some swell in southerly winds may be avoided by anchoring close to the head of the bay in the southeast corner but this bay is infested with thongweed.

At the head of the loch anchor east of the islet, or at neap tides northeast of the islet which gives better shelter from seaward than Tob Bhrollum.

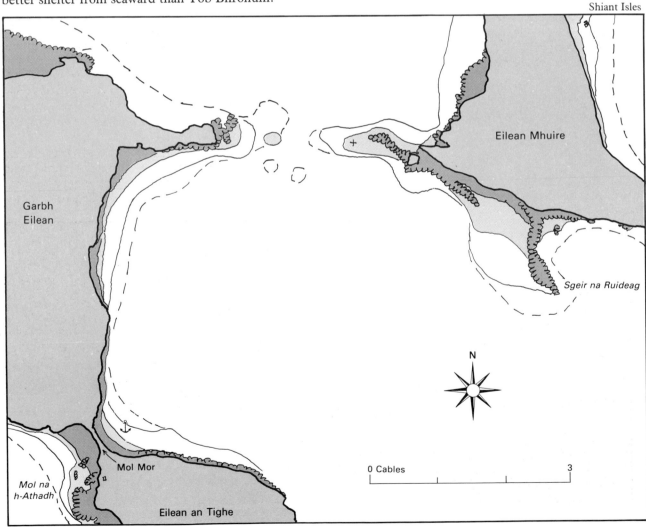

Shiant Isles

Shiant Isles

57°54′N 6°21′W

Tides

For tidal streams around Shiant Isles see above, page 131.

Constant (for Loch Shell) −0016 Ullapool (−0436 Dover)

Height in metres

MHWS	MHWN	MTL	MLWN	MLWS
4·8	3·6	2·8	1·9	0·7

Directions

A dramatic group of islands to visit in settled weather; the usual anchorage in moderate westerly winds is on the east side of Mol Mor, a stony isthmus between the two western islands. In moderate easterly winds it is possible to anchor in a similar position west of Mol Mor, but there are drying rocks off its south end on that side.

A drying reef extends 1½ cables south from a point in the western half of Eilean Mhuire, the northeast island. Another drying reef extends 1½ cables west from the same island into the passage between that island and Garbh Eilean, the northwest island, with a submerged rock at its outer end. Another drying reef extends less than ½ cable east from Garbh Eilean into the same passage. The clear passage is 1½ cables wide, but it should be taken to the west of mid-channel.

Loch Shell

58°00′N 6°27′·5W

The main fairway of the loch southwest of Eilean Iuvard (Iubhard) is clear of dangers, but rocks northwest of the island affect the approach to Tob Orinsay. The principal anchorage is Tob Limervay (Lemreway), north of Eilean Iuvard.

Tides

Constant −0016 Ullapool (−0436 Dover)

Height in metres

MHWS	MHWN	MTL	MLWN	MLWS
4·8	3·6	2·8	1·9	0·7

Tob Limervay

58°00′·8N 6°26′·2W

Directions

The entrance may be difficult to identify as in some conditions of light Eilean Iuvard merges with the background.

Sgeir Phlathuig, which dries 0·9 metre, lies on the northeast side of the approach; its west side is cleared by keeping the east side of Galta Mor at the west end of the Shiant Islands in line with the southeast point of Eilean Iuvard 178° astern. The south side of the rock is cleared by keeping Rubha Buidhe in line with Sron Chrom bearing 272°.

A drying rock lies ¼ cable southwest of the east point of the entrance to Tob Limervay (on which a wooden shed stands).

Anchorage

Anchor off the east side of the inlet, taking care to leave swinging room clear of drying reefs inshore. Shelter in southerly winds may be found on a narrow shelf close to Eilean Iuvard south of Sgeir Fraoich.

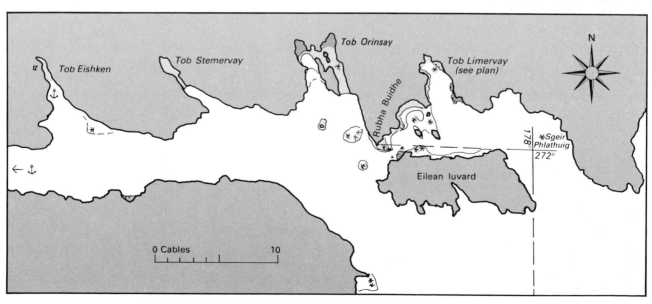

Loch Shell

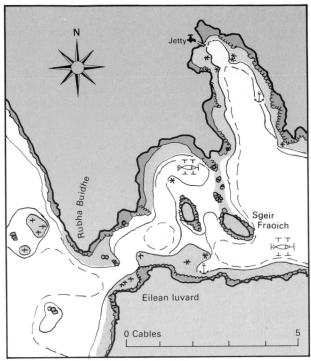

Tob Limervay

Sgeir Leum, 2 metres high, stands 4 cables WNW of Rubha Buidhe, the west point of Eilean Iuvard; a submerged rock at a depth of 0·3 metre lies ½ cable west of Sgeir Leum.

Severe gusts occur in strong winds from west and southwest in the inner part of Loch Shell. Several of the inlets are encumbered by fish cages but anchoring is still possible.

Tob Orinsay, a mile NNW of the west end of Eilean Iuvard, lies on the west side of Orinsay Island. Between the island and a promontory on the west side the bottom appears to be shingle with a depth of 3 metres. Depth in the inlet east of the island is mostly less than 1 metre.

Tob Stemervay, 1¼ mile WNW of Eilean Iuvard, has depths of 5 metres 2 cables from the entrance.

Tob Eishken, 1½ miles from the head of the loch on the north side, has a drying rock ¾ cable from the northeast shore in the entrance; a rock awash lies ¼ cable from the west shore about 3 cables north of the west point of the entrance.

The head of the loch dries off 3 cables, and there is a reasonable area with a depth of 5–10 metres.

Supplies

Post office, telephone. Water tap beside shed at the jetty.

Tob Limervay from northeast.

Dangers and marks in the main part of Loch Shell

Sgeir na Caorach, close southwest of the west end of Eilean Iuvard, is 1 metre high.

Sgeirean Dubha, 2 cables southwest of Rudha Buidhe, a sloping promontory on the north side of the west end of Caolas Tuath, dry 2·4 metres.

Bogha Ruadh, 2 cables WNW of Rubha Buidhe, dries 4 metres; submerged rocks lie 1 cable north and east of Bogha Ruadh.

East coast of Lewis – Gob na Milaid to Tiumpan Head

Chart

1794 (1:100,000). OS map *14*.

Tides

Tides off Kebock Head, 1½ miles north of Gob na Milaid, run at up to 3 knots at springs. The north-going stream begins −0405 Ullapool (+0400 Dover). The south-going stream begins +0220 Ullapool (−0200 Dover).

Between Kebock Head and the Eye Peninsula, east of Stornoway, the tides are weak.

Dangers

The shore as far as Stornoway is free from dangers but Dubh Sgeir, a detached islet 8 metres high, stands 3 cables northeast of Torray (Eilean Thoraidh), south of the entrance to Loch Erisort.

Lights

Gob na Milaid light beacon Fl.15s14m10M
Arnish Point Fl.WR.10s17m19/15M
Eitshal Radio Mast (58°10'·7N 6°35'·0W) 4F.R(vert) 237-357m
Tiumpan Head Fl(2)15s55m25M

Shelter

Loch Odhairn, Camas Orasaidh or Tob Cromore (Loch Erisort), Stornoway.

Loch Odhairn, 58°03'N 6°24'W. There are no dangers within the loch and even in easterly winds the sea rarely disturbs the inner part of the loch. Anchor east of a promontory on the south side opposite the jetty which is on the north side, a mile and a half from the entrance, to gain some shelter from westerly winds.

Supplies

Shop near jetty. Post office and telephone at Gravir, 1 mile.

Loch Mariveg (Mharabhig)

58°05'·4N 6°23'·5W

The sound behind Torray (Eilean Thoraidh) and other islands off the south side of the entrance to Loch Erisort leads to several sheltered bays and inlets around Loch Mariveg.

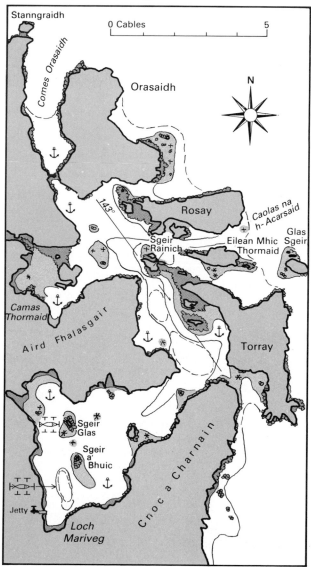

Approaches to Loch Mariveg

Charts

2529 (1:25,000), *1154* (1:14,300, depths in fathoms). OS map *14*.

Tides

Constant −0010 Ullapool (−0430 Dover)

Height in metres

MHWS	MHWN	MTL	MLWN	MLWS
4·8	3·7	2·9	2·0	0·7

Directions

The passage southwest of Torray is no more than ½ cable wide and less than 2 metres deep, and is further constricted by a rock well off the shore of Torray which covers at half tide but shows white below the water. A drying reef extends ¼ cable north of Cnoc a Charnain, the west point of the entrance.

Caolas na h-Acarsaid, the passage between Rosay (Eilean Rosaidh) and Eilean Mhic Thormaid, the island north of Torray, is identified by Dubh Sgeir, an 8-metre islet ¼ mile east of the larger islands. An uncharted rock at a depth of 1·2 metres lies ¼ cable southeast of Rosay, and a submerged reef extends ½ cable north of Sgeir Rainich at the inner end of the passage. On entering from seaward keep in the southern third of the channel between Eilean Mhic Thormaid and Rosay until north of the former island, then mid-channel, and towards the west end of the passage keep north of mid-channel until the north pool opens up.

Anchorages

Loch Mariveg is obstructed by several rocks above water and drying, and fish cages are moored along much of the west side of the loch. A submerged reef has been found between Sgeir a' Bhuic and Sgeir Ghlas. The best anchorages are southeast of Sgeir a' Bhuic and in the northwest corner. The jetty in the southwest corner dries; there is a water tap at the head of the jetty and a telephone nearby.

Torray, on its west side, east of lines of buoys of mussel farms there and clear of drying reefs which extend 50 metres southeast of an islet there.

Aird Fhalasgair, in the bay ¼ mile south of the point. A drying rock lies ¼ cable off the south point of the bay.

Camas Thormaid (the Witches' Pool to local yachtsmen), northwest of Aird Fhalasgair. Keep 20 metres from the south shore to avoid a drying rock 60 metres off, and anchor southwest of the 20-metre islet, where the bottom is heavy clay. There are submerged rocks north of the drying rock.

In the basin south or southwest of Orasaidh. A drying rock ¾ cable from the west shore is cleared by keeping the west side of Sgeir Rainich in line the east side of Cnoc a Charnain 143°.

Loch Mariveg approaches from northwest. Rosay is on the left and
Torray right of centre, beyond Aird Fhalasgair.

Camas Orasaidh from south, showing the boat passage at high water.

Loch Erisort

58°07′N 6°24′W

The shores of Loch Erisort and Loch Leurbost are fringed with scattered settlements, and several bays are suitable for anchoring.

Tides

Tidal streams are insignificant.

Constant −0010 Ullapool (−0430 Dover)

Height in metres

MHWS	MHWN	MTL	MLWN	MLWS
4·8	3·7	2·9	2·0	0·7

Dangers and marks

Tavay islands, Tabhaidh Mhor and Tabhaidh Bheag, stand in the middle of the entrance.

Barkin Islands, of which the main island is Tannaraidh, stand in the mouth of Loch Leurbost, northwest of Tavay.

Sgeirean Dubha Tannaraidh, a reef above water and drying, lie over a cable southwest of Tannaraidh, with a channel 10 metres deep between the reef and Tannaraidh.

Tanneray (note different spelling on the chart to distinguish from Tannaraidh, above; to confuse us further it appeared on older charts as Eilean Glas) at the northeast point of Eilean Chaluim Chille, and the north point of Cromore anchorage, is a little over a mile WSW of Tabhaidh Bheag.

The passage northwest of Eilean Chaluim Chille needs particular care: Sgeir nan Lus, a rock 2 metres high 1½ cables NNE of Eilean Chaluim Chille, has a drying reef ½ cable southwest of it. Plaideag, an extensive reef which dries 2·9 metres lies southeast of mid-channel, 3 cables beyond Sgeir nan Lus.

The islets on the northwest side of the passage, Eilean Chalaibrigh on which is an inconspicuous light beacon, and Eilean a' Bhlair, have drying rocks between them although there is a passage 1½ cables wide between the rocks. The passage west of Eilean a' Bhlair is clear, as is the passage north of Eilean Chalaibrigh. A submerged rock lies about ½ cable south of Eilean a' Bhlair. Transits can be picked off the chart or sketch plan to pass these dangers and it is best to plot them before approaching.

Sgeir nan Lus in line with Stac Tabhaidh, south of Tabhaidh Mhor 083° leads north of Plaideag, as well as through the passage between Chalaibrigh and Eilean a' Bhlair.

Sgeir nan Lus in line with a 13-metre Stac at the north point of the entrance to Loch Erisort 060° leads southeast of Plaideag, which is the most straightforward course to take at this point.

Tob Cromore from southwest.

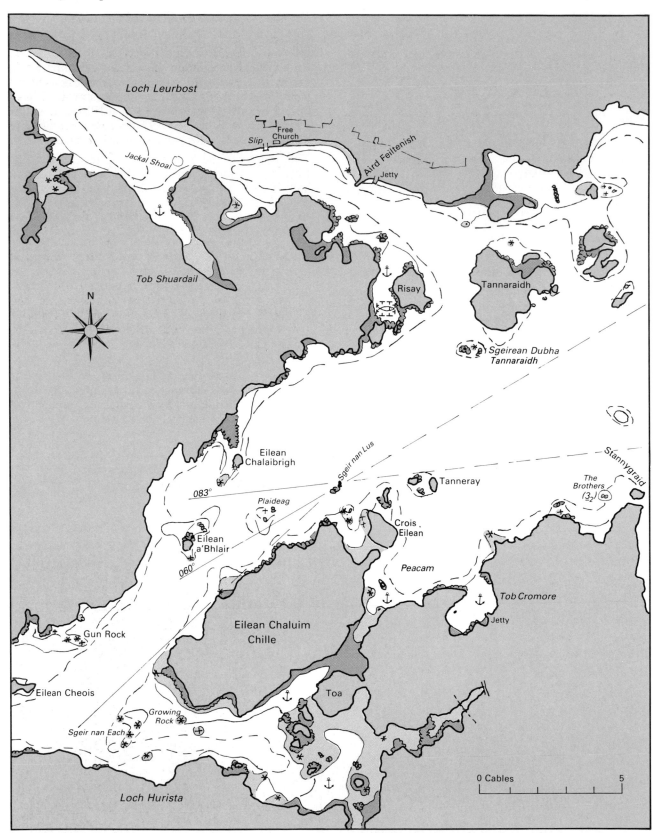

Loch Erisort and Loch Leurbost

Leading line 083° – Loch Erisort

Lights

The following are still listed but may not be lit:
Tabhaidh Bheag Fl.3s13m3M 260°-obscd-295°
Eilean Chalaibrigh Q.G.5m3M

Anchorages

Camas Orasaidh 58°06'·5N 6°23'·8W, is between Eilean Orasaidh and Stanngraidh, the south point of the entrance to Loch Erisort. The depth is 6 metres close to head of the inlet, which connects by a shallow, boulder-strewn channel at high water with the passages leading to Loch Mariveg (see above, page 151).

Peacam (Cromore) 58°06'·5N 6°25'W, on the east side of Eilean Chaluim Chille. On the south side of the approach the Brothers, a rock about a cable west of of Stanngraidh, dries 3·2 metres. Anchor south of Sgeir Peacam.

Tob Cromore, an enclosed basin on the southeast side of Peacam has a depth of 2–3 metres over most of its area, with a few moorings for inshore fishing boats, leaving plenty of space to anchor. A drying rock lies on the northwest side of the basin.

Water tap at the jetty, which dries; the southwest face is the most convenient to go alongside.

Anchorages in the inner part of the loch

Loch Hurista (Thorasdaidh) 58°06'N 6°26'W, south of Eilean Chaluim Chille. Rocks dry ½ cable southwest of Eilean Chaluim Chille, and Sgeir nan Each, a reef about a cable across with several rocks which dry on it, lies a cable from the south shore. A rock which dries 3·2 metres lies about ¾ cable from the south shore a cable ESE of the south end of Sgeir nan Each. Growing Rock ¾ cable southwest of Eilean Chaluim Chille dries 1·7 metres, and a submerged rock lies in mid-channel ¾ cable ESE of Growing Rock.

The most easterly rock of Sgeir nan Each dries 4·2 metres so that it seldom covers; if it can be identified without doubt, pass at least a cable west of Eilean Chaluim Chille then steer to pass ½ cable east of the rock which dries 4·2 metre until near the south shore and then turn to head for the anchorage chosen. Otherwise keep Sgeir nan Lus in sight astern until close to the south shore and turn to follow the south shore eastwards keeping ¼ cable off the shore until past Rubh' an Tanga, its most northerly point.

Leading line 060° – Loch Erisort

Peacam (Cromore Bay) from south.

Anchor in the passage southeast of Eilean Chaluim Chille or pass south and east of the islets in the middle of Loch Hurista and anchor south of Toa, a peninsula in the northeast corner of the loch. Drying rocks lie up to ¾ cable off the southwest side of the loch.

Keose, 58°06′N 6°29′W, on the north shore 1 mile west of Eilean Chaluim Chille. The channel north of Eilean Cheois is navigable, although there are several fish cages. Gun Rock and a reef, part of which uncovers, extends a cable ESE from the north shore NNE of Eilean Cheois. Anchor southwest of the jetty in the northwest corner of the bay.

Loch Erisort is navigable for a further 3 miles and several bays on either shore are suitable for anchoring. A rock ½ cable off the north shore ¾ mile west of Keose dries 0·2 metre. Two miles west of Keose two rocks above water stand on a drying reef which extends up to 1½ cables from the south shore. Bogh' a' Chaolais which dries 1·7 metres lies a cable north of these rocks.

Loch Leurbost

58°08′N 6°25′W

Danger

Sgeirean Dubha Tannaraidh is a drying reef with a rock 2 metres high about a cable southwest of Tannaraidh. A rock 1 cable from the north shore 1 cable NNW of Tannaraidh covers at HWS.

Directions

Loch Leurbost may be entered either by the north or southwest side of Tannaraidh. The loch narrows to less than 1 cable 1 mile from Tannaraidh; Jackal Shoal, ¾ cable northwest of the south point of the narrows has a depth of 1·8 metres over it.

Anchorages

Risay, the basin west of Risay, on the south side of the entrance to Loch Leurbost, has depths of 2–3 metres, soft mud, and can only be entered from the north.

Tob Shuardail on the south side of the loch, immediately west of the narrows. Jackal Shoal, on the south side of the narrows lies at a depth of 1·8 metres.

Head of the loch south of Orasaigh; the head of the loch is shoal for about 3 cables.

Off the jetty at Aird Feiltanish, or off the slip beside the Free Church at Crossbost.

Loch Grimshader

58°09′N 6°23′W

Sgeir a' Chaolais which dries 3·7 metres lies south of mid-channel about ¾ mile inside the loch opposite a bay on the north side. The south point of the entrance kept in sight open of the south shore 102°

clears this rock. In the southwest branches of the loch the bottom is soft mud; Loch Beag, the northwest arm, is crossed by a power cable with a safe clearance of 14 metres.

Stornoway Harbour

58°12′N 6°22′W

A sheltered natural harbour with heavy fishing-boat and ferry traffic and little shelter for a yacht free from disturbance. Most services and supplies are available, but yachts have to take their chance with the fishing boats. Under the bye-laws all anchors must be buoyed and the harbourmaster has authority to have a boat moved.

Chart

2529 (1:25,000 and 1:10,000).

Tides

Tidal streams are negligible but seiches, which are rapid rises or falls of 0·5 metre in 10 minutes, occur usually during unsettled weather.

Constant −0010 Ullapool (−0430 Dover)

Height in metres

MHWS	MHWN	MTL	MLWN	MLWS
4·8	3·7	2·9	2·0	0·7

Dangers and marks

The sheds at Arnish Point are conspicuous.

The Beasts of Holm are rocks a cable SSE of Holm Point at the east side of the entrance which dry up to 2·3 metres and are marked by a green beacon 5 metres high.

Drying reefs extend up to a cable northeast of Arnish Point, marked by a red can light buoy, and up to a cable north of the northwest part of the point, marked by a metal framework beacon 5 metres high near its outer end, although this may have collapsed.

Drying reefs extend up to a cable from the east shore; Sgeir Mhor Inaclete extends two cables from the north shore opposite Arnish Point, marked by a beacon 5 metres high near the outer end. There is some doubt about the colour of this beacon.

Beyond this there are no dangers in the fairway.

Lights

Arnish Point Fl.WR.10s17m19/15M
Sandwick Oc.WRG.6s10m9M
Stoney Field Fl.WRG.3s8m11M
Eilean na Gobhail Fl.G.6s8m
Slip jetty, NW end of Eilean na Gobhail 2F.G(vert)
No. 1 Pier Q.WRG.5m11M
Ferry terminal leading lights F.G

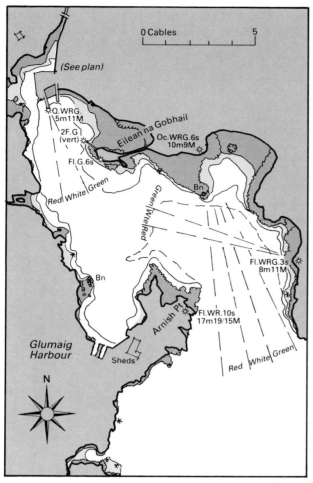

Stornoway

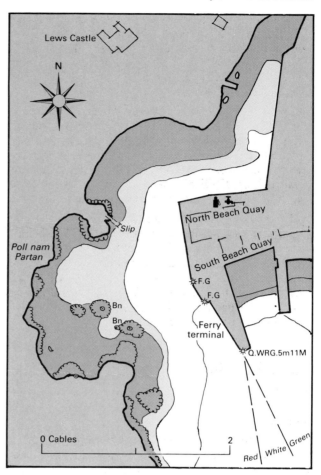

Stornoway Harbour

At night approach in the white sector of Arnish Point light and in turn the white sector of Sandwick light beacon, the white sector of Stoney Field light beacon astern, and the white sector of the light at No. 1 Pier.

Anchorages

Anchorages are all subject to disturbance from passing traffic. Yachts may go alongside quays for water or fuel but it isn't advisable to stay if it can be avoided, especially on Friday and Sunday nights.

Poll nam Portan has drying rocks well off the south-west side marked by lattice beacons with spherical topmarks. Most of the space is taken up with private and lifeboat moorings. If anchoring, avoid swinging into the fairway.

Glumaig Harbour, west of Arnish Point, is sheltered but the industrial surroundings and the distance from the town detract from it. A drying reef on the west side of the entrance is marked by a green beacon with a cage topmark, and other drying rocks lie ¾ cable south of the beacon. The bottom is foul with scrap steel and discarded equipment and the anchor should be buoyed.

Services and supplies

Shops, post office, telephone, hotels, bank. Showers at Fishermen's Mission on quay, or Nicholson Sports Centre (also swimming baths). Petrol at garage, water and diesel at North Beach Quay. *Calor Gas* and fishermen's chandlery at North Beach Quay. Car hire. Doctor.

Harbourmaster

VHF Ch 12 (24 hour watch), ☎ (0851) 3012.

Coastguard

Coastguard station is above a bank on South Beach Quay, ☎ (0851) 2013.

Customs

Customs clearance is available (in case you arrive from Faeroe or North America) ☎ (0851) 3626/3576.

The coast north of Tiumpan Head is described in Chapter VIII as it is only likely to be of interest to a yacht on passage round the Butt of Lewis.

Stornoway Harbour from southwest. Poll nam Partan on the left.

Shillay, Monach Isles, from WSW.

VIII. West side of the Outer Hebrides

The Atlantic coast of the Outer Hebrides has little shelter and in heavy westerly weather it would be dangerous to run for any of the passages between the islands, especially with a west-going tide when there would be heavy overfalls at the entrance to each sound. In clear visibility some of the lochs on the west side of Lewis provide accessible shelter. Strong tides and heavy seas occur off both Barra Head and Butt of Lewis.

For through passages between islands south of Barra see Chapter I.

The west side of Barra and the Uists

Charts

2769 and *2770* (1:30,000) cover the west coast of Barra with the passages through the sounds. Chart *2722* (1:200,000) gives small-scale coverage from Skerryvore to St Kilda, but Imray chart *C66*, perhaps used in conjunction with OS map *31*, is sufficient for a passage along this coast, although there are many hazards.

The distance from Flodday, at the northwest end of Sound of Pabbay to Monach Isles is 37 miles.

Sound of Vatersay

It is not yet known whether the inlet at the west end of the sound which is in the process of being blocked by a causeway will provide any shelter. There are several dangerous rocks up to ½ mile west of the entrance and the leading line is not easily distinguished. The traditional line is two houses on Vatersay in line 135°; the front house is stone-coloured, the rear one has a red roof and a road runs close northeast of them. Once within the entrance steer for the 50-metre hill east of the rear house to avoid Bo Leahan on the southwest side of the line. A slip is to be built into the west side of the new causeway.

There are no hazards on a direct line from Vatersay Sound to Greian Head at the northwest of Barra.

For the passage through the Sound of Barra see Chapter I.

Dangers and marks

Off the west side of South Uist drying rocks extend up to a mile from the shore and at the north end of South Uist Ardivachar Rocks which dry 3·2 metres are 1½ miles from the shore. The 20-metre contour avoids these dangers by a reasonable margin. Rubha Ardvule, 7 metres high, which lies 8 miles north of the Sound of Barra is prominent.

An inshore danger area extends 5 miles seaward from 2 miles south of Rubha Ardvule to Ardivachar Point and is in frequent use for short range rocket firing throughout the year Monday to Saturday, 1000–1700. Red lights, visible by day, are shown at Rubha Ardvule, Falconet Tower 7½ miles north, and at Ardivachar Point, from 1 hour before firing begins, changing to Iso.R.2s, 15 minutes before firing. Two safety boats patrol the range while firing is in progress. Radio information about range activity is broadcast on VHF Ch 8 daily at 1000. Information may also be had by phoning Benbecula ☎ (0870) 2384 and asking for the Range Safety Officer (extension 441), or the duty officer (extension 255) at weekends or in the evening.

An extended range is used for long range firing a few times each year and information can be found as above.

Bo Ruag which dries 1·2 metres, lies 3 miles west of the northwest end of Benbecula, close to the 20-metre line, and its position is usually revealed by breakers. There is no clearing mark for this rock on a passage along the coast and the best course when heading north is to steer for the disused lighthouse at Shillay at the west end of the Monach Isles, or to keep closer inshore.

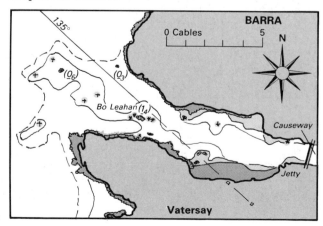

Sound of Vatersay

159

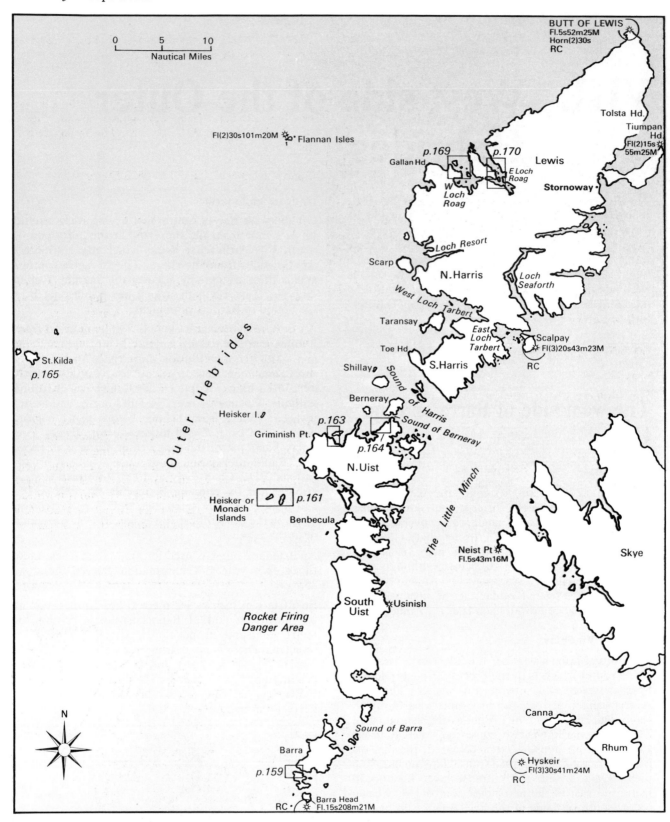

BUTT OF LEWIS
Fl.5s52m25M
Horn(2)30s
RC

Tolsta Hd.

Tiumpan
Hd.
Fl(2)15s
55m25M

Lewis

Fl(2)30s101m20M ☆ Flannan Isles

p.169 *p.170*

Gallan Hd.
W
Loch
Roag

E Loch
Roag

Stornoway

Loch Resort

Scarp

N.Harris

Loch
Seaforth

West Loch Tarbert

Taransay

East
Loch
Tarbert

Scalpay
☆ Fl(3)20s43m23M

Toe Hd.

RC

Shillay

S.Harris

O u t e r   H e b r i d e s

Berneray

St.Kilda
p.165

Heisker I.

p.163

Griminish Pt.

Sound of Harris

Sound of Berneray

p.164

N.Uist

Skye

Heisker or
Monach
Islands

p.161

Benbecula

Neist Pt ☆
Fl.5s43m16M

The Little Minch

South
Uist

☆ Usinish

Rocket Firing
Danger Area

Canna

N

Sound of Barra

Rhum

Barra

p.159

☆ Hyskeir
Fl(3)30s41m24M

RC

Barra Head
RC ☆ Fl.15s208m21M

St Kilda Peak 352° distant about 3 miles

The west end of what used to be Vatersay Sound; there should be less tidal effect now, but there are still plenty of rocks.

Monach Isles

57°31′N 7°38′W

The Monach Isles consist of Ceann Ear, Shivinish and Ceann Iar which are joined at low water; Shillay to the west on which is a disused lighthouse 40 metres high with a reasonably sheltered pool between that island and the main group, and Stockay which stands on a drying reef northeast of Ceann Ear. Rocks above water, drying and submerged are scattered over an area between 2½ miles northwest of Shillay and the coast of North Uist northeast of Stockay, to Causamul, which is 8 metres high, 1½ miles west of Aird an Runair, the west point of North Uist.

Charts

2722 (1:200,000). Imray chart *C66* (best). OS maps *22, 18*. Obsolete chart *2805* (1:24,300).

Tides

The north-going stream begins −0420 Ullapool (+0345 Dover). The south-going stream begins +0205 Ullapool (−0215 Dover). The spring rate in each direction is 2 knots.

Constant −0103 Ullapool (−0523 Dover)

Height in metres

MHWS	MHWN	MTL	MLWN	MLWS
4·2	3·0	2·4	1·3	0·4

Dangers and marks

They are too numerous to mention individually and navigation around the Monach Isles depends on good visibility as some of the clearing marks are at a distance of more than 10 miles. It may be helpful to plot the leading lines on the chart before approaching. The whole area around the Monach Isles and the west end of the Sound of Harris is strewn with fishing tackle with buoys and floating lines, up to 10 miles from the land.

Sound of Monach lies between Stockay and North Uist, but its navigable width is reduced by East Rock, 6 cables east of Stockay, drying rocks up to 2 miles southwest of North Uist and a submerged rock (which is not shown on Imray chart *C66*) at a depth of 1·8 metres further southwest, 1½ miles northeast of Stockay. A leading line for Sound of Monach is the west side of Causamul under the west part of Haskeir 333°.

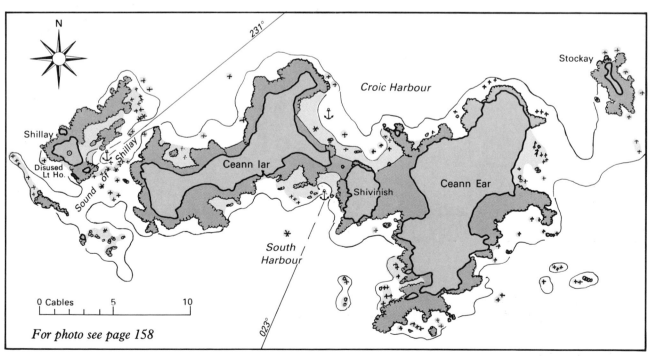

For photo see page 158

Monach Isles

Charlotte Rocks parts of which dry south of Causamul are close west of this line and the usual passage north is Sound of Causamul for which the leading line is Griminish Point just open of Aird an Runair 029°, see View A below.

Deasker, 3 metres high, about 2 miles north of Ceann Ear, is prominent.

In the passage west of Shillay drying reefs extend ½ mile south and ¼ mile west of Shillay, and the southeast end of Huskeran an extensive drying reef lies 9 cables northwest of Shillay. Ray Sgeir, 6 metres high which lies ½ mile south of Shillay, is a useful reference mark.

John's North Channel to the northwest of Monach Isles is the other main channel among all these hazards, and would be taken by a boat on a passage between Monach Isles and St Kilda. The leading line for John's North Channel is the north point of Stockay in line with Rueval, the highest hill on Benbecula 116°, see View B below. West Dureberg, a reef parts of which dry, lies between ½–1 mile north of Huskeran, an extensive reef 1½ miles northwest of Shillay. Clearing marks for West Dureberg are the northeast point of Ceann Ear in line with Rueval 114°, and Ray Sgeir in line with the west side of Shillay 157°, although this leads very close to West Dureberg.

The dangers described by no means exhaust the inventory, and such charts as there are should be carefully studied.

Anchorages

Anchorages at Monach Isles are used by lobster fishermen, some of whom have laid moorings there, and creels are left with buoys attached. The islands may be approached by any of the channels described above; from Sound of Causamul pass east of Deasker, 3 metres high, which is nearly 2 miles north of Ceann Ear.

Sound of Shillay, the best anchorage at the Monach Isles, lies between Shillay and Ceann Iar. It is entered from northeast between Edward Rock which dries 3·4 metres at the end of a reef ¼ mile north of the west point of Ceann Iar, and Stallion Rock which dries 2·1 metres 4 cables northeast of Shillay; other rocks lie up to 3 cables NNW of Stallion Rock. Stone beacons 4 metres high on Eilean Siorruidh (Eternal Isles), which are 1½ cables ESE of the disused lighthouse, in line 231° lead in to Sound of Shillay. In westerly winds anchor in Poll Bane east of the jetty but the bottom shoals abruptly from 7 metres to less than 2 metres about a cable off the jetty.

Croic Harbour (Cnoc Harbour in Admiralty *Pilot*), the bay on the north side of the main islands, provides shelter from east to northwest with a bottom of sand, but with clay in places, and isolated rocks in depths of less than 2 metres.

South Harbour lies between the south side of Ceann Iar and the west side of Shivinish. Several drying rocks lie up to ½ mile from the shores of each island; approach with middle of the isthmus between Ceann Iar and Shivinish bearing 023°.

Passage notes – Causamul to Pabbay

Charts

2841 (1:50,000) and *2642* (1:30,000) cover Sound of Pabbay etc.

Dangers and marks

Pabbay lies at the west end of Sound of Harris, 14 miles northeast of Causamul. Boreray is 3 miles southwest of Pabbay and Spuir, 12 metres high, lies a mile north of Boreray. The clearest course between Griminish Point and the Sound of Harris is outside Pabbay and through the Sound of Shillay.

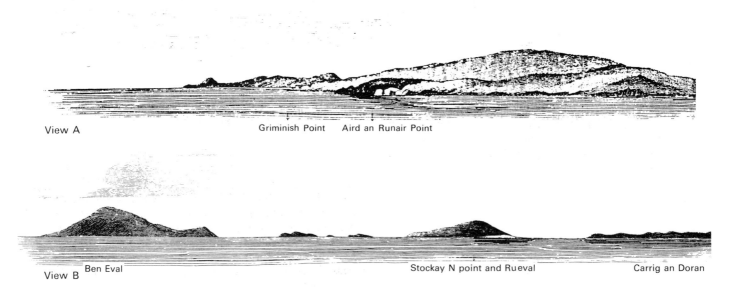

View A   Griminish Point   Aird an Runair Point

View B   Ben Eval   Stockay N point and Rueval   Carrig an Doran

Bo Lea which is awash, lies 1½ miles offshore 3 miles northeast of Griminish Point. Causamul in line with Griminish Point 221° and Spuir in line with the southeast side of Pabbay 058° lead northwest of Bo Lea.

To pass south of Pabbay, use these transits to clear Bo Lea then pass north of Spuir, and head for the north side of Berneray. Bo Leac Caolas, which seems to extend further than the chart shows and dries about 0·5 metre, lies in the middle of the Sound of Pabbay. When within ½–1 mile of Berneray steer for the north tip of Ensay bearing about 060° to avoid a shoal spit which extends ½ mile north of Berneray.

Griminish Harbour

57°39′N 7°26′W

In Valley Sound, Griminish Harbour, a shallow inlet west of Valley, a tidal island, is used as a base for lobster fishing boats during the summer, but the sound is obstructed by drying rocks and it is not recommended for yachts. A light column stands on the northwest side of Sgeir Dubh Mor on the northwest side of the entrance, but it is low-lying and may be difficult to pick out among breakers at high tide. If it is necessary to attempt it approach at about half tide as follows.

The plan and the directions are based on information provided by the harbourmaster for the Western Isles Council, but I know of no yacht which has visited Griminish. If it is necessary to attempt it approach at about half tide as follows. Pass close northeast of Sgeir Dubh Mor heading for Eilean nan Lus, until a cottage south of Callernish House, which is a circular building about 60 metres in diameter, is open east of Callernish House. There are shoal and drying patches in the channel but a place to anchor out of the tide may be found south of Valley. Diesel may be available from fishermen.

Lights

Sgeir Dubh Mor Q(2)G.10s4m4M
Jetty on southwest shore 2F.G(vert) April–October

Caolas a' Mhorain (Ardavuran Channel)

This channel is the approach to Sound of Berneray between Boreray and Ardavuran (Aird a' Mhorain), a mile to the southwest. Gairgrada, a mile west of Ardavuran dries 1·8 metres. To clear Gairgrada and reefs off Ardavuran steer with Boreray touching Leac Bhan on North Uist 095°, then the summit of Lingay under Beinn Mhor 123°. The area south and east of Boreray is shoal but does provide some shelter from the swell.

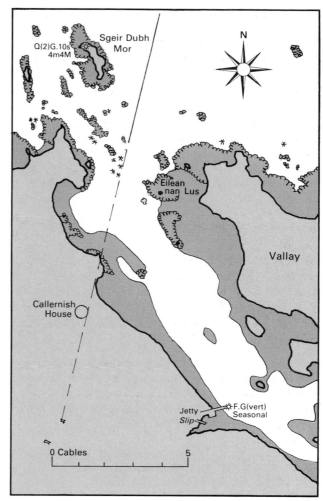

Griminish

Sound of Berneray

57°42′N 7°11′W

The approach from the west – the open Atlantic – is over sand with a depth of less than 2 metres so that conditions are rare when it is quiet enough to be used by a yacht. However the only Admiralty chart is at a scale of 1:200,000 (Imray's C66 is at 1:150,000) and the passage may be of occasional use.

Tides

The east-going stream begins +0550 Ullapool (+0130 Dover). The west-going stream begins −0020 Ullapool (−0440 Dover).

Directions

From east to west, from *No. 3* buoy pass a cable north of Eilean Fuam and then midway between Leac Bhan on North Uist and Berneray to avoid drying and submerged rocks. When the shore on the west side of Leac Bhan opens up steer SSW to follow a cable off the shore; if Newton farm can be identified keep it under the left slope of Crogary Mor 202°; pass ½ cable north of Suisnish and steer for the north point of Lingay.

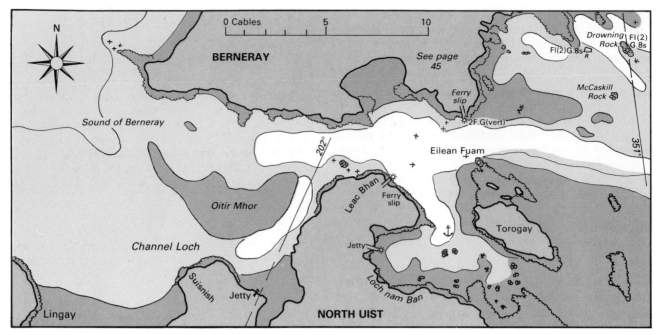

Sound of Berneray

To approach Bay's Loch from Sound of Berneray bring Drowning Rock beacon under Moor hill at the north end of Berneray 351° and keep on that bearing until 1 cable from Drowning Rock, then turn to port to pass northeast of the breakwater.

Lights

Eilean Fuam light beacon Q.6m2M
Berneray ferry slip 2F.G(vert)6m3M
Leac Bhan ferry slip 2F.R(vert)6m3M
Loch nam Ban ferry jetty 2F.G(vert)9m8M
No. 3 light buoy Fl.G.5s

Anchorage

In the mouth of Loch nam Ban, southeast of Leac Bhan or, at neaps, further in. A reef dries for a cable off the west point of the entrance and the shore of Torogay, on the east side of the loch, also dries 1 cable, and drying rocks lies in the middle of the loch.

St Kilda

57°48′N 7°35′W

The St Kilda group of islands lies 42 miles west of Pabbay at the west end of Sound of Harris. The main island was inhabited until 1930 and is now owned by the National Trust for Scotland, part of it being leased to the army for tracking missiles from the rocket range on North Uist, and the remainder leased to the Nature Conservancy Council. Apart from the area used by the army, the island is managed by a warden on behalf of NTS and NCC, who lives at the 'Factor's House', a white house just above the army buildings. The warden's permission must be obtained to go beyond the village.

Permission must also be obtained from the army commanding officer to use any of the army facilities, which are not public and only open to visitors at the CO's discretion.

Visibility and weather suitable for visiting St Kilda do not occur frequently and a yacht must be prepared to clear out at short notice. *Kilda Radar* keeps watch on VHF Ch 16. For passages through Sound of Harris see Chapter II.

Charts

2721 (1:200,000) or *2720* if coming from south; plan on *2524* (1:25,000). OS map *18*.

Tides

Around St Kilda the northeast-going stream begins +0545 Ullapool (+0125 Dover). The southwest-going stream begins −0030 Ullapool (−0450 Dover). Close to the islands streams run at up to 3 knots, and heavy tide rips extend right across the channel between Dun and Levenish when wind and tide are opposed.

Constant −0055 Ullapool (−0515 Dover)

Height in metres

MHWS	MHWN	MTL	MLWN	MLWS
3·3	2·5	1·8	1·2	0·4

Dangers and marks

Levenish, over a mile east of Dun at the southeast point of Hirta, is 55 metres in height. Rocks which dry 1·5 metres extend a short distance from Levenish, but there are no other hidden dangers.

Directions

Departure for St Kilda might be taken from Berneray (49 miles), Monach Isles (34 miles) or Vaccasay (53 miles), and in clear settled weather an overnight passage could be made, but there are no lights to assist such a passage except the leading lights at St Kilda which have a range of 3 miles.

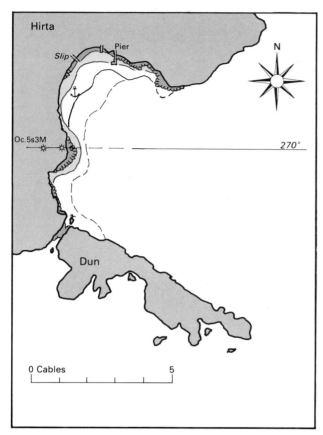

Village Bay, St Kilda

Lights

Leading lights 270° Oc.5s26/38m3M

Anchorage

Anchor in Village Bay at the southeast side of Hirta, the main island of the group, southwest of the pier or northeast of the front leading light. Keep clear of the approach to the slip on the northwest side of the bay, which is used by supply vessels, sometimes at night. There is almost always some swell and landing, at the west side of the pier, is tricky. In southerly and easterly winds which are any more than light the anchorage becomes untenable.

As a last resort in heavy weather from south or east shelter might be found in Loch a' Ghlinne (Glen Bay) on the north side of Hirta but depths are too great for anchoring except very close to the shore, and winds are accelerated by the cliffs.

Supplies

Small shop and pub at MOD camp; water, showers at MOD commander's discretion.

The west side of Harris and Lewis

The first 8 miles north of the entrance to Sound of Harris are fairly free from concealed hazards. Further north there are several areas of submerged and drying rocks with few marks by which to avoid them and a visit to the west coast of Harris and Lewis should only be undertaken in clear settled weather. There are no lights on this coast except at East Loch Roag, and at Flannan Islands which are 17 miles from the shore.

Chart

2841 (1:50,000) is essential for navigating in this area, although you could manage as far as Taransay with Imray chart *C66*. OS maps *13, 18*.

Tides

The north-going stream, with the east-going stream towards the Sound of Harris begins +0550 Ullapool (+0130 Dover). The south-going stream, with the west-going stream from the Sound of Harris begins −0020 Ullapool (−0440 Dover).

Passage notes – Toe Head to Gallan Head

Dangers and marks

Scarp island lies 11 miles north of Toe Head. Taransay Glorigs, an extensive area of rocks above water, drying and submerged, lie 3 miles off the mouth of West Loch Tarbert, and Old Rocks lie between Taransay Glorigs and Scarp. For clearing marks see West Loch Tarbert, below.

Gasker, 30 metres high, lies 4 miles WSW of Scarp. Obe Rocks, drying and submerged, extend up to 6 cables west of Scarp. Drying, submerged and above-water rocks lie up to 1¾ miles north and northwest of Scarp. Old Rocks and Obe Rocks almost always break in the swell.

Bomore Rock, 5½ cables offshore, 1¾ miles north of Mealasta, nearly dries.

Ard More Mangersta has radio masts and Gallan Head, 4 miles NNE, has a radio mast 177 metres in height. Sgeir Gallan, 3 cables NNW of Gallan Head, dries 3·4 metres.

Directions

From Toe Head steer toward Gasker, and pass midway between Gasker Beg and Scarp. 3 miles past Scarp a course can be steered towards Ard More Mangersta.

From north head for Gasker; a direct course from Ard More Mangersta to Gasker passes ¾ mile west of Bomore Rock (5 miles north of Scarp) and a mile

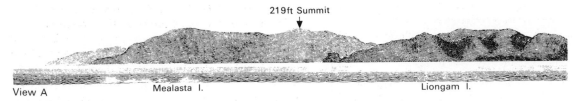

219ft summit of Mealasta I. open west of Liongam Island clears Bo Thorcuil to the westward.

Creagan Gorra Cleite open south of north side of Loch Tealasavay clears Bo Thorcuil to the southward.

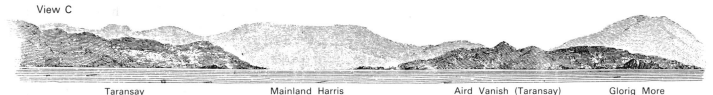

To clear Bo More bring one third of Aird Vanish (Taransay) open to the westward of Glorig More.

west of rocks northwest of Scarp, so that position checks have to be carefully kept. When Scarp is abeam a course can be steered direct for the passage between Coppay and Toe Head, but the position relative to Old Rocks and Taransay Glorigs still needs to be watched. From Toe Head to Caolas an Scarp pass east of Taransay Glorigs.

Radio

VHF cover does not reach the coast from Toe Head to beyond Scarp, extending about 2 miles west of Scarp.

Taransay

57°54′N 6°59′W

Tides

Constant −0053 Ullapool (−0513 Dover)

Height in metres

MHWS	MHWN	MTL	MLWN	MLWS
4·2	3·2	2·3	1·3	0·4

Dangers and marks

Drying rocks lie up to 7 cables south of Taransay; if passing through Sound of Taransay keep the summit of Coppay in line with Toe Head 244° to pass southeast of Bo Usbig (it is quite easy to confuse Shillay with Coppay). When Aird Nisabost is abeam on the starboard side take a mid-channel course through the sound. In Sound of Taransay Corran Raah and Luskentyre Banks reduce the navigable passage to ½

mile wide. Bo Raah lies 2 cables off Taransay, 4 cables south of Corran Raah, at a depth of 1 metre.

Anchorages

Northside Sands, 57°50′N 7°04′W, is an occasional anchorage at the west side of Borve Bay (Camus nam Borgh) 2 miles east of Toe Head. Drying reefs extend 1½ cables off the west point of the bay. Good holding and shelter in strong southerly winds can be found 1½ cables SSE of Sgeir Leomadal 7 cables west of Northside Sands.

Loch na h-Uidhe, Taransay, 57°53′·5N 7°03′W, on the south side of sandy isthmus joining the two parts of the island. Approaching from Toe Head steer for the south side of Aird Vanish, the west part of the island, to avoid Old Rocks (not to be confused with rocks of the same name south of Scarp) which dry 0·5 metre, 7 cables offshore. Steer towards Ben Raah, the highest point of Taransay until past the middle of the entrance, to clear a rock 1 metre high 2 cables from the west side of the inlet; a reef awash extends northeast from this rock which should be given a wide berth. Langaraid which dries 2·9 metres lies nearly 4 cables off the southwest shore of Taransay and, with Bo Usbig, is in the way when passing between Loch na h-Uidhe and Sound of Taransay.

Traigh Nisabost, 57°52′N 6°58′W, is an occasional anchorage off a sandy bay east of Aird Nisabost at the south side of Traigh Luskentyre on Harris; like any other sandy beach on the west side of the Outer Hebrides it should be treated with great caution because of the swell and even if you can get ashore you may have difficulty getting off again.

Sound of Taransay, 57°54′N 6°59′W. For passage notes see above. Anchor close inshore at the north side of Corran Raah, or in northwest wind, south of the spit, but look out for Bo Raah.

West Loch Tarbert

57°56′N 7°00′W

Tides

The in-going stream begins +0550 Ullapool (+0130 Dover). The out-going stream begins −0020 Ullapool (−0440 Dover).

Constant −0053 Ullapool (−0513 Dover)

Height in metres

MHWS	MHWN	MTL	MLWN	MLWS
4·2	3·2	2·3	1·3	0·4

Dangers and marks

In the main channel north of Taransay, the Taransay Glorigs, a patch of rocks above and below water lie up to 3 miles from the northeast side of the entrance. Gloruig More (Gloruig Sgoillte), the highest of these is 12 metres high, and the most southerly rock is 1·5 metres high. A submerged rock, Bo Molach, lies 6 cables WSW of Gloruig More.

Old Rocks, which dry up to 2·3 metres, lie up to 3 miles NNW of the Taransay Glorigs. A clearing mark for the most westerly of these, Bo More which dries 0·8 metre, is as follows. Aird Vanish, the west part of Taransay, appears from a distance of several miles to be a separate island, and keeping one third of the width of Aird Vanish open west of Gloruig More 330° leads clear west of Bo More, see View C opposite. Gasker, 30 metres high, lies 6 miles WNW of Gloruig More with Gasker Beg a mile ESE of it. Drying rocks lie up to 2 cables north of Taransay.

Soay Mor and Soay Beag, both 35 metres high, lie ½ mile from the northeast side of Loch Tarbert with Duisker, 2 metres high 9 cables ESE of Soay Mor. Many drying rocks lie between Duisker and Soay Mor and the shore.

Isay, 17 metres high, lies in the middle of the loch 1½ miles ESE of Duisker with a reef also named Duisker ½ mile NNE of it.

In clear visibility the approach to West Loch Tarbert presents no problem.

Anchorages

Loch Leosavay, 57°57′N 7°00′W, is 1 mile northwest of Soay Beag. Glas Sgeir, 8 metres high, stands on a drying reef a cable wide near the northeast side of the entrance of the loch. A drying rock lies off the northeast shore south of the jetty and the north and northwest arms are partly drying. Keep towards the west side of the loch and anchor off the jetty.

Loch Meavaig, 57°56′N 6°55′W, NNE of the outer Duisker is entered by the southeast side of that rock and east of Bo Harainish which dries 1·1 metres, west of a direct line from Duisker to the entrance. The head of the loch dries off 4 cables and it is prone to swell.

Loch Bun Abhainn-eader (Bunaveneadar), 57°56′N 6°52′W, 1 mile northeast of Isay, is identified by a conspicuous chimney. It may be entered either side of the east Duisker, but if passing north of it keep closer to the north shore of the loch as a reef with a depth of 0·1 metre extends up to 2 cables north of Duisker. Anchor to suit wind direction, clear of fish cages.

Head of West Loch Tarbert Anchor west of the jetty on the south side; this anchorage is subject to squalls in southerly winds.

Supplies

At Tarbert, ½ mile, see Chapter VII, page 143.

Scarp

58°01′N 7°08′W

Dangers and marks

Taransay Glorigs and Old Rocks, south of Scarp, together with a clearing mark for their west side, has been described at West Loch Tarbert, above.

Hushinish Glorigs, above water and drying, lie 6 cables south of Hushinish Point, on Harris south of Scarp. Hushinish Point in line with the right fall of the summit of Scarp 350° leads east of Old Rocks and Taransay Glorigs, but close west of Hushinish Glorigs, but this line is not clearly defined.

Caolas an Scarp separates the island from Harris, with a sandbar ¼ mile north of the narrowest part of the passage, on which the charted depth, near the Scarp side of the channel, is 1 metre but there seems to be less water. A northerly swell would make this passage dangerous. Several drying rocks lie between Fladday, north of Caolas an Scarp, and Harris. Anchor either north or south of the sandbar.

Braigh Mor

58°02′N 7°05′W

Braigh Mor is the sound between Lewis and the northeast side of Scarp, leading to several sheltered lochs.

Tides

Tidal streams are slight.

Constant −0053 Ullapool (−0513 Dover)

Height in metres

MHWS	MHWN	MTL	MLWN	MLWS
4·2	3·2	2·3	1·3	0·4

Dangers and marks

Obe Rocks, submerged and drying, lie up to 6 cables west of Scarp.

A patch of rocks lies up to 1½ miles north and northwest of Scarp with yet another rock named Duisker, 6 metres in height, at the east end.

In the passage between Duisker and Kearstay, an islet north of Scarp, rocks which dry 2·3 metres lie up to 1½ cables from both sides, leaving a clear passage 3 cables wide, but there are no leading marks.

There is a clear passage 1½ miles wide between Duisker and Mealasta, at the north side of the entrance.

Anchorages

An attractive anchorage, sheltered from the open sea, lies between Kearstay and Scarp.

Loch Resort is entered 2 miles east of Scarp. Greine Sgeir, an islet 6 metres high with reefs drying 1 cable off all sides, lies in mid-channel. A drying rock lies 2 cables off the south shore, west of Loch Cravadale where there is an occasional anchorage at the head of the bay. Loch Resort is 4 miles long and generally no more than ¼ mile wide. Anchor near the head of the loch, or at Diriscal, 2½ miles from the entrance on the south side with good holding on black smelly mud.

Loch Tealasavay, a mile north of Loch Resort, has only a small area at the south side of the head with moderate depths in which to anchor, but the sea comes straight in so that it is only an occasional anchorage.

Loch Hamnaway (Tamanavay on the chart) is entered north of Loch Tealasavay. Bo Thorcuil is a patch of submerged rocks 3 cables from the north shore west of the entrance. Creagan Gorra Cleite, at the head of Loch Tealasavay, showing in the middle of the entrance 079° (View B page 166), and the right-hand summit of Mealasta open west of Liongam 322° (View A page 166) lead south and southwest of Bo Thorcuil. In Loch Hamnaway anchor close to the head of the loch, or at the east side of the promontory on the south side.

Mealasta lies ½ mile from Lewis at the north side of the entrance to Braigh Mor. Caolas an Eilean, between Mealasta and Lewis, provides a tenuous anchorage in settled weather. Bo Caolas which dries extends 2 cables from the Lewis shore at the north end of the sound. Islands and rocks lie over a mile offshore for more than a mile north of Mealasta, with a reasonably clear channel inshore.

Bomore Rock 5½ cables offshore, 1¾ miles north of Mealasta, nearly dries.

Camas Uig (58°12′N 7°05′W) provides an occasional anchorage, particularly in a well sheltered pool in 3 metres, behind two small islets in the southeast corner off Carnish. Enter by the southwest side of the more southerly islet.

Flannan Islands

58°17′N 7°35′W

A group of rocky islands 17 miles west of Lewis with a lighthouse, occasionally visited by yachts although there is no anchorage. The bottom is bare rock and the large-scale Admiralty chart shows few soundings. Of the two landing places the concrete steps of the western one have been washed away.

Chart

Plan (1:15,000) on chart *2524*.

Flannan Isles landing place   *Photo:* Wallace Clark

Loch Roag

58°15′N 6°54′W

A remarkable group of lochs which could occupy a fortnight of exploring with a small boat if it were not for the difficulty of getting there.

Charts

3381, 3422 (1:12,500). OS map *13*.

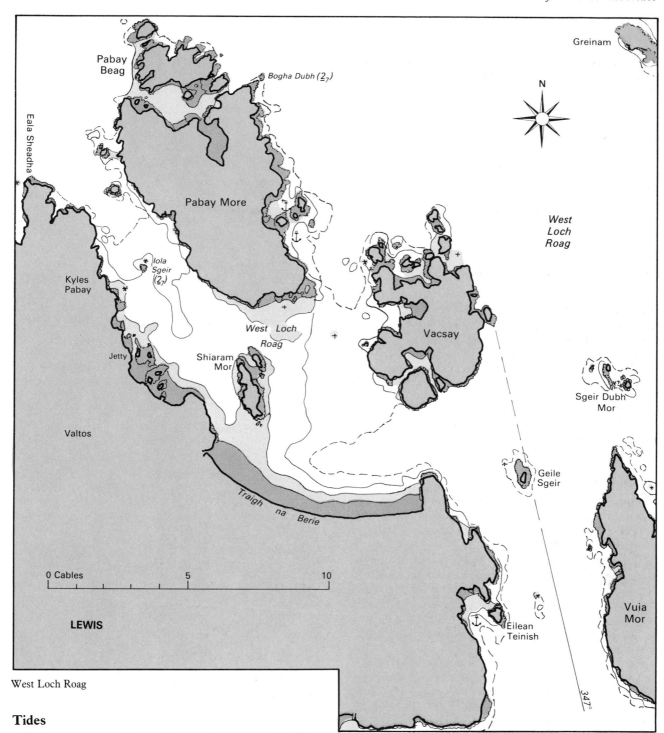

West Loch Roag

Tides

Off the entrance the northeast-going stream begins −0420 Ullapool (+0345 Dover). The southwest-going stream begins +0205 Ullapool (−0215 Dover). The spring rate is ¾ knot.

The in-going stream begins +0600 Ullapool (+0140 Dover). The out-going stream begins −0010 Ullapool (−0430 Dover); streams reach 1 knot in the narrower channels.

Constant −0053 Ullapool (−0513 Dover)

Height in metres

MHWS	MHWN	MTL	MLWN	MLWS
4·2	3·2	2·3	1·3	0·4

Dangers and marks

The entrance is 7 miles wide between Gallan Head, on which stands a conspicuous radio mast 170 metres in height, and Aird Laimishader, on which stands a small light beacon, a white hut 5 metres in height at about 60 metres above sea level. Sgeir Gallan, which dries 3·4 metres, lies ¼ mile NNW of Gallan Head. Between these points are scattered many islets, and the two parts of Loch Roag are separated by Great Bernera.

169

Old Hill, an islet 92 metres high shaped like a loaf of bread, and Mas Sgeir, 21 metres high, each lie 1½ miles northwest and north respectively of Little Bernera.

Lights

The radio mast on Gallan Head has red aero warning lights.
Aird Laimishader LFl.12s61m8M

West Loch Roag

Entered between Pabay Mor on its west side and Harsgeir, 12 metres high, 1¼ miles ENE of Pabay Mor. An anchorage which could be reached without the large-scale chart is on the east side of Pabay Mor, in the inlet northwest of Sgeir na h-Aon Chaorach which has a sandy beach at its head. Bogha Bhealt, which dries 2·4 metres, and is about ½ cable across, lies a cable southeast of Sgeir na h-Aon Chaorach and an alternative anchorage lies southwest of this rock, although it may be troubled by swell when the rock covers.

A submerged rock lies in the middle of the south end of the sound on the east side of Pabay Mor, and a rock which dries 2·7 metres lies in the middle of Kyles Pabay. Many other anchorages may be found with chart *3381*.

East Loch Roag

Entered between Sgeir Dhearg, 2 metres in height 3 cables southeast of Mas Sgeir, and Craigeam off Aird Laimishader. There is also a clear passage 3 cables wide south of Sgeir Dhearg. Loch Carloway, described below, is easy to enter but exposed to west. Several other anchorages can be approached without difficulty.

The fairway of East Loch Roag is clean as far as Greinam, an islet 1 cable across about 5 miles within the loch in the middle of the fairway, with a white light beacon 5 metres high at its south end. Rocks over which the depth is less than 2 metres lie up to 2 cables from either shore, but the clear passage is still 4 cables wide.

Keava lies ¼ mile south of Greinam light beacon and drying rocks lie up to a cable from its northeast shore. In Kyles Keava between Keava and Great Bernera drying rocks lie on both sides of the north entrance. A conspicuous cairn on Eilean Kearstay in line with the west side of Keava 166° leads between these rocks.

Kearstay lies ¼ mile south of Keava, with a passage ½ cable wide on its east side and a passage 1 cable wide on its west side. In the east passage a submerged rock lies a cable north of a promontory on the east side of the channel, and a drying rock lies ¼ cable northwest of the same promontory. The west passage has rocks awash and drying up to ¼ cable from its west side.

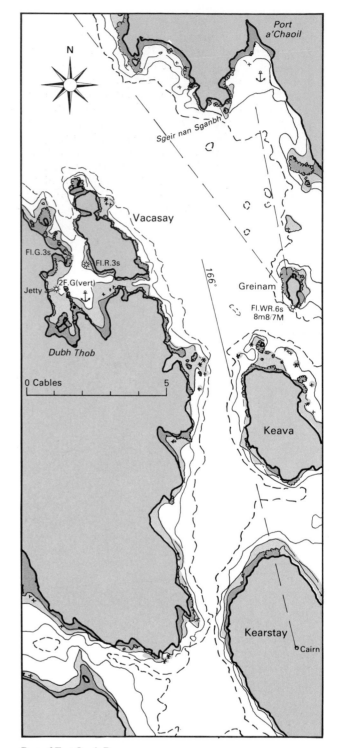

Part of East Loch Roag

Lights

Aird Laimishader LFl.12s61m8M
Greinam Fl.WR.6s8m8/7M
Breasclete Pier (west of Keava) 2F.R(vert)10/7m4M

There are also lights in Loch Carloway and at Dubh Thob.

Anchorages

Loch Carloway, 58°16'·5N 6°49'W, on the east side of the entrance of East Loch Roag is entered ½ mile south of Aird Laimishader light beacon. Tin Rocks, in the middle of the loch, are marked on their north side by a green conical buoy. Dunan Pier stands at the north side of the head of the loch and a shoal patch with a depth of 1 metre lies in the middle of the loch 1½ cables WSW of the pier. The depth alongside the pier is no more than 0·3 metre but the pier is being extended, and work is to be completed in spring 1991. The arm of the loch northeast of the pier is shoal, but provides shelter at neaps or for shallow-draught boats. A slip in the southeast corner of the loch is convenient for landing to visit the broch of Dun Carloway.

A light 2F.R(vert) stands at the head of Dunan Pier.

Shop, post office; water at the pier.

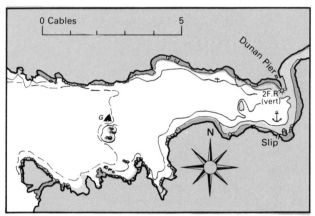

Loch Carloway

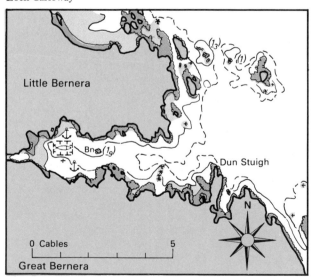

Bernera Harbour

Bernera Harbour, 58°15'·5N 6°52'W, (Kyles of Little Bernera) is on the west side of East Loch Roag about 2 miles south of Mas Sgeir. Cruitir, 3 metres high on an extensive reef, lies nearly 4 cables east of Little Bernera with drying rocks inshore of it.

Rocks which dry 0·7 metre on the south side of the inlet within the entrance extend to mid-channel. Further in, Sgeir a' Chaolais which dries 1·9 metres is marked on its south side by a beacon with a black and white cage topmark, a fish cage is moored west of Sgeir a' Chaolais, and a submerged rock lies ½ cable from the south shore 1 cable west of Sgeir a' Chaolais.

Keep to the north of mid-channel on entering, pass south of Sgeir a' Chaolais and anchor off the ruin on the northwest side of the inlet.

Dubh Thob 58°13'N 6°48'W (Kirkibost), between Great Bernera and Vacasay Island, which lies ½ mile northwest of Greinam is an enclosed basin with a narrow and shallow entrance from the east by the south side of Vacasay, and another with rocks marked by light beacons, from the north. A metal column 2 metres high marks a drying rock on the east side of the passage, and another stands on the shore on the west side, but reefs dry beyond this mark, and the clear channel is about a third of a cable wide. A jetty stands on the west side of the basin and a reef extends from the south shore to within ½ cable east of the jetty.

Fl.R.3s2m2M light on the drying rock west of Vacasay. Fl.G.3s2m2M light on shore on the west side of the channel. Kirkibost jetty 2F.G(vert).

Port a' Chaoil, 58°14'N 6°46'·5W, on the east shore of East Loch Roag, ¾ mile north of Greinam, is sheltered from seaward. Sgeir nan Sgarbh which dries 1·9 metres lies a third of a cable south of the west point of the bay, and a rock which dries 1·3 metres lies about ½ cable off the middle of the head of the bay, with a submerged rock further south. Rocks submerged and drying lie on a line between the east side of the bay and Greinam.

Breasclete, 58°13'N 6°45'W, east of Keava. Anchor south of old jetty which is east of the conspicuous abandoned fish-processing factory and new pier at Rubha Arspaig. Shop 200 metres left at crossroads. Water at the new pier.

Callanish, 58°11'·5N 6°45'W, anchor east of Bratanish islands which are about ¼ mile east of the south end of Kearstay. The passage ¼ mile southeast of the islands is crossed by power cables with headroom of 5·7 metres. A submerged rock lies a third of a cable south of Bratanish Mor, the west island, and another lies a third of a cable off the east shore of the inlet.

Passage notes – Gallan Head to Butt of Lewis and Tiumpan Head

A point about 1½ miles north of Aird Laimishader is named Tiumpan; in case any confusion should arise, Tiumpan Head is at the end of the Eye Peninsula, east of Stornoway on the east side of Lewis.

Tides

At the Butt of Lewis the northeast, east and south-going stream begins −0435 Ullapool (+0335 Dover). The north, west and southwest-going stream begins +0150 Ullapool (−0230 Dover). The spring rate in each direction is 4 to 5 knots close to the point, with eddies on the downstream side of the point. About a mile offshore the streams run at 3 knots; unless the wind is both fair and moderate, and the tide is going in the same direction the point should be given a berth of at least 5 miles, which must be added to the length of the passage.

Tidal streams on the northwest side of Lewis turn 15 minutes later and run at 1½ knots at springs.

Tidal streams on the east side of Lewis turn about an hour earlier and the maximum spring rate is 2 knots.

Dangers and marks

From Gallan Head to the Butt of Lewis is about 30 miles, 17 from the Butt of Lewis to Tiumpan Head, and a further 13 to Stornoway. The Butt of Lewis is completely exposed to weather between southwest and southeast and there is no shelter between Loch Roag and Stornoway except Broad Bay, north of Eye Peninsula, the head of which gives some shelter from southwest, and Port of Ness, but the latter is subject to swell even in calm conditions.

Aird Laimishader lies 7 miles northeast of Gallan Head, with the islets in the mouth of Loch Roag in between. Hen Shoal lies a mile offshore, 7 miles southwest of the Butt of Lewis, at a depth of 9 metres.

On the east side of Lewis, Port of Ness, 2 miles southeast of the lighthouse, provides some shelter from the west in a sandy bay with moderate depths. A drying boat harbour stands on the north side of the bay.

Braga Rock which dries 3·4 metres lies 2 cables offshore 3½ miles southeast of the lighthouse. Tolsta Head open of Cellar Head 180° leads east of the rock.

Tolsta Head is prominent with a vertical cliff 66 metres high at its end.

Tiumpan Head is marked by a white lighthouse tower 21 metres in height.

Lights

Aird Laimishader LFl.12s61m8M
Flannan Islands Fl(2)30s101m20M
Butt of Lewis Fl.5s52m25M
Tiumpan Head Fl(2)15s55m25M

By night these lights are sufficient for a coastal passage in good visibility.

For Stornoway see Chapter VII.

Appendix

I. GLOSSARY OF GAELIC WORDS WHICH COMMONLY APPEAR IN PLACE NAMES

Many varieties of spelling are found, so it is as well to search for possible alternatives; variations of the same word are listed together but usually at least have the same initial letter. Many words beginning with a consonant take an 'h' after the initial letter in certain cases; notably in adjectives the genitive and the feminine gender and genitive cases of nouns, so that most of the words below could have an 'h' as the second letter.

There is no possibility of guiding the reader on pronunciation except to say that consonants followed by an 'h' are not often pronounced, and that 'mh' and 'bh' at the beginning of a word are pronounced as (and of course in anglicised versions often spelt with) a 'v'. *Mhor* is pronounced – approximately – *vore*; *claidheamh* is something like *clayeh*, and *bogha* is *bo'a*.

Some names, particularly those of islands ending in 'a' or 'ay', are of Norse origin. Anyone at all familiar with French and Latin will see correspondences there, for example Caisteil – also Eaglais and Teampuill.

Many words are compounds made up of several often quite common parts, frequently linked by *na/nam/nan*. The following are the most usual forms of words which commonly occur in Gaelic place names. They often set out to describe the physical features and so give some clues to identification. Some of them occur almost everywhere; most lochs have a Sgeir More and an Eilean Dubh, or vice versa.

Gaelic	*English*
a, am, an, an t-	the
abhainn (avon)	river
acairseid	harbour (acair = anchor)
achadh (ach, auch)	field
aiseag, aiseig	ferry
allt	stream, burn
ard, aird	promontory
aros	house
ba	cattle
bairneach	limpet
bagh ('bay')	bay
ban	white, pale; female (ban-righ = queen), as noun: woman
bealach	narrow passage
beg, beag, beaga	small
ben, beinn	mountain
beul (bel)	mouth of (belnahua = mouth of the cave)
bodach	old man
bogha (bo')	a detached rock, usually one which uncovers
breac	speckled (as noun: trout)
buachaille	shepherd
buidhe (bhuidhe, buie)	yellow (also: pleasing)
bun	mouth of a river
cailleach	old woman
caisteil	castle
camas	bay
caol (a' chaolais)	narrow passage (kyle)
caora, caorach	sheep
carnan, charnain	small heap of stones
ceall, cille (kil...)	monastic cell, church
ceann (kin...)	head
clachan	usually a group of houses (clach = stone)
claidheamh	sword (hence 'claymore' = great sword)

cnoc (knock)	rounded hill
coire (corrie)	cauldron, hollow among hills, whirlpool
corr (adj)	tapering, peaked, pointed, uneven, odd. (n) heron
corran	tapering point of land
craobh	tree
creag	cliff, rock (crag)
cudag, cudaig	coalfish
darroch	oak tree
dearg ('jerrig')	red
deas	south
dobhran	otter
donn	brown (dun)
druim	ridge
dubh (dhu)	black, dark, (disastrous)
dun, duin	fortified place, usually prehistoric
each	horse
ear	east
eilean (or eileach)	island
fada	long
fir, fear	man
fraoch, fraoich	heather
garbh	rough
geal	white
gille	boy
glas	grey (sometimes green)
gobhar (gour)	goat (gabhar = she-goat)
gorm	blue
gamhna	stirk, year-old calf
iar	west (easily confused with Ear)
iolair	eagle
keills, kells	church
kin... (ceann)	head of
liath	grey
luib, Lub	bay, corner, fold
maol	bald lump; a bluff, a high rounded headland (Mull)
mara	sea
meadhonach	middle-sized
meall	lump, knob
mol	shingle beach
mor (more, mhor, vore)	large, great (often only relative)
muc, muck	pig (often a sea-pig = porpoise or a whale)
na, na h-, nam, nan	of (the)
naomh (nave, neave)	holy, saint
...nish (ness)	point of land
poll, puill	pool
righ ('ree')	king
ron, roin	seal
ruadh, rudha	red, reddish
rubha (rhu)	point of land, promontory
sailean	creek
sgeir, sgeirean (skerry)	rock, above water or covering
sron	nose (as a headland)
sruth	stream, current
taobh	side
tigh	house
tober	well
traigh	beach
tuath (or tuadh)	north
uamh	cave
uidhe	isthmus

II. CHARTS AND OTHER PUBLICATIONS

The Imray charts *C65* and *C66* at a scale of 1:150,000 cover much of the waters referred to in this volume. They are available at most chandlers and from the Clyde Cruising Club, usually folded, but for any boat which has a large enough chart table it is better to order a flat copy, or one laminated in plastic.

A general chart for the whole west coast of Scotland is Admiralty chart *2635* at a scale of 1:500,000.

The following Admiralty charts relate to the waters covered by this volume. Some of these are essential, and the more you have, the less your pilotage will be fraught with anxiety. The relevant Ordnance Survey maps are also listed.

Chart	Title – areas in Chapter I	Scale
1796	Ardnamurchan to Barra Head	1:100,000
1795	The Little Minch	1:100,000
2769	Barra Head to Greian Head	1:30,000
2770	Sound of Barra and Loch Boisdale	1:30,000
2825	Lochs on the east coast of Uist	various
2904	Usinish to Eigneig Mor	1:25,000
OS 31	Barra and surrounding islands	1:50,000
OS 22	Benbecula	1:50,000
OS 18	Sound of Harris	1:50,000

Chart	Title – areas in Chapter II	Scale
1795	The Little Minch	1:100,000
2825	Lochs on the east coast of Uist	various
2642	Sound of Harris	1:20,000
OS 18	Sound of Harris	1:50,000

Chart	Title – areas in Chapter III	Scale
2208	Mallaig to Canna Harbour	1:50,000
1795	The Little Minch	1:100,000
2533	Lochs Dunvegan and Snizort	1:25,000
OS 32		1:50,000
OS 23	North Skye	1:50,000
OS	Outdoor Leisure Map – The Cuillin and Torridon Hills	1:25,000

Chart	Title – areas in Chapter IV	Scale
2208	Mallaig to Canna Harbour	1:50,000
2209	Inner Sound	1:50,000
2541	Lochs Nevis, Hourn and Duich	1:25,000
2540	Loch Alsh	1:25,000
OS 33	Loch Alsh and Glen Shiel	1:50,000

Chart	Title – areas in Chapter V	Scale
2209	Inner Sound	1:50,000
2210	Approaches to Inner Sound	1:50,000
2534	Plans in the Inner Sound	1:25,000
2528	Loch Carron and Loch Gairloch	1:25,000
2498	Inner Sound, Southern Part	1:25,000
2479	Inner Sound, Middle Part	1:18,000
2480	Inner Sound, Northern Part	1:25,000
OS 33	Loch Alsh and Glen Shiel	1:50,000
OS 24	Raasay and Loch Torridon	1:50,000

Chart	Title – areas in Chapter VI	Scale
1785	North Minch, Northern Part	1:100,000
1794	North Minch, Southern Part	1:100,000
2509	Rubha Reidh to Cailleach Head	1:25,000
2500	Loch Broom and Approaches	1:25,000
2501	Summer Isles	1:26,000
2502	Eddrachillis Bay	1:25,150
2503	Lochs Laxford and Inchard	1:25,000
2504	Approaches to Loch Inver	1:25,000
3146	Loch Ewe	1:12,500
OS 19	Gairloch and Ullapool	1:50,000
OS 15	Loch Assynt	1:50,000
OS 9	Cape Wrath	1:50,000

Chart	Title – areas in Chapter VII	Scale
1785	North Minch, Northern Part	1:100,000
1794	North Minch, Southern Part	1:100,000
2905	East Loch Tarbert	1:10,000
2529	Approaches to Stornoway	1:25,000
OS 8	Stornoway and North Lewis	1:50,000
OS 14	Tarbert and Loch Seaforth	1:50,000

Chart	Title – areas in Chapter VIII	Scale
2722	Skerryvore to St Kilda	1:200,000
2721	St Kilda to the Butt of Lewis	1:200,000
2841	Sound of Harris to Ard More Mangersta	1:50,000
3381	West Loch Roag	1:12,500
3422	East Loch Roag	1:12,500
2524	Islands off the NW Coast of Scotland	various
OS 31	Barra and surrounding islands	1:50,000
OS 22	Benbecula	1:50,000
OS 18	Sound of Harris	1:50,000
OS 13	West Lewis and North Harris	1:50,000

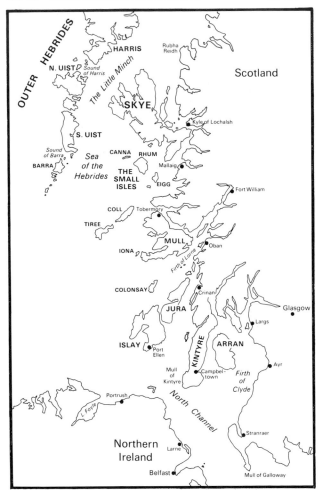

Index of Imray charts for the west coast of Scotland

OS *Outdoor Leisure Map – The Cuillin and Torridon Hills* (1:25,000) provides much more detail, especially for southwest Skye and the southwest side of the Inner Sound, than a chart is able to do.

The Yachtsman's Almanac – Malin, Hebrides and Minches Edition, published annually, is available from chandlers or post free from the publishers, Clyde Marine Press, Westgate, Toward, Argyll PA23 7UA.

Charts should be ordered early so that you have time to order more, if it looks as though your first choice is not enough. There are Admiralty chart agents throughout Britain, and in most other countries. Chart agents on the West Coast are:

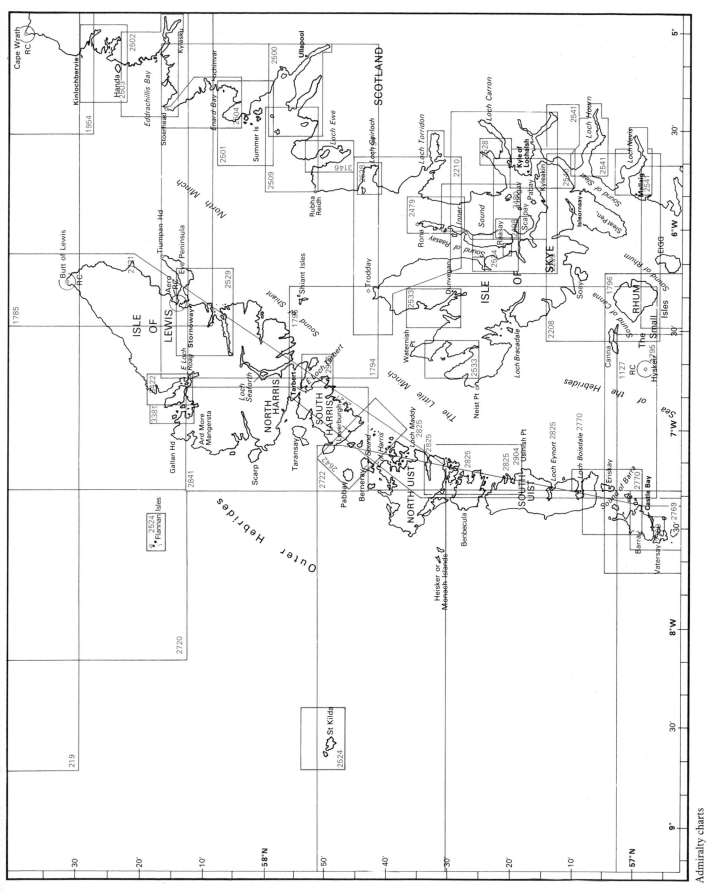

Kelvin Hughes, Glasgow ☎ 041-221 5452
Christie and Wilson, Glasgow ☎ 041-552 7137
Johnston Brothers, Mallaig ☎ (0687) 2215
Bridgend Stores, Aultbea ☎ (044 582) 204
Ullasport, Ullapool ☎ (0854) 2621
Duncan McIver, Ltd, Stornoway ☎ (0851) 2012

Imray, Laurie, Norie & Wilson Ltd are Admiralty chart agents and will supply charts by post; Wych House, The Broadway, St Ives, Huntingdon, Cambridgeshire PE17 4BT, ☎ (0480) 62114, telex 329195 Imrays G, fax (0480) 496109. They can arrange for charts to be laminated.

Some charts which have long been discontinued provide much more detail, at a larger scale, than any now published for the same area. All older charts, particularly the fine Victorian engravings, show more detail inshore and on land than the current publications, although they may be less accurate. Old charts should only be used to supplement current ones, not as a substitute for them.

Photocopies of old charts – of editions not less than 50 years old, for copyright reasons – may be obtained from the National Library of Scotland Map Room Annexe, 137 Causewayside, Edinburgh 9, ☎ (031) 226 4531.

Current charts show less detail ashore than older charts, and Ordnance Survey maps at a scale of 1:50,000, or Bartholomew maps at 1:100,000 help to fill in the picture.

A set of 50 sketch charts published by the Clyde Cruising Club is available from chandlers or direct from the CCC at SV *Carrick*, Clyde Street, Glasgow G1 4LN. These charts are convenient to use because of their size, but the relevant Admiralty charts should also be carried.

The Clyde Cruising Club *Sailing Directions and Anchorages* are also available from the CCC at the above address.

The Admiralty *West Coast of Scotland Pilot* (*NP 66*), with supplements up to date, is a most valuable publication.

The Admiralty *Tidal stream atlas for the North Coast of Ireland and West Coast of Scotland* (*NP 218*) is very useful.

Tide tables are essential, preferably for Ullapool giving heights of each high and low water.

The Yachtsman's Almanac – Malin, Hebrides and Minches Edition is available from chandlers, from the publishers, Clyde Marine Press, Westgate, Toward, Argyll PA23 7UA, or from Imrays (above).
Alternatively there are the full *Admiralty Tide Tables Vol. 1* (*NP 201*) or Brown's, Macmillan's or Reed's Almanacs.

Pilotage books

Scottish West Coast Pilot, Mark Brackenbury, Stanford 1981
Outer Hebrides Sailing Directions, Clyde Cruising Club, 1987
Ardnamurchan to Cape Wrath Sailing Directions, Clyde Cruising Club, 1984

General books

Scottish Lighthouses, R. W. Munro, Thule Press, 1979
The Islands of Western Scotland, W. H. Murray, Eyre Methuen, 1973
Companion Guide to the Western Highlands of Scotland, W. H. Murray, Collins
Exploring Scotland's Heritage – Argyll and the Western Isles Graham Ritchie and Mary Harman, HMSO 1985
Exploring Scotland's Heritage – The Highlands, Joanna Close-Brooks, HMSO 1986
The Islands of Scotland including Skye, Scottish Mountaineering Trust, 1989 (for climbers and hillwalkers)

III. QUICK REFERENCE TABLE OF PROVISIONS, SERVICES AND SUPPLIES

Columns

1	Water	A	Alongside, by hose
		T	Tap on jetty or quay
		N	Nearby tap
2	Shop	S	Several, or supermarket
		L	Local, well stocked village store
		B	Basic
3	Diesel	A	Alongside, by hose
		M	Marine diesel, near
		G	Garage
4	Petrol	P	(usually needs to be carried some distance)
5	Calor Gas	C	
6	Repairs	H	Hull
		M	Marine engine
		E	Electronics (engineer may need to come from a distance)
7	Chandlery	Y	Yacht
		F	Fishermen's chandlery
		I	Ironmonger, hardware store, which may be better than nothing
8	Visitors' moorings	V	(including those provided by hotel for customers)
9	Conveniences	R	Restaurant
		B	Bar
		S	Showers
10	Bank	£	
11	Rubbish disposal	D	

Page	Place, grouped in sequence of chapters	1	2	3	4	5	6	7	8	9	10	11
16	Castlebay	A	S	G	P	C	.	FI	V	RBS	£	D
23	Eriskay	T	L1½	.	.	C1½	.	I1½	V	RB1½	£	.
25	Lochboisdale	A	S	G	P	.	.	I	.	RB	.	D
32	Kallin	T	.	A	.	.	H	F	.	.	.	D
35	Locheport	.	L	.	.	.	.	.	.	.	.	.
40	Lochmaddy	A	L	G	.	C	.	.	V	RBS	£	D
41	Lochportain	.	B	.	.	.	.	.	.	.	.	.
46	Berneray	A	L	A	.	C	.	.	.	.	.	.
50	Leverburgh	T	L	.	P	C	.	.	.	.	.	.
60	Loch Harport											
	Loch Beag	.	L	.	.	.	.	.	.	RB	.	.
	Port na Long	.	L	.	.	.	.	.	.	RB	.	.
	Carbost	N	L	.	.	.	.	.	.	RB	.	.
64	Dunvegan	.	S	G	P	C	E	I	V	RBS	.	D
65	Stein	.	B	.	.	.	ME	Y	V	RBS	.	.
66	Edinbane	.	S	G	P	.	.	.	.	RB	.	.
66	Uig	T	L	G	P	.	.	.	.	.	.	D
71	Inverie	.	L	.	.	.	.	.	.	RB	.	.
73	Armadale	T	L	M	.	.	HM	.	V	RB	.	D
75	Isleornsay	N	B	.	P	.	.	.	.	RB	.	.
78	Glenelg	.	L	.	P	C	.	.	.	RB	.	.
79	Dornie	.	S	.	P	C	.	.	.	RB	.	.
81	Kyleakin	A	S	G	P	C	.	.	.	RBS	.	D
81	Kyle Of Lochalsh	A	S	G	P	C	E	I(Y)	.	RBS	£	D
85	Ardarroch	.	L	G	P	.	.	.	.	.	.	.
86	Plockton	(A)G	S	M	.	C	.	.	.	RBS	.	.
87	Lochcarron	.	S	G	P	C	.	I	.	RB	.	D
89	Poll Creadha	.	B	.	P	.	.	.	.	.	.	.
93	Shieldaig	.	S	.	.	C	.	.	.	RB	.	D
93	Torridon	.	L	.	.	.	.	.	.	RB	.	.
94	Badachro	A	L	A	.	.	.	Y	V	RBS	.	D
96	Gairloch	A	S1	G1	P1	C	M	.	.	RB	£	D
96	Broadford	.	S	G	P	.	.	.	.	RB	.	.
100	Portree	A	S	M	P	C	M	YFI	V	RB	£	D
105	Staffin	.	L	.	.	.	.	.	.	.	.	.
109	Aultbea	T	S	.	P	C	(ME)	.	.	RB	.	.
109	Poolewe	.	L	G	P	C	.	.	.	RB	.	.
110	Ullapool	A	S	A	P	C	ME	YFI	.	RB	£	D
112	Achiltibuie	.	S	.	.	.	.	.	.	RB	.	.
116	Lochinver	A	S	A	P	C	.	.	.	RB	.	D
120	Drumbeg	T	B	.	.	.	.	.	.	RB	.	.
122	Kylesku	T	L	A	P	.	.	.	.	RB	.	.
124	Scourie	.	L	.	P	.	.	.	.	RB	.	.
127	Kinlochbervie	A	S	A	P	C	HME	F	.	RBS	.	D
134	Finsbay	.	B	.	.	.	.	.	.	.	.	.
141	Scalpay	T	S	.	P	.	.	.	.	.	.	D
143	Tarbert	T	S	G	P	C	.	.	V	RBS	£	D
157	Stornoway	A	S	A	P	C	HME	F	V	RBS	£	D
	West Loch Tarbert	(see Tarbert, above)										
171	Breasclete	T	L	.	.	.	.	.	.	.	.	.
171	Carloway	T	L	.	.	.	.	.	.	.	.	.

Notes

Figures following reference letter indicate the distance in miles from the landing place.

Caley Marine at Inverness ☎ (0463) 236539 operate a mobile repair service.

IV. CONVERSION TABLES

metres–feet

m	ft/m	ft
0·3	1	3·3
0·6	2	6·6
0·9	3	9·8
1·2	4	13·1
1·5	5	16·4
1·8	6	19·7
2·1	7	23·0
2·4	8	26·2
2·7	9	29·5
3·0	10	32·8
6·1	20	65·6
9·1	30	98·4
12·2	40	131·2
15·2	50	164·0
30·5	100	328·1

centimetres–inches

cm	in/cm	in
2·5	1	0·4
5·1	2	0·8
7·6	3	1·2
10·2	4	1·6
12·7	5	2·0
15·2	6	2·4
17·8	7	2·8
20·3	8	3·1
22·9	9	3·5
25·4	10	3·9
50·8	20	7·9
76·2	30	11·8
101·6	40	15·7
127·0	50	19·7
254·0	100	39·4

metres–fathoms–feet

m	fathoms	ft
0·9	0·5	3
1·8	1	6
3·7	2	12
5·5	3	18
7·3	4	24
9·1	5	30
11·0	6	36
12·8	7	42
14·6	8	48
16·5	9	54
18·3	10	60
36·6	20	120
54·9	30	180
73·2	40	240
91·4	50	300

kilometres–statute miles

km	M/km	M
1·6	1	0·6
3·2	2	1·2
4·8	3	1·9
6·4	4	2·5
8·0	5	3·1
9·7	6	3·7
11·3	7	4·3
12·9	8	5·0
14·5	9	5·6
16·1	10	6·2
32·2	20	12·4
48·3	30	18·6
64·4	40	24·9
80·5	50	31·1
120·7	75	46·6
160·9	100	62·1
402·3	250	155·3
804·7	500	310·7
1609·3	1000	621·4

kilograms–pounds

kg	lb/kg	lb
0·5	1	2·2
0·9	2	4·4
1·4	3	6·6
1·8	4	8·8
2·3	5	11·0
2·7	6	13·2
3·2	7	15·4
3·6	8	17·6
4·1	9	19·8
4·5	10	22·0
9·1	20	44·1
13·6	30	66·1
18·1	40	88·2
22·7	50	110·2
34·0	75	165·3
45·4	100	220·5
113·4	250	551·2
226·8	500	1102·3
453·6	1000	2204·6

litres–gallons

l	gal/l	gal
4·5	1	0·2
9·1	2	0·4
13·6	3	0·7
18·2	4	0·9
22·7	5	1·1
27·3	6	1·3
31·8	7	1·5
36·4	8	1·8
40·9	9	2·0
45·5	10	2·2
90·9	20	4·4
136·4	30	6·6
181·8	40	8·8
227·3	50	11·0
341·0	75	16·5
454·6	100	22·0
1136·5	250	55·0
2273·0	500	110·0
4546·1	1000	220·0

Index